Intellectual Disability and the Death Penalty

Intellectual Disability and the Death Penalty

Current Issues and Controversies

Marc J. Tassé and John H. Blume

 PRAEGER™

An Imprint of ABC-CLIO, LLC

Santa Barbara, California • Denver, Colorado

Library of Congress Cataloging-in-Publication Data

Names: Tassé, Marc J., author. | Blume, John H., author.
Title: Intellectual disability and the death penalty : current issues and
    controversies / Marc J. Tassé and John H. Blume.
Description: Santa Barbara, California : Praeger, 2018. |
    Includes bibliographical references and index.
Identifiers: LCCN 2017037271 (print) | LCCN 2017045921 (ebook) |
    ISBN 9781440840159 (ebook) | ISBN 9781440840142 (hardcopy : alk. paper)
Subjects: LCSH: Capital punishment—United States. | Offenders with mental
    disabilities—Legal status, laws, etc.—United States. | People with
    mental disabilities and crime—United States. | Mentally ill—Commitment
    and detention—United States. | Insanity (Law)—United States.
Classification: LCC KF9227.C2 (ebook) | LCC KF9227.C2 T37 2017 (print) |
    DDC 345.73/0773—dc23
LC record available at https://lccn.loc.gov/2017037271

ISBN: 978-1-4408-4014-2 (print)
ISBN: 978-1-4408-4015-9 (ebook)

22 21 20 19 18   1 2 3 4 5

This book is also available as an eBook.

Praeger
An Imprint of ABC-CLIO, LLC

ABC-CLIO, LLC
130 Cremona Drive, P.O. Box 1911
Santa Barbara, California 93116-1911
www.abc-clio.com

This book is printed on acid-free paper ∞

Manufactured in the United States of America

Contents

Preface

In its 2002 landmark decision in *Atkins v. Virginia*, the Supreme Court of the United States held that the execution of people with intellectual disability was a "cruel and unusual punishment" barred by the Eighth Amendment to the United States Constitution. In doing so, the Court, implicitly and at times explicitly in its opinion, recognized the lesser culpability of this vulnerable population. While the *Atkins* Court gave states some latitude to develop appropriate mechanisms for assessing intellectual disability in capital cases and thus implementing the new constitutional exclusion against capital punishment for people determined to have intellectual disability, some jurisdictions have mistakenly interpreted *Atkins* as allowing them to deviate, in some instances markedly, from the generally recognized national professional consensus regarding the determination of intellectual disability. At bottom, intellectual disability remains a clinical diagnosis, and the states and their courts must recognize and apply existing nationally accepted clinical definitions to guide their decisions in determining whether the individual in any *Atkins'* hearing has intellectual disability. This was reiterated in the most recent Supreme Court rulings in *Hall v. Florida* (2014) and *Moore v. Texas* (2017).

Determining whether a particular capital defendant or death row inmate has intellectual disability in many death penalty cases has been far from a simple clinical exercise. This is so for a number of reasons, including (1) resistance to the Supreme Court's decision in *Atkins* itself; (2) the use of scientifically unsound definitions of intellectual disability and assessment methods for its determination; (3) judge, juror, and attorney stereotypes of people who have an intellectual disability; (4) the use of "expert" witnesses who lack familiarity with and clinical judgment in intellectual disability; and (5) racial and ethnic bias. Despite being informed by more than a decade and a half of experience since the Court's decision in *Atkins*, many issues remain controversial and unsettled for judges, prosecutors, defense attorneys, jurors, as well as mental health experts called upon to make determinations of intellectual disability in capital cases.

Drawing upon our different experiences as a psychologist who has worked for decades with people with intellectual disability and a legal academic who has devoted a significant amount of his career to studying the legal treatment of persons with a variety of mental impairments, this book reviews the major clinical and legal issues and controversies surrounding the matter of the death penalty in America when the defendant is suspected of having intellectual disability. We have attempted to do so as thoroughly and objectively as possible as we intend for this book to be a valuable resource for mental health experts, attorneys, investigators, mitigation specialists, and other members of legal teams, as well as judges who, willingly or unwillingly, become involved in an *Atkins* hearing and want to better understand the relevant issues at hand.

Acknowledgments

We would like to thank ABC-CLIO/Praeger Publishers for the forethought and invitation to write this book. We also thank Debbie Carvalko, Senior Acquisitions Editor, Psychology and Health, at ABC-CLIO/Praeger Publishers, for her guidance and support throughout the process of bringing this book to fruition.

We extend our warmest gratitude to Wesley R. Barnhart, Kelsey L. Bush, Kristin Dell'Armo, Stoni L. Fortney, Dr. Susan M. Havercamp, Emily Paavola, and Lindsey Vann (alphabetical order) for reviewing and providing insightful comments on earlier drafts of the chapters contained in this book. We also wish to thank Monica A. Sandoval for her assistance with formatting of the chapters into APA publication style, and Charlie Sim and Jackie Newman for research assistance.

Marc Tassé extends warm thanks to Professor Ruth Luckasson for her encouragement more than a decade ago to dive into the criminal justice issues associated with intellectual disability and to become involved in *Atkins* cases, it has been an intellectually stimulating journey to say the least. He also extends his warmest gratitude to his spouse and colleague, Dr. Susan M. Havercamp, who is the first peer reviewer he seeks input from and who is always patient and understanding.

John Blume would like to thank Professors Ruth Luckasson and Jim Ellis who first introduced him 30 years ago to the special challenges persons with intellectual disability face when charged with a capital crime or sentenced to death. He would also like to thank the clients with intellectual disability whom he has interacted with over the years for the lessons they have imparted. And, last but not least, he would like to thank his spouse, Drucy Glass, for her patience and support.

Marc J. Tassé and John H. Blume

Intellectual Disability and How It Is Diagnosed

Intellectual disability is a multifaceted and complex condition that comes in a wide range of clinical presentations but has historically been defined by three long-standing criteria and/or prongs related to (1) significantly subaverage intellectual functioning, (2) significant subaverage adaptive behavior as expressed in conceptual skills (language, reading, and writing, and money, time, and number concepts), social skills (interpersonal skills, social responsibility, self-esteem, social problem solving, following rules and obeying laws, avoiding being victimized, and wariness), and practical skills (personal hygiene, safety, healthcare, travel/transportation, following schedule, home-living skills, and occupational skills), and (3) if the individual's impaired functioning originated during the developmental period (see American Psychiatric Association (APA), 2013; Schalock et al., 2010). Although the developmental period is not operationally defined in the *DSM-5* (APA, 2013), the developmental period is generally considered to be from birth through the age of 18 years (Schalock et al., 2010). The causes or risk factors leading to impaired functioning typically associated with intellectual disability can originate prenatally (e.g., genetic or chromosomal factors, maternal alcohol or drug consumption during pregnancy, trauma or insult during fetal development, etc.), perinatally (e.g., anoxia, infection transmission, trauma, etc.), and/or postnatally (e.g., deprivation, brain injury, exposure to teratogens, etc.). Intellectual disability can be the result of any number of known genetic syndromes or risk factors. Establishing the exact etiology associated with intellectual disability is not needed to make a diagnosis. Knowing the cause or causes can be of value to the individual and/or his or her family, especially for the purposes of family planning and counseling.

Before continuing any further, we will briefly define intellectual disability, adaptive behavior, and age of onset. The definition and description of these terms are defined in more detail in Chapters, 5, 6, and 7, respectively.

Intellectual functioning is defined as a wide-ranging set of cognitive skills that include reasoning, problem solving, planning, abstract thinking, and learning (APA, 2013). Adaptive behavior is a separate and independent construct that involves the abilities that are learned and performed to meet one's community or society's expectations relative to one's chronological age and cultural group (Schalock et al., 2010). Intellectual disability has always been conceptualized as a developmental disorder, meaning that its origins are found either prior to/during conception or fetal development (e.g., chromosomal, genetic, metabolic disorders), during birthing, or in the years following birth during which an individual's development progresses toward maturity. The precise chronological age at which all human development (e.g., brain development) has reached its full-blown maturity can be debated; for some time now, the end of the developmental period has been generally accepted to be at the age of 18 years (see Schalock et al., 2010).

Common Characteristics, Severity Levels, and Etiology

There are no universally distinctive personality traits, physical or dysmorphic features, common to all cases of intellectual disability (ID). There is no "ID look" or "ID talk" or "ID mannerisms" or "ID personality." There is only a level of human functioning that, when present, leads to establishing a diagnosis of intellectual disability. The clinical presentation of a person with intellectual disability (i.e., level of functioning or independence, ease of adjustment in mainstream settings, intensity of support needs) will be dependent on a number of factors associated with the individual's human functioning. Human functioning includes not only intellectual functioning and adaptive behavior but also physical health, mental health, intrinsic motivation, and behavior.

Although the *Diagnostic and Statistical Manual for Mental Disorders* (*DSM*), currently in its fifth iteration (*DSM-5*), has continued to use a system of severity levels for intellectual disability, it has recently abandoned the use of IQ scores as the determinant of these ID severity levels (APA, 2013). In lieu of using the individual's overall IQ score, the *DSM-5* now recommends using the individual's level of adaptive functioning across conceptual, social, and practical skills. The American Association on Intellectual and Developmental Disabilities (AAIDD) recognized more than 25 years ago (see Luckasson et al., 1992) that the clinical presentation of intellectual disability was far too complex and varied to impose a severity metric on the basis of one, sole determinant. Hence, AAIDD abandoned the severity levels for "intellectual disability" in 1992 and recommended in its place the use of severity levels of human functioning (see Schalock & Luckasson, 2015), as well as a multifactorial metric of intensity of support needs (see Schalock et al., 2010).

We will discuss in greater detail in Chapters 5, 6, and 7 how the three prongs of intellectual disability are assessed. For the purpose of making an intellectual disability determination, establishing the presence of "significant subaverage" intellectual functioning or adaptive behavior requires clinical judgment (Luckasson & Schalock, 2015; Schalock & Luckasson, 2013) and rigorous individualized assessment. The generally accepted scientific definition of the term "significant subaverage" is performance that is at least two standard deviations below the average level for the individual's peers (see APA, 2013; Schalock et al., 2010). Intellectual disability has always been defined as a condition that originated either before birth or during the developmental period and has thus long been differentiated from causes and risk factors (e.g., brain injuries, neurological diseases, etc.) that occur outside of the developmental period. For example, a brain tumor that occurs in a child at age 3 years and results in the child's intellectual functioning and adaptive behavior to become severely impaired (as previously defined) may then result in a clinician diagnosing the child with intellectual disability. The same brain tumor occurring in an adult at age 33 years and resulting in comparable significant subaverage intellectual functioning and adaptive behavior would not be diagnosed as intellectual disability because the condition originated outside of the developmental period. Thousands of potential causes and risk factors can lead to an individual's intellectual functioning and adaptive behavior being significantly impaired, with many more causes, risk factors, and interactions of risk factors that remain unknown. A formal diagnosis of intellectual disability can be made, as is made in approximately 40–50% of all cases, in the absence of a clearly established etiology.

Prevalence

Before we discuss prevalence, we should define a few terms: mean and standard deviation. *Mean* is a statistical term used to represent the average performance of an individual or group. A standard deviation (SD) is used as a unit of variability in the observed scores and is a measure used to mark off segments of performance or scores that are either above or below the mean/average of the group or population. A customary approach with some standardized tests, such as tests of intelligence and adaptive behavior, is to set the population mean at 100 and the standard deviation in increments of 15. For example, if we were to plot all the scores on an ability test (e.g., test of intelligence or adaptive behavior) of the entire population onto a metric where the x-axis is the person's performance or standard score and the y-axis is the probability of getting a specific score/performance, we would find that the dispersion of these scores would result in what is called the normal distribution, with the shape of the curve of these scores reflecting a bell (see Figure 1.1). When looking at the normal distribution, we see that there is a 68% probability that people would score at or near the mean and that this probability decreases equally on either side of the population mean as you move away from it (e.g., 16% of the scores are +/–1 SD from the mean, 2.3% of the scores are +/–2 SD from the mean).

The theoretical prevalence of intellectual disability (ID), assuming scores that are two standard deviations below the population mean, should equate to approximately 2.3% of the population (Urbina, 2014). This theoretical 2.3% is derived from the proportion of the U.S. population that is functioning approximately two standard deviations or more below the population's average performance (see Figure 1.1). However, to have a diagnosis of intellectual disability, you must present significant deficits in two separate constructs: intellectual functioning and adaptive behavior. Therefore,

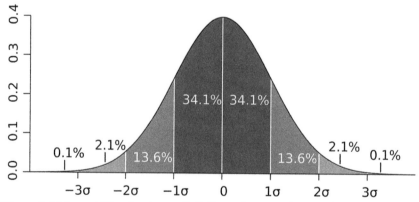

Figure 1.1 Normal Distribution or Bell-Shaped Curve. (Drawn by M. W. Toews)

the actual estimated prevalence (i.e., number of people who have ID) is closer to 1.04% (Maulik, Mascarenhas, Mathers, Dua, & Saxena, 2011).

Having a low IQ does appear to correlate with an increased risk of being involved with the criminal justice system as an offender, and this risk increases when combined with growing up socially disadvantaged, having struggled with substance abuse, and/or having a family member with a criminal background (Holland, Clare, & Mukhopadhyay, 2002). People with ID who are interfacing with the criminal justice system are almost exclusively individuals with mild deficits in intellectual functioning and adaptive behavior (Holland et al., 2002; Lyall, Holland, Collins, & Styles, 1995). It should be emphasized that people with intellectual disability are more likely to be victims of crime than perpetrators. In fact, according to a study by Sobsey (1994) people with intellectual disability are 4–10 times more likely than people without an intellectual disability to be a victim of crime. People with ID are known to be more gullible, easily duped, and easier victims of crime who are often considered unreliable witnesses by law enforcement.

The prevalence of inmates who have intellectual disability is difficult to ascertain for a number of reasons. The methods used to assess functioning in prison settings are often only screening tools. Many studies estimating the prevalence of ID in prisons report data only on tests of intellectual functioning and are not inclusive of an assessment of adaptive behavior. In many prevalence studies, inmate participation in the screening for intellectual disability was voluntary. Having laid out all these concerns, the consensus in the scientific community remains that people with intellectual disability are overrepresented in prisons (Fazel, Xenitidis, & Powell, 2008). One prevalence study of prison inmates in the United Kingdom reported that approximately 7% of prisoners had an intellectual disability (Hayes, Shackell, Mottram, & Lancaster, 2007); whereas, an estimate of U.S. prison populations found the prevalence of intellectual disability ranging between 4% and 10% (Petersilia, 2000).

Intellectual Disability Is a Lifelong Condition

When Schalock and his colleagues (2010) assert the assumption/aspiration, "With appropriate personalized supports over a sustained period, the life functioning of the person with intellectual disability generally will improve" (p. 1), what they are talking about is the person's adaptive behavior. With proper intervention and supports, a person will learn and improve his or her ability to meet society's expectations. This is important because it means that we can teach new adaptive skills to all those with intellectual disability, no matter their level of disability, and can contribute to their improved independence and resulting quality of life. Improved functioning may also be seen in inmates after a number of years of incarceration because they now have access to educational materials and activities, as well as time to focus on learning new skills.

Although intensive educational and therapeutic interventions received in infancy and early childhood may alleviate some of the child's deficits in intellectual functioning and adaptive behavior, intellectual disability is generally considered a lifelong condition (APA, 2013).

Misconceptions and Erroneous Beliefs

The general population will often hold beliefs and stereotypes of persons with an intellectual disability that are often founded on Hollywood characterizations rather than on known facts about the condition. These beliefs and misconceptions may also be from an experience with one family member, neighbor, or acquaintance who had Down syndrome and generalizing that individual's functioning to all persons with intellectual disability.

The overall functioning of the majority (i.e., approximately 85%) of persons with intellectual disability falls in what has historically been defined as the "mild" range of ID. Harris (2006) accurately summarized the overall functioning of individuals with mild intellectual disability as follows:

> In the early months of life, these individuals may not be distinguishable from normal children: they may only be recognized at school entry or in the preschool years (0–5) when social and communication skills develop. Persons with mild intellectual disability may acquire academic skills up to a fifth- or sixth-grade level by their late teenage years. During their adult years, mildly intellectually disabled persons may develop sufficient social and vocational abilities to work and live independently or in supervised apartments and group homes and need a minimum of external support. Still, ongoing guidance is needed under stressful social conditions or during economic hardship. Their developmental achievements allow them to engage others in conversation and participate in clinical interviews. Their learning difficulties may become evident in academic work. Socioculturally, when academic achievement is not required, their problems may be minimal. Yet there may be a noticeable degree of social and emotional immaturity, leading to difficulties in coping in a community setting. There may be difficulty in coping with the demands of marriage or child rearing or to meet specific cultural expectations. Still, for the most part, behavioral, emotional, and social problems of persons with mild intellectual disability

and their need for psychosocial and behavioral treatment and support are similar to those of persons with normal intelligence. (p. 53)

Laypeople (who may include attorneys, judges, psychiatrists, and psychologists) have some unfounded misconceptions and erroneous beliefs about what people with intellectual disability are able or unable to do or achieve. Although there is scant high-quality research on the U.S. population's attitudes towards people with intellectual disability (Scior, 2011), a study by Musso, Barker, Proto, and Gouvier (2012) of 890 college students illustrated many of the common misconceptions seen by the authors of this book, among professionals and jurors in *Atkins* hearings. Musso and her colleagues reported that a plurality of college students in their survey reported being able to tell someone had mild intellectual disability by looking at them, as well as believing that most adults with mild intellectual disability needed caretakers throughout their lives, are always happy, were placed in special education classrooms, or are more aggressive than people without intellectual disability. Other common mistaken beliefs about the ability or inability of people with intellectual disability include the following areas:

- **Graduating from high school.** The U.S. Department of Education (2011) reports that approximately 35–37% of students being served in special education under the label of intellectual disability leave high school with a regular high school diploma. This statistic holds constant over the last decade or more according to reporting from the U.S. Department of Education.
- **Getting a driver's license.** The U.S. Department of Education funded a large national longitudinal study of the outcomes of students who had been served in special education under various disability categories (including intellectual disability). The National Longitudinal Transition Study-2 (NLTS2) (Newman et al., 2011) tracked and surveyed students and their parents at 2-year intervals post high school. The NLTS2 report of survey students with intellectual disability up to 8 years post high school (age ranging from 22 to 26 years) reported that 29% had a learner's permit or driver's license.
- **Getting and keeping a job.** The NLTS2 reports show that 76% had a job at some point after leaving high school and that 39% had a job at the time of the survey.
- **Getting married.** One out of 10 young adults with intellectual disability reported being married at the time of interview.
- **Having children.** One out of 4 (25.3%) of individuals with ID reported having had a child.
- **Managing money.** Forty-two percent reported having a savings account, 29% reported having a checking account, and 19% reported having a credit card.

Almost all of the *Atkins* claims will be dealing with individuals who have intellectual functioning and adaptive behavior levels that are at or near (within 1 standard deviation of the approximate cutoff score) 2 standard deviations below the population mean. These people either have intellectual disability with mild deficits of intellectual functioning and/or adaptive behavior or are in what was formerly called the "borderline intellectual functioning" range. Very few of these *Atkins* claims will be people who are in the profound, severe, or even moderate range of deficits in intellectual and adaptive behavior. These cases in the mild range of intellectual and adaptive functioning represent the most difficult cases to rule in or rule out intellectual disability, making it even more important to keep one's misconceptions and erroneous assumptions in check because these men and women look like anyone else and will most likely present a wide range of relative strengths and abilities. As listed in Schalock and colleagues (2012; see p. 26), the following all-encompassing stereotypes have no scientific basis or grounding in reality:

- People with ID look and talk differently than people without ID.
- People with ID are completely incompetent and dangerous.
- People with ID cannot accomplish complex tasks.
- People with ID cannot get a driver's license, buy a car, or drive a car.
- People with ID do not (and cannot) support their families.
- People with ID cannot romantically love or be romantically loved.
- People with ID cannot acquire work and social skills needed to live independently.
- People with ID are characterized only by limitations and don't have strengths that coexist with their limitations.

A rigorous assessment of intellectual functioning, adaptive behavior, and determination of age of onset supporting a diagnosis of intellectual disability cannot be set aside because the person diagnosed with intellectual disability has one or more discrete abilities that confound your conception of what people with intellectual disability can or should be able to do.

Stigma

The condition known as "intellectual disability" has long-held significant stigma in our societies. So much so that the name of the condition itself has had to be changed over the years because of the acquired stigma of the label itself (see Tassé & Mehling, in press). Old medical/professional terms once used to identify the condition (e.g., moron, imbecile, idiot, mentally retarded) are part of the everyday vernacular to insult and hurt people rather than diagnose for the purpose of providing care and assistance. Hence, most people with intellectual disability will make every effort to "fit in" and "pass" for someone who does not have a disability. The use of different strategies to mask their deficits (e.g., pretending to read a newspaper or book, acquiescing to questioning, avoiding situations that require academic skills that might be a deficit, etc.), or outright denial of a disability has often been coined "cloak of competence," following the important work done by Edgerton (see Edgerton, 1967, 1993).

Edgerton (1967, 1993) followed a group of adults with intellectual disability who were integrated into community settings after having lived most of their lives in an institution. Edgerton's (1993) research showed that adults with ID, when moved into more typical community settings, will show improvements in their adaptive behavior, independence, community engagement, and overall quality of life. In addition, these individuals often do not advertise their disability and, when possible, find benefactors who can help them in areas that they have deficits (e.g., banking, bill paying, budgeting, organization, job searches, etc.). Like many others, when effective supports are in place, the person's overall functioning will generally improve (see Schalock et al., 2010) and appear to the naïve observer as being more adapted and skilled. However, if these supports (e.g., benefactors) are lost, the person's adjustment and stress levels will be significantly impacted. Hence, when conducting a comprehensive assessment for the purpose of making an intellectual disability determination, one must be cautious when using self-reported information from an individual being assessed for intellectual disability.

Atkins v. Virginia

The Supreme Court of the United States ruled in 2002 that people with intellectual disability needed special protections because of their disability and that their execution would be a violation of the Eighth Amendment of the U.S. Constitution, barring cruel and unusual punishment (*Atkins v. Virginia*, 2002). The Supreme Court of the United States did not bar the execution of people with intellectual disability because they do not understand the difference between right and wrong or because murder is unacceptable in any civilized society. Because people with intellectual disability for the most part understand right from wrong and they understand that hurting people is wrong, they are generally "competent" in the eyes of the law. The Supreme Court of the United States ruled in this manner because it acknowledged that people with ID are less culpable due to their impaired ability to engage in logical reasoning, to understand and process information, to learn from their mistakes and experiences, and to communicate, control their impulses, and understand the reactions of others (Blume, Johnson, Marcus, & Paavola, 2014). Blume and his colleagues further explained that the court was also moved by the fact that people with intellectual disability are by the very nature of their disability and associated impairments (1) at a greater risk of wrongful execution given the greater likelihood of false confessions, (2) limited in their ability to effectively communicate with their attorneys and provide them with facts and details related to the crime that might be instrumental in their defense, (3) limited in providing effective testimony in their own case because of difficulties with communication, and (4) at a greater risk to be perceived as lacking in empathy and remorse because of their courtroom behavior and demeanor.

Intellectual disability is not a legal concept in the same sense that "criminally insane" is a legal term. *Atkins v. Virginia* ruled that "intellectual disability" was a clinical condition for which people with this condition warranted a constitutional protection from the death penalty and that the determination of intellectual disability should be based on some generally accepted principle of the clinical definition of intellectual disability. The fact that intellectual disability is a clinical definition that should be defined according to the proper professional and clinical standards held by the field of intellectual disability was reiterated by the Supreme Court of the United States in *Hall v. Florida* (2014) and *Moore v. Texas* (2017). Hence, understanding the proper clinical definition and recommended practice in determining intellectual disability is crucial to any death penalty case involving an *Atkins* claim. We will present in the following chapters how intellectual disability is assessed, along with the existing recommended practices for assessing intellectual functioning, adaptive behavior, and age of onset for the purpose of making an intellectual disability determination.

State Definitions of Intellectual Disability

The Supreme Court of the United States decision in *Atkins v. Virginia* left the responsibility of defining intellectual disability up to each individual state. Of course, being a protected class of people, the clinical definition of intellectual disability in each state should bear some resemblance to the clinically accepted definition of intellectual disability, such that a person diagnosed with intellectual disability in New York City should be equally likely to be diagnosed with intellectual disability were he or she living in Anchorage, Biloxi, Columbus, or Boston. The Supreme Court justices in *Atkins v. Virginia* directed states to two existing national treatises (i.e., American Association on Intellectual and Developmental Disabilities, American Psychiatric Association's *DSM*) as guidance for the definition and diagnostic criteria for intellectual disability. There is a consensus between these two national treatises in their definition and diagnostic criteria for diagnosing intellectual disability. The necessity of anchoring state definitions and statutes of intellectual disability to accepted medical/professional practices was reiterated in both recent Supreme Court decisions in this matter (see *Hall v. Florida*, 2014, and *Moore v. Texas*, 2017).

The American Association on Intellectual and Developmental Disabilities (AAIDD) is an interdisciplinary professional society founded more than 140 years ago and has been a leader in establishing the definition and terminology of intellectual disability (see Tassé & Grover, 2013). The American Psychiatric Association (APA) has been publishing the *Diagnostic and Statistical Manual of Mental Disorders* since the late 1950s and has had diagnostic criteria for intellectual disability since then. Both AAIDD in its 11th edition of its *Terminology and Classification Manual* (see Schalock et al., 2010) and APA in its fifth edition of the *DSM* (see APA, 2013), define intellectual disability as originating during the developmental period and being characterized by significant impairments in both intellectual functioning and adaptive behavior. Significant impairments in adaptive behavior are defined by the presence of conceptual, social, or practical skills that are approximately 2 standard deviations or more below the population mean. AAIDD and *DSM-5* recommend that the determination of intellectual disability be accomplished using a careful approach inclusive of records review, standardized individual assessments, comprehensive clinical interviews of the person and other significant informants, and clinical judgment. These are discussed at greater length in Chapters 5, 6, and 7.

Several excellent sources cover in great detail the federal and state statutes defining intellectual disability in states that have the death penalty (DeMatteo, Marczyk, & Pich, 2007; Wood, Packman, Howell, & Bongar, 2014). A review of existing state statutes defining intellectual disability confirms that, since 2002, there continues to be substantial differences from state to state in how intellectual disability is being defined. All states with the death penalty have a statute that includes the three prongs, but the operationalization (e.g., specifying a definition for significant deficits; defining adaptive behavior as conceptual, social, and practical skills; specifying an age of onset) of these three prongs is far from consistent across the country. Woods and her colleagues (2014) concluded that a national uniform definition of intellectual disability is needed to ensure consistent application across states of the protections guaranteed under *Atkins v. Virginia*. Until then, most cases continue to use the state statutes as a guide and then rely heavily on the AAIDD and *DSM-5* systems for the operationalization of the state definition, since AAIDD and *DSM-5* establish national consensus on clinical standards of practice in defining and diagnosing intellectual disability.

References

American Psychiatric Association (APA). (2013). *Diagnostic and Statistical Manual of Mental Disorders* (5th Edition) (*DSM-5*). Arlington, VA: American Psychiatric Publishing.

Atkins v. Virginia, 536 U.S. 304 (2002).

Blume, J. H., Johnson, S. L., Marcus, P., & Paavola, E. C. (2014). A tale of two (and possibly three) Atkins: Intellectual disability and capital punishment twelve years after the Supreme Court's creation of a categorical bar. *William & Mary Bill of Rights*, 23, 393–414.

DeMatteo, D., Marczyk, G., & Pich, M. (2007). A national survey of state legislation defining mental retardation: Implications for policy and practice after *Atkins*. *Behavioral Sciences and the Law*, 25, 781–802.

Edgerton, R. B. (1967). *The Cloak of Competence: Stigma in the Lives of the Mentally Retarded*. Berkley: University of California Press.

Edgerton, R. B. (1993). *The Cloak of Competence: Revised and Updated*. Berkley: University of California Press.

Fazel, S., Xenitidis, K., & Powell, J. (2008). The prevalence of intellectual disabilities among 12,000 prisoners—A systematic review. *International Journal of Law and Psychiatry*, 31(4), 369–373.

Hall v. Florida, 134 S. Ct. at 1986 (2014).

Harris, J. C. (2006). *Intellectual Disability: Understanding Its Development, Causes, Classification, Evaluation, and Treatment*. New York: Oxford University Press.

Hayes, S., Shackell, P., Mottram, P., & Lancaster, R. (2007). The prevalence of intellectual disability in a major UK prison. *British Journal of Learning Disability*, 35, 162–167.

Holland, T., Clare, I. C. H., & Mukhopadhyay, T. (2002). Prevalence of "criminal offending" by men and women with intellectual disability and the characteristics of "offenders": implications for research and service development. *Journal of Intellectual Disability Research*, 46(s1), 6–20.

Luckasson, R., Coulter, D. L., Polloway, E. A., Reiss, S., Schalock, R. L., Snell, M. E., Spitalnik, D. M., & Stark, J. A. (1992). *Mental Retardation: Definition, Classification, and Systems of Supports* (9th Edition). Washington, DC: American Association on Mental Retardation.

Luckasson, R., & Schalock, R. L. (2015). Standards to guide the use of clinical judgment in the field of intellectual disability. *Intellectual and Developmental Disabilities*, 53(3), 240–251.

Lyall, I., Holland, A. J., Collins, S., & Styles, P. (1995). Incidence of persons with a learning disability detained in police custody: A needs assessment for service development. *Medicine, Science and the Law, 35,* 61–71.

Maulik, P. K., Mascarenhas, M. N., Mathers, C. D., Dua, T., & Saxena, S. (2011). Prevalence of intellectual disability: A meta-analysis of population-based studies. *Research in Developmental Disabilities, 32,* 419–436.

Moore v. Texas, 137 S. Ct. 1039 (2017).

Musso, M. W., Barker, A. A., Proto, D. A., & Gouvier, W. D. (2012). College students' conceptualizations of deficits involved in mild intellectual disability. *Research in Developmental Disabilities, 33,* 224–228.

Newman, L., Wagner, M., Knokey, A. M., Marder, C., Nagle, K., Shaver, D., & Wei, Xin. (2011). *The Post-High School Outcomes of Young Adults with Disabilities up to 8 Years After High School. A Report from the National Longitudinal Transition Study-2 (NLTS-2)* (NCSER 2011–3005). Menlo Park, CA: SRI International. Source: www.nlts2.org

Petersilia, J. (2000). *Doing Justice? Criminal Offenders with Developmental Disabilities.* CPRC Brief, 12 (4), California Policy Research Center, University of California.

Schalock, R. L., Buntinx, W. H. E., Borthwick-Duffy, S., Bradley, V., Craig, E. M., Coulter, D. L., Gomez, S. C., Lachapelle, Y., Luckasson, R. A., Reeve, A., Shogren, K. A., Snell, M. E., Spreat, S., Tass, M. J. Thompson, J. R., Verdugo, M. A., Wehmeyer, M. L., & Yeager, M. H. (2010). *Intellectual Disability: Definition, Classification, and System of Supports* (11th Edition). Washington, DC: American Association on Intellectual and Developmental Disabilities.

Schalock, R. L., Luckasson, R. A., Bradley, V., Buntinx, W. H. E., Lachapelle, Y., Shogren, K. A., Snell, M. E., Tass, M. J., Thompson, J. R., Verdugo, M. A., & Wehmeyer, M. L. (2012). Intellectual Disability: Definition, Classification, and System of Supports (11th Edition)—User's Guide. Washington, DC: American Association on Intellectual and Developmental Disabilities.

Schalock, R. L., & Luckasson, R. (2013). *Clinical Judgment* (2nd Edition). Washington, DC: American Association on Intellectual and Developmental Disabilities.

Schalock, R. L., & Luckasson, R. (2015). A systematic approach to subgroup classification in intellectual disability. *Intellectual and Developmental Disabilities, 53,* 358–366.

Scior, K. (2011). Public awareness, attitudes, and beliefs regarding intellectual disability: A systematic review. *Research in Developmental Disabilities, 32,* 2164–2182.

Sobsey, D. (1994). *Violence and Abuse in the Lives of People with Disabilities.* Baltimore: Paul H. Brookes Publishing.

Tassé, M. J., & Grover, M. D. (2013). American Association on Intellectual and Developmental Disabilities (pp. 122–125). In F. R. Volkmar (Ed.), *Encyclopedia of Autism Spectrum Disorders.* New York: Springer.

Tassé, M. J., & Mehling, M. H. (in press). Mental retardation [intellectual disability]: Historical changes in terminology. In E. Braaten (Ed.), *The SAGE Encyclopedia of Intellectual and Developmental Disorders*. Thousand Oaks, CA: Sage Publications.

Urbina, S. (2014). *Essentials of Psychological Testing* (2nd Edition). Hoboken, NJ: John Wiley & Sons.

U.S. Department of Education, Office of Special Education and Rehabilitative Services, Office of Special Education Programs. (2011). *30th Annual Report to Congress on the Implementation of the Individuals with Disabilities Education Act—2008*. Washington, DC: Author.

Wood, S. E., Packman, W., Howell S., & Bongar, B. (2014). A failure to implement: Analyzing state responses to the Supreme Court's directives in *Atkins v. Virginia* and suggestions for a national standard. *Psychiatry, Psychology and Law, 21(1)*, 16–45.

CHAPTER TWO

A Brief History of and Introduction to the Modern American Death Penalty

The death penalty is as old as civilization itself. Laws authorizing the death penalty as a punishment for crime go back to at least the Code of Hammurabi of the eighteenth century BCE, which authorized capital punishment for 25 different offenses. All ancient cultures used the death penalty, often unsparingly, and executed persons for a variety of offenses including blasphemy, witchcraft, sexual offenses (such as bestiality and sodomy), as well as robbery, rape, murder, and other more traditionally understood crimes of violence (Ruggiero, 1978). Widespread use of the death penalty as a punishment for crime (and as an instrument of social control) continued throughout antiquity, the Middle Ages, the Renaissance, and the Early Modern Period (Ruggiero, 1978).

Capital punishment made its way to the *"New World"* as part and parcel of the English legal system, which was imported in large part by most of the original colonies of North America. The first legal execution took place in Virginia in 1608 when George Kendall was put to death by hanging for espionage. Kendall was found guilty of being a Spanish spy. All told, approximately 14,500 executions have been carried out in the colonies and then by various states and the federal government after the nations' founding. This number does not include the thousands of individuals who were executed by lynching following nonjudicial proceedings.

When discussing the American death penalty, it is important to bear in mind that, throughout American history, there have been significant regional differences in the administration and application of capital punishment. For example, during the colonial period, the Puritanically rooted Northern colonies frequently imposed the death penalty for a number of crimes against morality (e.g., the Salem Witch Trials), while the Southern slaveholding colonies had more capital offenses (and carried out more executions) involving violations of property laws. Regional disparities persist to this day, with a majority of death sentences and executions being imposed and carried out in states that were formerly members of the Confederacy. In fact, if anything, the disparity is more pronounced today than at any other time in our nation's history. Not surprisingly, in all regions and at all times (including the present), the death penalty has been disproportionately used against black offenders, especially in cases involving white victims (an effect even more pronounced in cases where the white victim is also female; see Blume & Johnson, 2012; Bright, 1995).

For most of our nation's history, the legality of the death penalty (as opposed to its utility or morality) went unchallenged. Even in the states that abolished capital punishment relatively early (e.g., Michigan in 1846, Rhode Island in 1852, and Wisconsin in 1953), the demise of the death penalty had to do with its perceived morality, wisdom, or utility as opposed to whether it was a legally permissible method of punishment. The first death penalty case to be heard by the Supreme Court of the United States was more than 100 years after the founding of the Republic when, in *Wilkerson v. Utah* (1878), the Court tackled not whether the death penalty itself was legal but only whether death by firing squad was cruel and unusual punishment banned by the Eighth Amendment to the Constitution (and concluded it was not).

In the early twentieth century, the Supreme Court began to show more interest in capital cases. For example, the High Court overturned a number of capital convictions on the basis that a death-sentenced inmate's confession was involuntary (i.e., that his "will was overborne" by coercive police interrogation practices; see *Blackburn v. Alabama*, 1960; *Spano v. New York*, 1959; *Withrow v. Williams*, 1993).Most of these cases involved black defendants accused of the murder of someone white, most arose in the South, and in most of them, the interrogation "techniques" used by law enforcement were quite brutal. For example, in *Brown v. Mississippi* (1936), the Court held that the defendant's confession should not have been admitted at his trial because it was literally beaten out of him with a bullwhip. The local sheriff admitted as much: When asked if he had whipped the defendant, he replied, "not too much considering he was a negro" (*Brown v. Mississippi*, 1936).

Other famous capital cases of the pre–World War II era also involved criminal procedure, as opposed to death penalty–related legal issues. The famous "Scottsboro Boys" case is illustrative (*Powell v. Alabama*, 1932). In that case, nine young black defendants were accused of raping two white females on a train near rural Scottsboro, Alabama (*Powell v. Alabama*, 1932). After narrowly escaping being lynched, the defendants were charged with the (then) capital offense of rape. Because there was no clear right to appointed counsel for indigent defendants at the time, the local judge appointed the entire county bar to represent the defendants (*Powell v. Alabama*, 1932). Proving the old adage that "everybody's job is nobody's job," no attorney did any work at all to investigate the alleged victims' allegations or prepare the case for trial, and no one showed up to represent the defendants on the scheduled trial date (*Powell v. Alabama*, 1932). Counsel, unfamiliar with the case and having no time to prepare, was pressed into service, and the trials proceeded immediately. Despite quite flimsy evidence that the individuals charged were the perpetrators (or that the rapes had even occurred), the defendants were found guilty and sentenced to death based upon the testimony of the two unreliable "victims." After the Alabama Supreme Court affirmed their convictions and death sentences, the U.S. Supreme Court agreed to hear the case and concluded that the defendants were denied due process based on the lack of an "effective appointment of counsel" (*Powell v. Alabama*, 1932). The defendants were eventually, after several more trials, all exonerated. Despite the closer judicial scrutiny that death penalty cases often received in the first half of the twentieth century, the constitutional legitimacy of the death penalty remained a given.

After World War II, the use of the death penalty worldwide began to decline dramatically. Many countries in Europe [e.g., England, France, and Germany (by international mandate)] abolished capital punishment altogether (Patterson, 2006). In the United States, the number of death sentences imposed nationally dropped by approximately half (see Patterson, 2006). Some, but not all, of the reluctance to execute citizens had to do with the atrocities associated with Nazi Germany, but—regardless of the reasons—the death penalty was no longer embraced with the same enthusiasm by Americans as it was prior to World War II. The decrease in the number of death sentences and executions in the United States was especially noticeable in the states outside the old Confederacy.

The postwar period also saw an increased focus on and legal challenges to segregation and other forms of racial discrimination. Thurgood Marshall (who went on to become a Supreme Court Justice himself) and his cohorts at the NAACP (National Association for the Advancement of Colored People) Legal Defense Fund (LDF) were the architects of most of this litigation. Through their efforts, the Supreme Court declared a number of forms of segregation and discrimination in education, public accommodations, voting, and other areas to be unconstitutional (see *Brown v. Board of Education*, 1954; *Powers v. Ohio*, 1991; *Runyon v. McCrary*, 1976). But Marshall was also a staunch opponent of capital punishment. He had seen, in many cases personally, how it was used by the white power structure as a form of legal lynching (Banner, 2002). Over time and with the assistance of a number of others, including the brilliant young University of Pennsylvania Law School professor Anthony G. Amsterdam, Marshall devised a strategy to persuade the Supreme Court of the United States to invalidate the American death penalty (Banner, 2002).

A major obstacle to such a legal argument was the language of the Constitution itself. Several provisions of the Bill of Rights, including the Fifth, Sixth, and Fourteenth Amendments, explicitly mention deprivation of life and capital crimes. For example, the Due Process Clauses of the Fifth and Fourteenth Amendments state that no one "shall be deprived of life, liberty or property without due process of law." Thus, the framers clearly operated under the assumption that the death penalty was a legally permissible punishment. Further complicating matters was a (then) relatively orthodox view that the Eighth Amendment's ban on "cruel and unusual punishments" only barred criminal sanctions deemed excessive at the time it was ratified by the states in 1791, when capital punishment was clearly constitutional. The death penalty was legal (and widely used) in every state in the early years of the Republic.

However, the Court, or at least a majority thereof, took a more expansive view of what was a cruel and unusual punishment in the early years of the last century. In 1910, in *Weems v. United States* (1910), for example, the Court ruled that a 15-year sentence of "cadera temporeal" (i.e., hard and painful labor) for falsifying a public document was a cruel and unusual punishment. The Court reasoned that the meaning of the Eighth Amendment was not frozen in time but acquired new meaning as "public opinion becomes enlightened by public justice." (*Weems v. United States*, 1910). Applying contemporary standards, the High Court found that Weems's punishment ran afoul of the Eighth Amendment. Several decades later, the Court used similar reasoning in *Trop v. Dulles* (1958) in finding that a sentence of expatriation (stripping a person of his American citizenship) following a conviction of desertion during the Korean War was cruel and unusual. In doing so, the Court stated that the Eighth Amendment's Cruel and Unusual Punishment Clause draws its meaning from the "evolving standards of decency that mark the progress of a maturing society" (*Trop v. Dulles*, 1958).

Drawing on these and other legal developments, Marshall, Amsterdam, and others at LDF launched a multifaceted attack on capital punishment as administered in the United States. While the challenge was initially confined to the death penalty for the crime of rape, a punishment reserved almost exclusively for black men accused of sexually assaulting or attempting to sexually assault white women, the attorneys decided relatively quickly that they would attempt to intervene in all capital cases (Banner, 2002).[1] Their efforts were aided in 1963 by a (then) rare dissent from the denial of certiorari in *Rudolph v. Alabama* (1963), authored by Justice Arthur Goldberg. Rudolph had been sentenced to death in Alabama, convicted of raping a white woman. After the Alabama Supreme Court affirmed Rudolph's conviction and death sentence, his lawyers asked the Supreme Court of the United States to examine his case (i.e., to grant certiorari). The Court declined to do so, but Justice Goldberg, joined by Justices William J. Brennan Jr. and William O. Douglas, took the unusual step of saying that they believed the Court should entertain the question whether the imposition of the death penalty for the crime of rape violated the Eighth and Fourteenth Amendments. Since it takes only four of the nine justices to agree to hear a case, and since three members of the Court appeared poised to entertain a constitutional challenge to the death penalty, the "game was afoot."

The Legal Defense Fund redoubled its efforts and attempted to intervene in all capital cases with an array of legal challenges including arguments that state death sentencing schemes were unconstitutional due to (1) racial discrimination (primarily in cases involving the crime of rape), (2) the systematic exclusion of jurors who had moral reservations about capital punishment, (3) the failure to provide standards for jurors to use in determining whether someone should be sentenced to death, and (4) a more core challenge to capital punishment itself (i.e., that the death penalty itself was unconstitutional in all cases because it was inconsistent with "evolving standards of decency"; see *Rudolph v. Alabama*, 1963). The LDF's strategy, sometimes referred to as the "moratorium" strategy, was designed to halt all executions in the United States while the legal attacks on individual death sentences and the death penalty itself played out (Banner, 2002). The rationale behind the strategy was that if executions could be temporarily halted, then the American people (including members of the Supreme Court) would realize that capital punishment was a thing of the past. The strategy was at least partially successful: 1968 marked the first year in the history of the nation that no one was executed (Banner, 2002).

The year of 1968 also saw LDF's first major success in the Supreme Court decision in *Witherspoon v. Illinois* (1968). The Court reversed

Witherspoon's death sentence because approximately half of the jury pool was excused from serving based on an Illinois statute providing that any potential juror who had "conscientious scruples against capital punishment" was not qualified to serve as a juror in a capital case (*Witherspoon v. Illinois*, 1968). After the jury pool was purged of the "conscientious objectors" (in the trial judge's words), Witherspoon was convicted of capital murder and sentenced to death (*Witherspoon v. Illinois*, 1968). While the Court rebuffed Witherspoon's argument that such a jury was more likely to find him guilty was not sufficiently supported by empirical data (even though it was), it did conclude that a death sentence imposed by such a jury did not express "the conscience of the community on the ultimate question of life or death" (*Witherspoon v. Illinois*, 1968). The Court noted that, given the large number of Americans who had qualms about capital punishment, a jury such as Witherspoon's spoke only for a "distinct and dwindling minority" (*Witherspoon v. Illinois*, 1968). Since many states used a similar practice, the *Witherspoon* decision resulted in the removal of a significant number of the nation's condemned inmates from death row (Banner, 2002).

The job not finished, LDF pressed on. In 1970, the Supreme Court granted certiorari to resolve the remaining two procedural challenges to various states' capital sentencing laws: (1) whether juries tasked with deciding whether a capital defendant should live or die must be provided with standards to guide the life or death decision and (2) whether the sentencing hearing needed to be separated from the determination of whether the defendant was guilty (or not guilty) of the charged offenses (i.e., whether capital trials must be bifurcated).[2] In the two cases raising the issues, *McGautha v. California* (1971) and *Crampton v. Ohio*, a majority of the Court said no to both. As for the alleged need for standards to shape the jury's life/death decision, the Court held that it was impossible to determine before the fact what factors jurors should consider in making the "awesome" determination of selecting which capital defendants should live or die (Banner, 2002). And on the need for the separation of the guilt-or-innocence and sentencing decisions into distinct proceedings, the Court held that while doing so might be a better method of structuring a capital trial, the Constitution did not require states to engage in the best practices identified by academic elites (Banner, 2002).

To most observers, this appeared to be the end of the road for LDF's legal assault on the American death penalty, and court watchers predicted that executions would soon resume. But then, to almost everyone's surprise, the Court almost immediately decided to address the issue of the constitutionality of the death penalty head-on, and in *Furman v. Georgia*

(1972), the Court ordered briefing and argument on the question of whether capital punishment, as then administered, violated the Eighth Amendment's Cruel and Unusual Punishment Clause (*Furman v. Georgia*, 1972).[3] And then, just a year after *McGuatha* and *Crampton*, the Court (*Furman v. Georgia*, 1972), by a bare 5–4 majority, invalidated all then existing death penalty statutes. However, each of the five justices in the majority wrote their own opinions, and no clear consensus emerged as to why the death penalty, which had been upheld against constitutional attack just the year before (see *McGautha v. California*, 1971),[4] was now unconstitutional. At the risk of oversimplification, the constitutional rub arose from the fact that the death penalty was imposed in only a fraction of cases in which it was legally available. Several of the justices could divine no rational basis explaining why some offenders were sentenced to death while others were spared. For this reason, the Court found that all state systems of capital punishment allowed for the arbitrary and capricious imposition of capital punishment (see *Gregg v. Georgia*, 1976).[5] Justice Brennan's concurring opinion captures this sentiment: "When the punishment of death is inflicted in a trivial number of the cases in which it is legally available, the conclusion is virtually inescapable that it is being inflicted arbitrarily. Indeed, it smacks of little more than a lottery system" (*Furman v. Georgia*, 1972; p. 293). There was, in short, no "rational basis that could differentiate in those terms the few who die from the many who go to prison" (*Furman v. Georgia*, 1972). Justices White and Stewart echoed similar concerns, with Stewart comparing being sentenced to death to being struck by lightning (*Furman v. Georgia*, 1972).[6] The fear that racial discrimination was playing a significant role in the death selection process was also of grave concern to several members of the Court, with Justice Douglas observing, for example, that the state capital punishment schemes were "pregnant with discrimination" (*Furman v. Georgia*, 1972).[7] If forced to find a ground of common agreement among the justices, it was that jurors had complete and unguided discretion in deciding whether a capital defendant should receive the death penalty or life in prison (*Gregg v. Georgia*, 1976).[8] This— in turn—led to the arbitrary imposition of capital punishment.

Furman was an enormously controversial decision. To many, it appeared that the Supreme Court had (once again) intruded on state's rights. Following other controversial and unpopular criminal procedure decisions in the High Court, such as *Gideon v. Wainwright* (requiring states to provide counsel to indigent defendants) (1963), *Mapp v. Ohio* (limiting states from conducting warrantless searches and seizures) (1961), and *Miranda v. Arizona* (requiring states to inform suspects being interrogated of the right to remain silent and to counsel) (1966), and not even taking into account resistance to the Court's school desegregation and other civil rights cases (*Brown v. Board of Education*, 1954), the Court's decision to invalidate all existing capital punishment laws solidified the majority public perception that the justices in Washington coddled violent criminals in disregard of public safety. *Furman* was the lead story in every major paper in the country the day after the Court's decision, with law enforcement officers and state and local politicians predicting murder and mayhem (Banner, 2002).

Despite predictions from many quarters that *Furman* marked the end of the American death penalty, states rushed to create capital sentencing schemes that they hoped would satisfy the new constitutional standard (or at least satisfy one of the justices in the *Furman* majority). The task, however, was not so simple. As described, different Supreme Court justices had identified different flaws in the various capital punishment schemes. States therefore took different approaches to try and remedy the legal problems identified by members of the Court.

Again, at the risk of oversimplification, the post-*Furman* statutes fell primarily into two broad categories: mandatory death penalty statutes and guided discretion statutes. Both types of new death penalty laws were intended to reduce the role of jury discretion. The mandatory statutes attempted to cure arbitrariness by eliminating jury discretion; if a defendant was found guilty of a capital offense, then the death penalty was imposed—no ifs, ands, or buts. The guided discretion statutes, on the other hand, attempted to reduce arbitrariness by creating new procedures. The central features of most guided discretion schemes included a bifurcated trial (separating the issues of guilt-or-innocence and punishment into two distinct phases of the trial), the creation of statutory aggravating circumstances limiting who could be sentenced to death (e.g., murder committed during the commission of burglary, rape, or robbery), permitting the jury to consider "mitigating" circumstances about the defendant's life or background,[9] and mandatory appellate review by the state's highest court (including proportionality review to determine whether the death penalty was excessive in light of sentences imposed in similar cases).

And then there was Texas. Texas enacted a "hybrid" scheme. If a defendant was convicted of capital murder, then at the punishment phase of the trial, the jury was asked to answer two questions. The first query asked whether the defendant committed capital murder deliberately (which given that intent to kill was an element of capital murder was not much of an impediment to sentencing a defendant to death). The second special issue asked whether the defendant posed a continuing threat to society (Texas Penal Code Annotated, 1974). If the jury answered the two questions in the affirmative, then the judge was required to sentence the defendant to death. By 1976, the new laws made their way back to the Supreme Court of the United States. The Court upheld the guided discretion statutes but held that the mandatory statutes violated the Eighth Amendment (*Gregg v. Georgia*, 1976; *Jurek v. Texas*, 1976; *Proffit v. Florida*, 1976; *Roberts v. Louisiana*, 1976; *Woodson v. North Carolina*, 1976).[10]

Gregg v. Georgia (1976) was the lead case. The Court first addressed the global question whether—regardless of the procedures used—the death penalty was a constitutionally permissible mode of punishment. Justice Potter Stewart, writing for the majority, found that it was, noting that "[d]espite the continuing debate, dating back to the 19th century, over the morality and utility of capital punishment, it is now evident that a large proportion of American society continues to regard it as an appropriate and necessary criminal sanction" (*Gregg v. Georgia*, 1976, p. 179).[11] Thus, the Court concluded the death penalty was not per se violative of the Eighth Amendment. Then turning to the Georgia statute itself, the Court found that it passed constitutional muster even though "some jury discretion still exists" because "the discretion to be exercised is controlled by clear and objective standards so as to produce non-discriminatory application." (*Gregg v. Georgia,* 1976).[12] The Court concluded:

> In summary, the concerns expressed in Furman that the penalty of death not be imposed in an arbitrary or capricious manner can be met by a carefully drafted statute that ensures that the sentencing authority is given adequate information and guidance. As a general proposition these concerns are best met by a system that provides for a bifurcated proceeding at which the sentencing authority is apprised of the information relevant to the imposition of sentence and provided with standards to guide its use of the information. (*Gregg v. Georgia*, 1976)[13]

The Court also emphasized the importance of appellate review:

> As an important additional safeguard against arbitrariness and caprice, the Georgia statutory scheme provides for automatic appeal of all death sentences to the State's Supreme Court. That court is required by statute to review each sentence of death and determine whether it was imposed under the influence of passion or prejudice, whether the evidence supports the jury's finding of a statutory aggravating circumstance, and whether the sentence is disproportionate compared to those sentences imposed in similar cases. (*Gregg v. Georgia*, 1976)

The mandatory statutes, on the other hand, did not fare so well. In *Woodson v. North Carolina* (1976), the Court reasoned that such statutes were out of step with "contemporary" standards of decency because they eliminated the jury's essential role in maintaining a "link" between "community values" and the capital punishment system (1976). In the Court's view, a capital jury must be allowed to take into account the "diverse frailties" of mankind (*Woodson v. North Carolina*, 1976). The Court also believed that the mandatory statutes only "papered over" the problem of unguided and unchecked discretion because juries would refuse to convict many defendants of murder if forced with such a Draconian choice (*Woodson v. North Carolina*, 1976). Due to the uniqueness of the death penalty, the Court held that the Constitution required that the sentencer could not be precluded from considering the "character and record of the individual offender and the circumstances of the particular offense" (*Woodson v. North Carolina*, 1976).

As for Texas's quasi-then-mandatory capital punishment scheme, which required a death sentence if the jury concluded that the murder was deliberate and that the murderer posed a future danger, the Court—in a decision many legal observers believe it ultimately regretted—held its nose and approved the statute despite grave reservations that the Texas scheme, like true mandatory schemes, did not allow for the consideration of most mitigating evidence. Those reservations proved to be true, and the Court has been forced on multiple occasions to revisit the workings of the Texas law (see *Penry v. Lynaugh*, 1989; p. 302; *Penry v. Johnson*, 2001).

Thus, the American death penalty was back in business.[14] The first few years after *Gregg* saw a Court highly engaged in managing—and in the view of some critics micromanaging—state capital punishment systems. Relying on the Eighth Amendment principle that "death is different," (1976) the Court considered and found wanting state rules limiting the presentation or consideration of a capital defendant's mitigating evidence (*Lockett v. Ohio*, 1978; *Eddings v. Oklahoma*, 1982),[15] invalidated overly broad and vague statutory aggravating circumstances (see *Godfrey v. Georgia*, 1980),[16] limited consideration of evidence in capital sentencing not disclosed to the defense (see *Gardner v. Florida*, 1977),[17] and struck down other procedures the Court believed created a risk of arbitrary and capricious imposition of the death penalty.

Beginning in the mid-1980s, however, the Court began to take a much more laissez-faire approach to the regulation of state death penalty laws, believing that, within fairly broad limits, states should have the authority to run their capital punishment systems without federal judicial oversight. This trend continued throughout the 1990s and remains, at least for now, as the dominant view. That being said, however, in the last 15 years, the Court has carefully examined the competency of counsel in capital cases, especially in regard to the development and presentation of mitigating evidence. In the majority of the cases it has reviewed on the issue, the Court has concluded that capital defendants were deprived of their Sixth Amendment right to the effective assistance of counsel (*Williams v. Taylor*, 2000; *Wiggins v. Smith*, 2003; *Rompilla v. Beard*, 2005).[18] For example, in *Porter v. McCollum* (2009), the Court concluded that George Porter's trial counsel failed to adequately represent him because by failing to gather and present evidence during his capital sentencing hearing of his heroism during his military service in the Korean War. In the course of ordering a new sentencing trial, the Court described Porter "as a veteran who was both wounded and decorated for his active participation in two major engagements during the Korean war; his combat service left him unfortunately a traumatized, changed man" (*Porter v. McCollum*, 2009). The Court has similarly found trial lawyers to perform incompetently for failing to discover and present evidence of sexual abuse, low intellectual functioning, and brain damage (*Wiggins v. Smith*, 2003).

Another more recent doctrinal development is the Court's recognition of the fundamental role that the jury plays in capital sentencing. Some states, such as Florida and Arizona, responded to *Furman* by allowing judges—as opposed to juries—to determine whether the prosecution had proven the existence of a statutory aggravating circumstance and whether the defendant should be sentenced to death (or life in prison). After initially approving such systems, the Court (eventually) reversed course and held that the Sixth Amendment right to jury trial requires that a jury— not a judge—be tasked with the responsibility for finding any factors that make the death penalty a possible punishment (see *Ring v. Arizona*, 2002; *Hurst v. Florida*, 2016). The still open question is whether juries (again as opposed to judges) must make the actual sentencing decision.

Finally, a theme in *Furman* and *Gregg*, reaffirmed repeatedly over the last 40 years and especially relevant to this book, is that capital punishment should be reserved for the most culpable offenders who commit the most heinous crimes. Justice Anthony Kennedy recently stated that "the death penalty is reserved for a narrow category of crimes and offenders" (*Roper v. Simmons*, 2005)—for the "worst of the worst" and not for the "average" murderer (*Furman v. Georgia*, 1972).[19] This worst-of-the-worst principle influenced the Court in *Gregg* to conclude that the death penalty was not disproportionate in all cases because while "[i]t is an extreme sanction, [it is] suitable to the most extreme of crimes" (*Gregg v. Georgia*, 1976).[20] Under the new Georgia statute requiring jurors to consider aggravating and mitigating circumstances, the Court found the jurors were forced to consider "the particularized nature of the crime and the particularized characteristics of the individual defendant" (*Gregg v. Georgia*, 1976). By doing so, the Court believed "[n]o longer can a jury wantonly and freakishly impose the death sentence" (*Gregg v. Georgia*, 1976). The Court has made clear on a number of occasions that capital punishment should be "reserved for those crimes that are 'so grievous an affront to humanity that the only adequate response may be the penalty of death'" (*Kennedy v. Louisiana*, 2008).[21]

The commitment to reserve capital punishment for the "worst of the worst" and conversely to prevent "average murderers" from being sentenced to death manifests itself most clearly in two discrete areas of the Court's capital punishment jurisprudence. First, the Court has—in theory—confined the imposition of the death penalty to "a narrow category of the most serious crimes" (*Atkins v. Virginia*, 2002). Thus the death penalty may not be imposed for nonhomicide offenses, such as armed robbery and rape (see *Coker v. Georgia*, 1977; *Enmund v. Florida*, 1982; *Kennedy v. Louisiana*, 2008).[22] Even for those found guilty of murder, the requirement that a state prove an aggravating circumstance before a defendant is eligible to be sentenced to death is intended to provide the required narrowing of the class of murderers eligible for the death penalty and reserve the sentence for only the worst or most extreme murders. Thus, states are required to "give narrow and precise definition to the aggravating factors that can result in a capital sentence" (*Roper v. Simmons*, 2005). Furthermore, it is not enough that an aggravating circumstance "genuinely narrow[s] the class of persons eligible for the death penalty"; it must also "reasonably justify the imposition of a more severe sentence on the defendant compared to others found guilty of murder" (*Zant v. Stephens*, 1983). Where the state fails to narrowly and precisely define an aggravating circumstance, it "fail[s] adequately to channel the sentencing decision" as required by *Gregg* (see *Godfrey v. Georgia*, 1980). As a result, the Court has invalidated aggravating circumstances broadly defined to allow the imposition of the death penalty upon a defendant whose "crimes cannot be said to have reflected a consciousness materially more 'depraved' than that of any person guilty of murder" (*Godfrey v. Georgia*, 1980). In *Godfrey v. Georgia*, for example, the Court considered the Georgia aggravating circumstance that made a murder that was found to be "outrageously or wantonly vile, horrible and inhuman" eligible for capital punishment. The Court concluded that "[a] person of ordinary sensibility could fairly characterize almost every murder as 'outrageously or wantonly vile, horrible and inhuman'" and thus held that the aggravating circumstance could not be used unless the state clarified its meaning (and the murders it was intended to apply to) (*Godfrey v. Georgia*, 1980).

The Court has also prohibited the imposition of the death penalty on those deemed less culpable than the worst offender, holding that its "narrowing jurisprudence . . . seeks to ensure that only the most deserving of execution are put to death" (*Atkins v. Virginia*, 2002). In order to do so, the Court has held that "[i]n any capital case a defendant has wide latitude to raise as a mitigating factor 'any aspect of [his or her] character or record' . . . as a basis for a sentence less than death" (*Roper v. Simmons*, 2005).[23] Thus, in capital cases, defendants may present virtually any kind of evidence they think will help persuade the jury to show mercy. Common types of mitigating evidence presented in capital cases include evidence of mental illness or impairment, low intellectual functioning, child abuse, intoxication, good behavior in prison, and the like. Additionally, the Court has barred the imposition of the death penalty on certain individuals deemed categorically undeserving of the death penalty. In *Enmund v. Florida* (1982) and *Tison v. Arizona* (1987), for example, the Court held that persons guilty of murder as an accessory but who did not actually kill could be sentenced to death only if they were major participants in the criminal offense and showed deliberate indifference to human life. Then, in *Atkins v. Virginia* (2002), as will be discussed in more detail in the next chapter, the Court created a categorical bar to execution for persons with intellectual disability (formerly classified as mental retardation), finding, "[i]f the culpability of the average murderer is insufficient to justify the most extreme sanction available to the State, the lesser culpability of the mentally retarded offender surely does not merit that form of retribution" (2002). Several years later, the Court similarly found that juvenile offenders "cannot with reliability be classified among the worst offenders" and barred the execution of offenders who committed a crime before turning 18 in *Roper v. Simmons* (2005). The Court has also determined that individuals who have become insane while on death row, even if they were completely sane at the time they committed the capital offense, cannot be executed unless their sanity is restored (*Ford v. Wainwright*, 1986).

In a similar vein, the Court has attempted to eliminate other forms of arbitrariness in the imposition of the death penalty, particularly arbitrariness resulting from racial discrimination. Multiple justices in *Furman* based their decision, at least in part, on the fact that the death penalty was disproportionately imposed on African Americans (*Furman v. Georgia*, 1972).[24] Since then, the Court has (in theory) "engaged in 'unceasing efforts' to eradicate racial prejudice" in the administration of capital punishment and the criminal justice system as a whole (*McCleskey v. Kemp*, 1987). For example, the Court has prohibited the exercise of prosecutorial discretion to seek the death penalty on the basis of race (*McCleskey v. Kemp*, 1987),[25] prohibited racially biased prosecutorial arguments (*McCleskey v. Kemp*, 1987),[26] prohibited prosecutors from exercising peremptory challenges to potential jurors on the basis of race (*McCleskey v. Kemp*, 1987),[27] and allowed defendants in capital cases to ask potential jurors about any racial biases they might harbor (*Turner v. Murray*, 1986).[28] However, the Court "blinked" when it was confronted with overwhelming statistical evidence of invidious racial discrimination at work in the Georgia capital punishment scheme. By a 5–4 vote, the Court determined that Warren McClesky's sophisticated (and unchallenged) statistical evidence that, controlling for other relevant factors, defendants charged with killing white victims were 4.3 times more likely to be sentenced to death and that black defendants convicted of the murder of a white victim were 2.4 times more likely to receive the ultimate punishment failed to prove a constitutional violation because it did not establish that the prosecutor or jury acted with a specific discriminatory purpose (*McCleskey v. Kemp*, 1987).

The attempts of the Court to make the administration of the death penalty more reliable and less arbitrary have been largely unsuccessful. The same types of arbitrariness identified by the Court's majority in *Furman* (infrequency, race and class discrimination, inconsistency of application) persist to this day. These failures have led former and current members of the Court who once supported capital punishment to question whether its attempts to regulate the capital punishment regimes were worth the candle. Justice Lewis Powell, for example, said after his retirement that if he could change one vote during his 15-year career as a Supreme Court justice, it would be his majority decision upholding the Georgia death penalty scheme in *McCleskey* (Jeffries, 2001).[29] Justice Powell later expressed that he had "come to think that capital punishment should be abolished" and that it "serves no useful purpose" (Mandery, 2013). Justice Harry Blackmun concluded late in his career that the Court's efforts to curb capital punishment's flaws had been an abject failure, and he stated he would no longer "tinker with the machinery of death" (*Callins v. Collins*, 1994).[30] Justice John Paul Stevens has made clear in a number of recent speeches that the death penalty is an irreparably flawed government program (Mandery, 2013; *Baze v. Rees*, 2008).[31] And most recently, Justice Stephen Breyer called for full briefing on the constitutionality of the death penalty as a whole (*Glossip v. Gross*, 2015).[32] In his dissenting opinion in a recent case involving lethal injection protocols, Justice Breyer, joined by Justice Ruth Bader Ginsburg, stated:

> In 1976, the Court thought that the constitutional infirmities in the death penalty could be healed; the Court in effect delegated significant responsibility to the States to develop procedures that would protect against those constitutional problems. Almost 40 years of studies, surveys, and experience strongly indicate, however, that this effort has failed. Today's administration of the death penalty involves three fundamental constitutional defects: (1) serious unreliability, (2) arbitrariness in application, and

(3) unconscionably long delays that undermine the death penalty's penological purpose. Perhaps as a result, (4) most places within the United States have abandoned its use. (*Glossip v. Gross*, 2015)

According to Justice Breyer, the first three considerations—unreliability, arbitrariness, and delays—make the punishment cruel; the widespread abandonment of the practice makes it unusual (*Glossip v. Gross*, 2015). Justice Breyer found that these unresolved and unresolvable issues make it "highly likely that the death penalty violates the Eighth Amendment" and tasked litigators to raise these issues with the Court (*Glossip v. Gross*, 2015).

Lawyers for condemned death row inmates, as they did after Justice Goldberg's dissent from the denial of certiorari in *Rudolph v. Alabama*, have taken up the Justice's challenge and are once again raising claims attacking the legal foundations of the modern American death penalty. It remains to be seen when or even if the Court will again agree to decide whether the death penalty is a constitutional punishment.

However, in closing, it is important to note that regardless of what the Supreme Court does, the death penalty appears to have fallen out of favor in the United States. Since the late 1990s, the number of states that retain the death penalty has dropped from 38 to 31. Four others currently have a moratorium in place imposed by governors (States Without the Death Penalty). Many of the states that still have capital punishment statutes on the books are "de facto" abolitionist jurisdictions having no one (or almost no one) on death row. The number of persons both sentenced to death and executed each year has also steadily dropped nationwide, with both—as this book goes to press—having reached their lowest numbers in several decades (Death Penalty Fact Sheet). Public opinion is also turning against capital punishment with support for the death penalty now hovering around 50 percent. Scholars and pundits debate the causes (and stability) of these trend lines, but it is important to note that the American people, not necessarily the Supreme Court, may have the final say on whether the death penalty is sound social policy.

Against this historical and doctrinal backdrop, we will next discuss in more detail the Supreme Court's decision in *Atkins v. Virginia* (2002), which—at bottom—is the reason this book exists.

Notes

1. While state practices varied, at that time the death penalty was a potential punishment for murder, rape, robbery, and kidnapping.

2. In most states, the question of sentencing in capital cases was settled in what was referred to as a "unitary" proceeding. After hearing the evidence and

receiving instructions from the trial judge, the jury would deliberate and decide whether the defendant was guilty of the capital offense. If the defendant was found guilty, the jury would decide whether or not they recommended mercy. A finding of guilt with a recommendation of mercy resulted in a life sentence; a finding of guilt without a recommendation of mercy meant that the defendant would be sentenced to death.

3. *Furman* was actually five consolidated cases from five different states, but in the legal lexicon, the cases are known as *Furman v. Georgia*, 408 U.S. 238 (1972).

4. *See McGautha*, p. 193: rejecting the argument that absence of standards to guide jury's discretion in death penalty sentencing was "fundamentally lawless" and violated the Fourteenth Amendment.

5. "Because of the uniqueness of the death penalty, Furman held that it could not be imposed under sentencing procedures that created a substantial risk that it would be inflicted in an arbitrary and capricious manner" (*Gregg v. Georgia*, 1976; p. 188).

6. Justice White stated: "the death penalty is exacted with great infrequency even for the most atrocious crimes and . . . there is no meaningful basis for distinguishing the few cases in which it is imposed from the many cases in which it is not" (*Furman v. Georgia*, 1972; p. 313). Justice Stewart concluded: "the Eighth and Fourteenth Amendments cannot tolerate the infliction of a sentence of death under legal systems that permit this unique penalty to be so wantonly and freakishly imposed" (p. 310). Stewart, concurring, went on to say:

> These death sentences are cruel and unusual in the same way that being struck by lightning is cruel and unusual. For, of all the people convicted of rapes and murders in 1967 and 1968, many just as reprehensible as these, the petitioners are among a capriciously selected random handful upon whom the sentence of death has in fact been imposed. My concurring Brothers have demonstrated that, if any basis can be discerned for the selection of these few to be sentenced to die, it is the constitutionally impermissible basis of race (pp. 309–310).

Justice White voiced similar objections to imposition of capital punishment, stating: "the death penalty is exacted with great infrequency even for the most atrocious crimes and that there is no meaningful basis for distinguishing the few cases in which it is imposed from the many cases in which it is not" (p. 313).

7. For example, in Justice Douglas's view, it was "incontestable that the death penalty inflicted on one defendant is 'unusual' if it discriminates against him by reason of his race, religion, wealth, social position, or class, or if it is imposed under a procedure that gives room for the play of such prejudices" (p. 242). Justice Marshall agreed:

> It is immediately apparent that Negroes were executed far more often than whites in proportion to their percentage of the population. Studies indicate that while the higher rate of execution among Negroes is partially due to a higher rate of crime, there is evidence of racial discrimination. Racial or other discriminations should not be surprising (pp. 364–365).

8. See *Gregg*, 428 U.S. at 189. ("Furman mandates that where discretion is afforded a sentencing body on a matter so grave as the determination of whether a human life should be taken or spared, that discretion must be suitably directed and limited as to minimize the risk of wholly arbitrary and capricious action.")

9. By "mitigating" circumstances, we refer to facts about the defendant's life and background that do not excuse the crime, that is, are not a legal defense to the capital offense, but that might (depending on the jury's assessment of the evidence) lessen or "mitigate" the punishment imposed. Common examples of mitigating circumstances are child abuse, substance abuse, mental illness, or impairment not rising to the legal level of insanity, and the like.

10. The Court granted certiorari in five cases. *Gregg v. Georgia*, 428 U.S. 153 (1976), *Proffit v. Florida*, 428 U.S. 242 (1976), and *Jurek v. Texas*, 428 U.S. 262 (1976) involved guided discretion statutes of various types that were deemed constitutional. *Woodson v. North Carolina* 428 U.S. 280 (1976) and *Roberts v. Louisiana*, 428 U.S. 325 (1976), involved mandatory statutes, which were invalidated.

11. Justice Stewart continued:

> The most marked indication of society's endorsement of the death penalty for murder is the legislative response to Furman. The legislatures of at least [thirty-five] States have enacted new statutes that provide for the death penalty for at least some crimes that result in the death of another person. And the Congress of the United States, in 1974, enacted a statute providing the death penalty for aircraft piracy that results in death. These recently adopted statutes have attempted to address the concerns expressed by the Court in Furman primarily (i) by specifying the factors to be weighed and the procedures to be followed in deciding when to impose a capital sentence, or (ii) by making the death penalty mandatory for specified crimes. But all of the post-Furman statutes make clear that capital punishment itself has not been rejected by the elected representatives of the people. (pp. 179–181)

12. *Id.* at 198 (quoting *Coley v. State*, 204 S.E.2d 612, 615 (Ga. 1974)).

13. *Id.* at 195. In short, Georgia's new sentencing procedures require as a prerequisite to the imposition of the death penalty, specific jury findings as to the circumstances of the crime or the character of the defendant. Moreover, to guard further against a situation comparable to that presented in *Furman*, the Supreme Court of Georgia compares each death sentence with the sentences imposed on similarly situated defendants to ensure that the sentence of death in a particular case is not disproportionate. On their face, these procedures seem to satisfy the concerns of *Furman*. No longer should there be "no meaningful basis for distinguishing the few cases in which [the death penalty] is imposed from the many cases in which it is not." *Id.* at 198 (alteration in original) (quoting *Furman v. Georgia*, 408 U.S. 238, 313 (1972) (White, J., concurring)).

14. Most states with mandatory statutes that were found wanting in *Woodson* (e.g., North Carolina and South Carolina) quickly enacted death penalty statutes modeled on Georgia's guided discretion system.

15. See *Lockett v. Ohio*, 438 U.S. 586, 604–05 (1978) (holding that the judge should not be precluded from considering, as a mitigating factor, anything about

the defendant's character or record that he argues is a basis for a lesser sentence); *Eddings v. Oklahoma*, 455 U.S. 104, 116–17 (1982) (holding that it is not enough for a court to consider only age as a mitigating factor but must take into consideration all those that are relevant).

16. See *Godfrey v. Georgia*, 446 U.S. 420, 431–33 (1980) (holding that a state must define aggravating circumstances in a manner that is not so broad as to encompass every or nearly every murder).

17. See *Gardner v. Florida*, 430 U.S. 349, 358 (1977) (holding that a defendant may not be sentenced to death on the basis of information he has no opportunity to meet or explain).

18. See *Williams v. Taylor*, 529 U.S. 362 (2000) (holding that the defendant was deprived effective assistance of counsel because the attorney failed to introduce evidence that he was "borderline mentally retarded," that he did not advance beyond the sixth grade, and that prison guards stated that he was nonviolent and would thrive in a more structured environment.); *Wiggins v. Smith*, 539 U.S. 510, 523 (2003) (holding that the relevant inquiry into effective assistance of counsel is whether or not counsel's investigation leading him to not introduce evidence of mitigation was itself reasonable); *Rompilla v. Beard*, 545 U.S 374, 393 (2005) (holding that the likelihood of a different result if the evidence would have come in is sufficient to undermine confidence in the outcome that was reached at sentencing).

19. In *Furman*, Justice Brennan responded to the states' argument that death sentences were inflicted only in extreme cases, saying "[i]nformed selectivity, of course, is a value not to be denigrated." However, the justice found that the low levels of infliction of capital punishment made it "highly implausible that only the worst criminals or the criminals who commit the worst crimes are selected for this punishment" (408 U.S. pp. 293–94 (Brennan, J., concurring)). In fact, he noted that if "Furman or his crime illustrates the 'extreme,' then nearly all murderers and their murders are also 'extreme'" (p. 294).

20. *Gregg*, 428 U.S. p. 187. The Court further found that the death penalty served the penological goal, or social purpose, of retribution when imposed for the worst crimes:

> Indeed, the decision that capital punishment may be the appropriate sanction in extreme cases is an expression of the community's belief that certain crimes are themselves so grievous an affront to humanity that the only adequate response may be the penalty of death. (*id.* p. 184)

21. *Kennedy v. Louisiana*, 554 U.S. 407, 437 (2008) (quoting *Gregg*, 428 U.S. pp. 184, 187).

22. See *Kennedy* 554 U.S. at 437 (2008) (prohibiting the imposition of the death penalty for the rape of a child); *Enmund v. Florida*, 458 U.S. 782, 797 (1982) (prohibiting the imposition of the death penalty for felony murder where the defendant did not kill, attempt to kill, or intend to kill); *Coker v. Georgia*, 433 U.S. 584 (1977) (prohibiting the imposition of the death penalty for the rape of an adult woman).

23. Quoting *Lockett v. Ohio*, 438 U.S. 586, 604 (1978).

24. 408 U.S. at 242 (Douglas, J., concurring) ("It would seem to be incontestable that the death penalty inflicted on one defendant is 'unusual' if it discriminates against him by reason of his race, religion, wealth, social position, or class, or if it is imposed under a procedure that gives room for the play of such prejudices."); *id.* at 310 (Stewart, J., concurring) ("My concurring Brothers have demonstrated that, if any basis can be discerned for the selection of these few to be sentenced to die, it is the constitutionally impermissible basis of race."); *id.* at 364–365 (Marshall, J., concurring) ("It is immediately apparent that Negroes were executed far more often than whites in proportion to their percentage of the population. Studies indicate that while the higher rate of execution among Negroes is partially due to a higher rate of crime, there is evidence of racial discrimination. Racial or other discriminations should not be surprising.").

25. *Id.* at 309, n. 30 (citing *Wayte v. United States*, 470 U.S. 598, 608 (1985)).

26. *Id.* (citing *Donnelly v. DeChristoforo*, 416 U.S. 637, 643 (1974)).

27. *Id.* (citing *Batson v. Kentucky*, 476 U.S. 79 (1986)).

28. *Turner v. Murray*, 476 U.S. 28, 36–37 (1986). Recognizing that the modern-era death penalty statutes continue to leave death sentences to the jury, the Court found capital sentencing proceedings are particularly susceptible to racial discrimination: "Because of the range of discretion entrusted to a jury in a capital sentencing hearing, there is a unique opportunity for racial prejudice to operate but remain undetected" (p. 35).

29. John Jeffries (2001), at 451–453 (reporting that Justice Powell said in 1991 that he would change his vote in *McCleskey v. Kemp*, 481 U.S. 279 (1987)).

30. *Callins v. Collins*, 510 U.S. 1141, 1145 (1994) (Blackmun, J., dissenting from the denial of certiorari).

31. Mandery, *supra* note 104, at 439–440 (describing multiple speeches in which Justice Stevens stated he regretted upholding Texas's post-*Furman* death penalty statute in *Jurek v. Texas*, 428 U.S. 262 (1976)); *see also Baze v. Rees*, 553 U.S. 35, 71 (2008) (Stevens, J., dissenting) (finding that, though it did not "justify a refusal to respect precedents that remain a part of our law," based on his own experience, "the imposition of the death penalty represents 'the pointless and needless extinction of life with only marginal contributions to any discernible social or public purposes'").

32. *Glossip v. Gross*, 135 S. Ct. 2726, 2755 (2015) (Breyer, J., dissenting).

References

Atkins v. Virginia, 536 U.S. 304, 319 (2002).

Banner, S. (2002). *The Death Penalty: An American History*. Cambridge, MA: Harvard University Press.

Baze v. Rees, 553 U.S. 35 (2008).

Blackburn v. Alabama, 361 U.S. 199, 210 (1960).

Blume, J. H., & Johnson, S. L. (2012). Unholy parallels between *McCleskey v. Kemp* and *Plessy v. Ferguson*: Why *McCleskey* (still) matters. *Ohio State Journal of Criminal Law, 10,* 37–63.

Bright, S. B. (1995). Symposium: Discrimination, death and Denial: The tolerance of racial discrimination in infliction of the death penalty. *Santa Clara Law Review, 35,* 433–483.

Brown v. Board of Education, 347 U.S. 483, 486, 495 (1954).

Brown v. Mississippi, 297 U.S. 278, 282, 284 (1936).

Callins v. Collins, 510 U.S. 1141, 1145 (1994).

Coker v. Georgia, 433 U.S. 584 (1977).

Crampton v. Ohio 402 U.S. 183 (1970).

Death Penalty Fact Sheet [nonperiodical web document]. https://deathpenaltyinfo .org/documents/FactSheet.pdf

Eddings v. Oklahoma, 455 U.S. 104, 116–117 (1982).

Enmund v. Florida, 458 U.S. 782, 797 (1982).

Ford v. Wainwright, 477 U.S. 399, 411 (1986).

Furman v. Georgia, 408 U.S. 238–240, 242, 293–294, 309–310, 313 (1972).

Gardner v. Florida, 430 U.S. 349, 358 (1977).

Gideon v. Wainwright, 372 U.S. 335, 340 (1963).

Godfrey v. Georgia, 446 U.S. 420, 428–429, 431–433 (1980).

Gregg v. Georgia, 428 U.S. 153, 179–181, 187–189, 195, 198, 206–207 (1976).

Hurst v. Florida, 136 S. Ct. 616, 619 (2016).

Jeffries, J. C. (2001). *Justice Lewis F. Powell: A Biography* (2nd Edition). New York: Fordham University Press.

Jurek v. Texas, 428 U.S. 262 (1976).

Kennedy v. Louisiana, 554 U.S. 407, 437 (2008).

Lockett v. Ohio, 438 U.S. 586, 604–605 (1978).

Mandery, E. J. (2013). *A Wild Justice: The Death and Resurrection of Capital Punishment in America.* New York: W.W. Norton & Co.

Mapp v. Ohio, 367 U.S. 643, 656–657 (1961).

McGautha v. California, 402 U.S. 193 (1971).

McClesky v. Kemp, 481 U.S. 249, 309 (1987).

Miranda v. Arizona, 384 U.S. 436, 461 (1966).

Patterson, K. L. (2006). Acculturation and the Development of the Death Penalty Doctrine in the United States. *Duke Law Journal, 55,* 1217–1246.

Penry v. Johnson, 532 U.S. 782 (2001).

Penry v. Lynaugh, 492 U.S. 302 (1989).

Porter v. McCollum, 558 U.S. 30, 41 (2009).

Powell v. Alabama, 287 U.S. 45, 49, 51, 71 (1932).

Powers v. Ohio, 499 U.S. 400, 404 (1991).

Proffit v. Florida, 428 U.S. 242 (1976).

Ring v. Arizona, 536 U.S. 584, 589 (2002).

Roberts v. Louisiana, 428 U.S. 325 (1976).

Rompilla v. Beard, 545 U.S. 374, 393 (2005).

Roper v. Simmons, 543 U.S. 551, 568–569 (2005).

Rudolph v. Alabama, 375 U.S. 889–890 (1963).

Ruggiero, G. (1978). Law and Punishment in Early Renaissance Venice. *Journal of Criminal Law & Criminology, 69,* 243–256.

Runyon v. McCrary, 427 U.S. 160, 170 (1976).

Spano v. New York, 360 U.S. 315, 321–22 (1959).

States Without the Death Penalty [nonperiodical web document]. Retrieved from https://deathpenaltyinfo.org/states-and-without-death-penalty.

Texas Penal Code Annotated. § 19.03 (1974).

Tison v. Arizona, 481 U.S. 137, 157 (1987).

Trop v. Dulles, 356 U.S. 86, 101–02 (1958).

Turner v. Murray, 476 U.S. 28, 35–37 (1986).

Wayte v. United States, 470 U.S. 598, 608 (1985)

Weems v. United States, 217 U.S. 349, 387 (1910).

Wiggins v. Smith, 539 U.S. 510, 523, 235 (2003).

Wilkerson v. Utah, 99 U.S. 130 (1878).

Williams v. Taylor, 529 U.S. 362 (2000).

Witherspoon v. Illinois, 391 U.S. 510, 512, 519–520 (1968).

Withrow v. Williams, 507 U.S. 680, 688–89 (1993).

Woodson v. North Carolina, 428 U.S. 280, 295, 302, 304 (1976).

Zant v. Stephens, 462 U.S. 862, 877 (1983).

CHAPTER THREE

The Supreme Court and the Categorical Exemption from Capital Punishment for Persons with Intellectual Disability: *Atkins v. Virginia*

On August 16, 1996, 18-year-old Daryl Atkins and his friend William Jones abducted Eric Nesbitt in York County, Virginia. The two men drove Nesbitt, an airman at Langley Air Force Base, to an ATM machine in his own car where they were captured on video making cash withdrawals (Olive, 2014). Atkins and Jones then took Nesbitt to an isolated location and killed him. After being apprehended, both Jones and Atkins were charged with kidnaping, robbery, and murder. When interrogated by law enforcement, both defendants acknowledged being involved in the crime, but each claimed the other was the "trigger-man." In Virginia, unlike many other jurisdictions that retain the death penalty, only the person who actually commits the homicide can be sentenced to death (except in cases of murder for hire) (VA Code Annotated, 2016). Thus, due to inconsistencies in Atkins' statements to law enforcement, the prosecution offered Jones a plea bargain in exchange for his testimony against Atkins. Jones took the deal and testified at Atkins' capital trial that Atkins was the one who shot and killed Nesbitt. Atkins also testified in his own defense and placed the blame back on Jones. The jury believed Jones, whose testimony was—on an objective analysis—more coherent than Atkins' version of the events, and found Atkins guilty of all three offenses. Following a sentencing hearing, where the defense presented evidence that Atkins was "mildly mentally retarded," the same jury sentenced Atkins to death.[1]

Following an appellate reversal on technical grounds related to a misleading verdict form, a new sentencing hearing was convened. At that proceeding, an expert witness for the defense testified (again) that Atkins was "mildly mentally retarded." The prosecution presented its own expert, who disagreed with the defense psychologist's opinion as to Atkins' intellectual functioning, concluding (and opining) that Atkins' sole diagnosis was antisocial personality disorder. Atkins was again sentenced to death. This time, the Virginia Supreme Court affirmed.

At his initial trial, at the second sentencing hearing, and in his appeals to the Virginia Supreme Court, Atkins maintained that he could not be sentenced to death because he had "mental retardation" (the term used by all courts at that time) and that the execution of any person with mental retardation violated the Eighth Amendment to the United States Constitution's ban on cruel and unusual punishment. There was, however, one significant obstacle to Atkins' legal arguments: the United States Supreme Court's decision in *Penry v. Lynaugh* (1989). Johnny Paul Penry, a Texas death row inmate, had made the identical claim years earlier. And, when his case reached the Supreme Court, a majority of its members surveyed state practices, identified only a few death penalty jurisdictions that barred capital punishment for persons with mental retardation, and concluded there was no national consensus barring the practice. Because the identification of such a consensus was a necessary prerequisite to a judicial finding that sentencing a discrete category of offenders to death was "cruel and unusual" as a matter of Eighth Amendment jurisprudence, the Court rejected Penry's claim. Thus, both prior to and following *Penry*, the legal significance of a capital defendant being a person with intellectual disability was left to the states; most of which, in turn, left it to juries in individual cases to consider the disability as a "mitigating circumstance," (i.e., as a reason it could—but did not have to—spare the defendant's life; see *People v. Smithey*, 1999). And frequently the jury did not use the presence of a diagnosis of intellectual disability as a mitigating factor leading to the barring of execution (see Keyes, Edwards, & Perske, 2002; List of Defendants, n.d.).

Working in Atkins' favor, however, was that—post *Penry*—a number of states had, through legislative enactment or judicial decision, concluded that the death penalty was indeed a disproportionate punishment for individuals with intellectual disability (see, e.g., *Rogers v. State*, Ind. 1998). This wave of legislation was largely a product of lobbying efforts organized by Professor James Ellis of the University of New Mexico School of Law, who had worked for years on behalf of persons with intellectual disability and mental illness. The new statutes created, arguably at least, a "dramatic shift in the state legislative landscape" in the aftermath of *Penry* (*Atkins v. Virginia*, 2002). Thus, after the Virginia Supreme Court rejected Atkins' contention that his death sentence was inconsistent with the "evolving standards of decency" that inform the Eighth Amendment's ban on cruel and unusual punishment, the Supreme Court of the United States granted his petition for a writ of certiorari to determine, for a second time, whether the execution of persons with mental retardation was cruel and unusual punishment under the Eighth Amendment (see *Atkins v. Virginia*, 2002; *McCarver v. North Carolina*, 2001; NC General Statutes Annotated, West 2015).[2] A 6–3 majority, in an opinion authored by Justice John Paul Stevens, ultimately concluded that it was.

The Court began by establishing that a fundamental "precept of justice [is] that punishment for crime should be graduated and proportioned to [the] offense" (*Atkins v. Virginia*, 2002; p. 311). This proportionality concept is—and was even before *Atkins*—an integral part of any Eighth Amendment analysis. The Court also made clear that determining whether a punishment is constitutionally excessive or cruel and unusual is judged by current standards, not by those that existed at the time that the Eighth Amendment was ratified. The core Eighth Amendment concept is the "dignity of man," and thus its constitutional content must be informed by "the evolving standards of decency that mark the progress of a maturing society" (*Atkins v. Virginia*, 2002; p. 311).[3] The "evolving standard, . . . should be informed by 'objective factors to the maximum possible extent'" (*Atkins v. Virginia*, 2002; p. 311).[4] Hence, the most reliable evidence of this evolving standard is found in state legislative enactments and jury verdicts. However, despite the importance of the objective evidence, the Court was adamant that "in the end [its] own judgment will be brought to bear on the question of the acceptability of the death penalty under the Eighth Amendment" (*Atkins v. Virginia*, 2002; p. 311).

Its course set, the Court first reviewed the lay of the legislative land. The Court was impressed with the fact that, at the time of its decision in *Penry* (1989), only two death penalty states and the federal government prohibited the death penalty for offenders who had mental retardation. Since that time, however, an additional 16 states had taken death off the punishment table for persons with mental retardation (*Atkins v. Virginia*, 2002). Moreover, the Court noted that "[i]t is not so much the number of these States that is significant, but the consistency of the direction of change" (*Atkins v. Virginia*, 2002; p. 315). The Court viewed these enactments, especially "[g]iven the well-known . . . [popularity of] anticrime legislation," as "powerful evidence that today our society views mentally retarded offenders as categorically less culpable than the average criminal" (*Atkins v. Virginia*, 2002; pp. 315–316). The Court also looked to the opinions of social and professional organizations (e.g., American Psychological Association) with "germane expertise," the opposition to the practice by "widely diverse religious communities," international practices rejecting the death penalty for persons with intellectual disability, and polling data (*Atkins v. Virginia*, 2002; p. 317). While not dispositive, these factors gave further support to the Court's opinion that there was a consensus opposing the practice "among those who have addressed the issue" (*Atkins v. Virginia*, 2002; p. 317). The Court also noted that even in those states that retained the death penalty for persons with mental retardation, only five had actually carried out the execution of these individuals since *Penry*. Thus, the Court concluded that "[t]he practice . . . has become truly unusual, . . . [and] it is fair to say, that a national consensus has developed against it" (*Atkins v. Virginia*, 2002; p. 317).

The Court then examined the underlying merits of the consensus, beginning with the observation that it reflected a "judgment about the relative culpability of mentally retarded offenders, and the relationship between mental retardation and the penological purposes served by the death penalty" (*Atkins v. Virginia*, 2002; p. 317). The Court noted that, due to their impairments, those with mental retardation "have diminished capacities to understand and process information, to communicate, to abstract from mistakes and learn from experience, to engage in logical reasoning, to control impulses, and to understand the reactions of others" (*Atkins v. Virginia*, 2002; p. 318). These deficiencies, while not justifying an exemption from criminal liability, did in the Court's view diminish the personal culpability of individuals with mental retardation to the extent that neither of the justifications advanced by states in support of the death penalty—retribution and deterrence—would be served by permitting their execution.

Because retribution (i.e., "just deserts") "depends on the culpability of the offender," the Court found that the death penalty, society's most extreme punishment, was excessive due to the "lesser culpability of the mentally retarded offender" (*Atkins v. Virginia*, 2002; p. 319). The Court also concluded that deterrence interests are not served by the execution of offenders with mental retardation because "capital punishment can [only] serve as a deterrent when [a crime] is the result of premeditation and deliberation," that is, when the threat of death, "will inhibit criminal actors from carrying out murderous conduct." The Court then stated that this type "of calculus is at the opposite end of the spectrum from [the] behavior of [the] mentally retarded" due to their cognitive and behavioral impairments (*Atkins v. Virginia*, 2002; pp. 319–320).

In addition to concluding that retaining the death penalty for persons with mental retardation would not further legitimate interests in retribution or deterrence, the Court also found that "[t]he reduced capacity of mentally retarded offenders provides a second justification for a categorical rule making such offenders ineligible for the death penalty" (*Atkins v. Virginia*, 2002; p. 320). Due to their impairments, there were a host of reasons, including the increased risk of false confessions, the likelihood of difficulties in communicating with counsel, and a lesser ability (due to limited communication skills) to effectively testify on their own behalf, that, "in the aggregate," offenders with intellectual disability were subject to an unacceptable "risk of wrongful execution" (*Atkins v. Virginia*, 2002; pp. 320–321). The Court also noted the possibility that an intellectually disabled person's "demeanor may create an unwarranted impression of lack of remorse for their crimes," which could enhance the likelihood that the jury would impose the death penalty due to a mistaken belief that they pose a future danger, a demonstrably important consideration in capital sentencing proceedings (*Atkins v. Virginia*, 2002; p. 321).

Thus, the Court determined that its "independent evaluation of the issue reveals no reason to disagree with the judgment of the legislatures that have . . . concluded that death is not a suitable punishment for a mentally retarded criminal" and that therefore "the Constitution 'places a substantive restriction on the State's power to take the life' of a mentally retarded offender" (*Atkins v. Virginia*, 2002; p. 321). The Court reversed the judgment of the Virginia Supreme Court and remanded for "further proceedings not inconsistent with this opinion" (*Atkins v. Virginia*, 2002; p. 321).

As previously noted, three members of the Court—Chief Justice William Rehnquist joined by Justices Antonin Scalia and Clarence Thomas—dissented. First, the dissenting justices accused the majority of creating a consensus against executing persons with mental retardation that did not in fact exist by considering states that had rejected the death penalty altogether, international law, and the views of professional and religious organizations and public opinion polls. The majority did so, according to the dissenters, as a "post-hoc rationalization for its subjectively preferred result rather than any objective effort to ascertain the content of an evolving standard of decency" (*Atkins v. Virginia*, 2002; p. 322). Second, the dissenters did not believe that the death penalty was an excessive punishment for all persons with intellectual disability. The dissenters rejected the view that any class characterizations regarding the diminished capacity of offenders with mental retardation could be made and thus believed that the decision whether to sentence a person with mental retardation to death should be made on a case-by-case basis. Finally, the dissenters believed that the Court's creation of a categorical exclusion would "turn the process of a capital trial into a game" due to the ease with which "the symptoms of this condition can be feigned" (*Atkins v. Virginia*, 2002; p. 353). The dissenters predicted that because death row inmates had nothing to lose if they malingered mental retardation, there would be numerous frivolous claims (*Atkins v. Virginia*, 2002; p. 354).

Two other aspects of the *Atkins* decision are worth discussing in more detail before turning to the Court's more recent decisions in this area. First, on the positive side of the ledger, the Court did, at least implicitly, embrace clinical definitions of intellectual disability and scientific means of assessing intellectual functioning. In footnote 3 of the majority opinion—in the course of discussing the trial evidence that Atkins was "mildly mentally retarded"—Justice Stevens relied upon both the American Association on Mental Retardation (now known as the American Association on Intellectual and Developmental Disabilities) and the American Psychiatric Association's virtually identical definitions of mental retardation set forth in *Mental Retardation: Definition, Classification and Systems of Supports* (9th Edition) (Luckasson et al., 1992) and the *Diagnostic and Statistical Manual of Mental Disorders (DSM-IV-TR)* (American Psychiatric Association (APA), 2000) respectively (*Atkins v. Virginia*, 2002; p. 308). Both definitions included the clinically accepted three prongs: (1) significantly subaverage intellectual functioning, existing concurrently with (2) significant limitations in adaptive functioning and (3) manifestation or onset prior to the age of 18. Similarly, the Court also recognized that the Wechsler Adult Intelligence Scales (WAIS) were the "standard instrument in the United States for assessing intellectual functioning" (*Atkins v. Virginia*, 2002; atn. 5).

Second, the Court observed that "[t]o the extent there is serious disagreement about the execution of mentally retarded offenders, it is in determining which offenders are in fact retarded" (*Atkins v. Virginia*, 2002; p. 318). While noting that the Commonwealth disputed that Atkins "suffers from mental retardation," the Court concluded, as it had done in a different death penalty context when it created a categorical bar to putting to death persons who were insane or incompetent at the time of their execution, that '"we leave to the State[s] the task of developing appropriate ways to enforce the constitutional restriction upon [their] execution of sentences'" (*Atkins v. Virginia*, 2002; p. 317). As we will see in this and other chapters of this book, this was an extremely poor choice of language and continues to produce unfortunate and, in our view, unintended results. Atkins' case was remanded to the Virginia state courts for a hearing on the question of whether he was protected by the Court's new categorical ban.

The Supreme Court has returned to the issue of intellectual disability and capital punishment on five subsequent occasions.[5] We will briefly discuss those decisions before offering some observations that will (hopefully) set the tone for the remainder of this book.

Schirro v. Smith

Three years after *Atkins*, the Court issued a short unanimous opinion reversing a decision of the United States Court of Appeals for the Ninth Circuit, which had ordered the Arizona state courts to convene a jury trial on the issue of whether Robert Douglas Smith was a person with intellectual disability (*Schirro v. Smith*, 2005). The Court held that the court of appeals "erred in commanding the Arizona courts to conduct a jury trial to resolve Smith's mental retardation claim" (*Schirro v. Smith*, 2005; p. 6). Relying on the language previously referred to regarding states having the freedom to develop ways to enforce the new restriction on capital sentencing, the Court noted that Arizona had developed a procedure entrusting the decision to a judge. While noting that the Arizona procedure might, "in its application, be subject to constitutional challenge," the Court reversed the following judgment because the state had not been provided an opportunity to even apply its new procedure when the Ninth Circuit "pre-emptively imposed its jury trial condition" (*Schirro v. Smith*, 2005; p. 6).

Schirro, in our view, is for the most part unremarkable. While we will return to the language about allowing states to determine how to enforce the *Atkins* rule, it does seem clear that the type of procedural decision at issue in *Schirro* (judge versus jury as decision maker) was the very kind of decision the *Atkins* Court had in mind. Thus it broke no new ground and also did not evidence any retrenchment by the Court. Smith is still an inmate on Indiana's death row.

Bobby v. Bies

The Court's next encounter with the death penalty and intellectual disability came in 2009 in *Bobby v. Bies*.[6] Michael Bies, an Ohio death row inmate, had been determined by the Ohio state courts to be a person with intellectual disability. The prosecutors in his case had also conceded as much. But the wrinkle was that the judicial determinations and prosecutorial concessions occurred prior to the Supreme Court's creation of the categorical bar in *Atkins*. At the time *Atkins* was decided, Bies' case was pending in the federal courts. His lawyers returned to the Ohio state courts asking that his death sentence be commuted to life imprisonment based on the combination of *Atkins'* new prohibition against executing persons with intellectual disability and the prior judicial determinations that he fell within the class of protected persons. The courts refused to do so and ordered that an evidentiary hearing be conducted to allow prosecutors to attempt to prove that, despite their prior concessions, Bies was not intellectually disabled. Claiming that the issue had already been decided in his favor by the state courts, Bies invoked the Fifth Amendment's Double Jeopardy Clause and asked the federal courts to prevent the state courts from revisiting the intellectual disability question. A federal district court judge and a panel of the United States Court of Appeals for the Sixth Circuit agreed with Bies, enjoining the state court hearing and ordering that Bies be resentenced to life imprisonment due to his intellectual disability. The Supreme Court granted certiorari and reversed, holding that the lower courts had "fundamentally misapplied the Double Jeopardy Clause and its issue preclusion (collateral estoppel) component" (*Bobby v. Bies*, 2009; p. 829).

While largely a "one-off" procedural case turning on nuances of the archaic collateral estoppel doctrine that itself is (way) outside the scope of this book, the Court—again—said several unfortunate things. First, in describing its own decision in *Atkins*, the Court stated that "[o]ur opinion did not provide procedural or substantive guides for determining when a person who claims mental retardation 'will be so impaired as to fall [within *Atkins*' compass]'" (*Bobby v. Bies*, 2009; p. 831). Again, the precise meaning of this is unclear, but it has led to state court mischief. The Court then reiterated its previous language from *Atkins*, previously noted, that it had "'left to the States the task of developing appropriate ways to enforce the constitutional restriction'" (*Bobby v. Bies*, 2009; p. 831). Finally, the Court, without additional explanation, stated that "[m]ental retardation as a mitigator and mental retardation under *Atkins* . . . are discrete legal issues" (*Bobby v. Bies*, 2009; p. 836). It did not say how (or why) they are different, and it is not obvious how or why they are different, but the Court did say it.

At the subsequent state court hearing, Bies was found to be a person with intellectual disability. The prosecution's retained expert agreed with the defense expert that Bies was intellectually disabled and thus consented to resentencing Bies to life imprisonment. Subsequently, the federal courts vacated Bies' conviction, finding that the prosecution failed to disclose evidence that Bies may not have been the perpetrator (*Bies v. Sheldon*, 2014), and a "plea-bargain" was ultimately reached for a term of years sentence. Thus the litigation that made its way to the Supreme Court turned out to be much ado about nothing.

Hall v. Florida

In 2014, in *Hall v. Florida*, the Court was confronted with a post-*Atkins* "gloss" placed on Florida's statutory definition of intellectual disability by its highest court. In *Cherry v. State* (2007), the Florida Supreme Court, relying on the language previously discussed about allowing the states to come up with "appropriate ways" to enforce *Atkins'* categorical exclusion, held that an individual with an intelligence quotient (IQ) score above 70— even if the score was within the 71–75 standard error of measurement (SEM)—is barred from claiming intellectual disability.[7] Thus, when Freddie Lee Hall, a Florida death row inmate for more than 30 years, sought the benefit of *Atkins*, the Florida Supreme Court rejected his claim because—and solely because—he had previously scored 71 on an IQ test. Furthermore, the state courts applied this "bright line" rule despite very strong evidence that Hall had significantly subaverage intellectual functioning, deficits in adaptive functioning, and clear onset before age 18. After previously denying certiorari several times to consider whether Florida's rule was consistent with *Atkins'* mandate, including *Cherry* itself, the Court decided to review Hall's case.

Justice Kennedy, writing for a 6–3 majority, concluded that Florida's rigid rule rejecting the SEM inherent in any IQ test "disregards established medical practice," both because it "takes an IQ score as final and conclusive evidence of a defendant's intellectual capacity" and also because it "relies on a purportedly scientific measurement of the defendant's abilities, his IQ scores, while failing to recognize that score is, on its own terms, imprecise" (*Hall v. Florida*, 2017; p. 1995). The Court's decision compelling states to acknowledge the SEM when determining whether a person has intellectual disability—a "no-brainer" as a matter of clinical practice—is significant because the Court repeatedly referred to the "views of the medical community," "established medical practice," the "professional community," "medical experts," and the "medical community's diagnostic framework" (*Hall v. Florida*, 2014; p. 1994). Recognizing that "[i]ntellectual disability is a condition, not a number" (*Hall v. Florida*, 2014; p. 2000), the Court made clear that Florida's refusal to take the SEM into account was inconsistent with those views, practices, and opinions, thus establishing, at least in this instance, that states are not free to define intellectual disability in a manner at odds with clinical consensus (*Hall v. Florida*,

2014; p. 2000). The Court stated at one point: "The Court agrees with the medical experts that when a defendant's IQ test score falls within the test's acknowledged and inherent margin of error, the defendant must be able to present additional evidence of intellectual disability, including testimony regarding adaptive deficits" (*Hall v. Florida*, 2014; p. 2001). The failure to do so, Justice Anthony Kennedy wrote, would allow states to "deny the basic dignity the Constitution protects" (*Hall v. Florida*, 2014; p. 2001). Thus Florida and other states that utilized a 70 IQ cutoff were forced to change their practice.

On remand, the Florida Supreme Court found that Hall had satisfied his burden of proof on all three prongs of the intellectual disability question and remanded to the trial court with instructions to impose a life sentence (*Hall v. State*, 2016).

Brumfield v. Cain

The very next term, in *Brumfield v. Cain* (2015), the Court was faced with another deviation from clinical consensus. Tried, convicted, and sentenced to death in Louisiana before *Atkins* was decided, Kevan Brumfield filed a state postconviction challenge to his death sentence. Brumfield relied on evidence presented at the sentencing phase of his capital trial that he had an IQ of 75, had a fourth-grade reading level, and had been in special education classes. Brumfield's postconviction lawyer asked the court considering his client's *Atkins* claim for funds for investigative and expert assistance and an evidentiary hearing to prove his contention that he fell within the category of persons protected by *Atkins*. The judge, however, summarily rejected Brumfield's assertion of intellectual disability without granting funds or providing a hearing on the bases that Brumfield (1) had an IQ of 75 and (2) had not "demonstrated impairment based on the record in adaptive skills" but rather had "anti-social personality" disorder.[8] The Supreme Court rejected the first basis, relying on *Hall's* repudiation of a state court's ability to reject the standard error of measurement and apply mandatory IQ cutoffs (*Brumfield v. Cain*, 2015). The Court found the second wanting as well, in part due to the fact that antisocial personality disorder (even if it was an accurate diagnosis) is not inconsistent with deficits in adaptive functioning or intellectual disability. Relying on the *DSM-IV-TR* (APA, 2000), the Court noted that the diagnostic criteria for intellectual disability does not include "'an exclusion criterion'" for persons with antisocial personality disorder or any other psychiatric diagnosis. The Court remanded the case for "further proceedings consistent" with this new understanding (*Brumfield v. Cain*, 2015; p. 2283). On remand, the United States Court of Appeals for the Fifth Circuit concluded that Brumfield was entitled to *Atkins*' protections, and he has subsequently been resentenced to life imprisonment.

Moore v. Texas

The Court's most recent foray into the intellectual disability and death penalty thicket involved a Texas death row inmate, Bobby James Moore. Moore was sentenced to death in Texas after being convicted—along with two other men—of the robbery and murder of a grocery store clerk (*Moore v. Texas*, 2017). Moore subsequently challenged the validity of his pre-*Atkins* death sentence in state postconviction proceedings, maintaining that he was a person with intellectual disability. A Texas state court judge, after hearing several days of testimony, agreed with Moore. The evidence of intellectual disability included a number of IQ scores ranging from 59 to 78 (the average of which was 70.66), and testimony that, as a teenager, Moore did not understand the days of the week or months of the year, could not tell time, or do rudimentary math. He failed every subject in the 9th grade and then dropped out of school. His father, who physically and emotionally abused Moore and ridiculed him as "stupid," threw him out of the house. Moore survived on the streets eating from trash cans (even continuing to do so after becoming almost deathly ill due to food poisoning). After considering all the evidence presented at the *Atkins* hearing, the state trial judge concluded that Moore had carried his burden of proof on the intellectual disability issue and recommended that his sentence be modified to life in prison (*Moore v. Texas*, 2017; pp. 1039, 1045).

The State appealed and (as is often the case) found a receptive audience in the Texas Court of Criminal Appeals (CCA) (*Moore v. Texas*, 2017; p. 1047). The CCA found fault with the lower court's assessment of both Prongs 1 and 2 of Moore's intellectual disability claim. On the issue of intellectual functioning, the CCA—considering only two of Moore's IQ tests (a 78 and a 74)—rejected Moore's contention that his IQ was in the lower range of the standard error of measurement on varying bases (i.e., he had a history of academic failure and depression, which could have deflated his scores). The CCA concluded that his IQ was "above the intellectually disabled range" (*Moore v. Texas*, 2017; p. 1047). On the second prong, the CCA concluded that what it perceived to be Moore's adaptive strengths (i.e., living on the streets, playing pool and mowing lawns for money, and fleeing after the crime) undermined the significance of any adaptive deficits.

The CCA further concluded that the trial court erred by not requiring Moore to prove that any alleged adaptive deficits were directly related to his low intellectual functioning as opposed to other potential causes, such as Moore's history of drug abuse, learning disorders, racially motivated harassment, academic failure, or the abuse he suffered at the hand of his father (*Moore v. Texas*, 2017).

Finally, the CCA considered each of the so-called *Briseño* factors. These warrant a more detailed discussion. As is true of many issues related to capital punishment, following the Supreme Court's decision in *Atkins*, Texas went its own way. While the general definition of intellectual disability embraced in the Texas legislature's Health and Safety Code was in line with clinical consensus (Texas Health and Safety Code), the CCA, in the first post-*Atkins* case to come before it, created out of whole cloth an anticlinical "gloss" on the deficits in the adaptive functioning prong of the judicial inquiry to be used in the *Atkins* context (*Ex Parte Briseño*, 2004). It did so after first noting that—in its view—it was required to determine "the level and degree of mental retardation at which a consensus of Texas citizens would agree that a person should be exempted from the death penalty" (*Ex Parte Briseño*, 2004; p. 6). While the CCA thought most Texans would agree that Lennie, of John Steinbeck's *Of Mice and Men*, was such a person, it questioned whether the life of every capital defendant in Texas who met the clinical definition of intellectual disability should be spared from the executioner (*Ex Parte Briseño*, 2004; p. 6). Turning to what it perceived to be the "exceedingly subjective" adaptive functioning prong, on which in the court's opinion experts in most cases would invariably disagree, the CCA came up with some "other evidentiary factors" that fact finders in capital trial should "focus upon in weighing evidence as indicative of mental retardation" (*Ex Parte Briseño*, 2004; p. 8), including:

- Did those who knew the person best during the developmental stage—his family, friends, teachers, employers, authorities—think he was mentally retarded at that time, and, if so, act in accordance with that determination?
- Has the person formulated plans and carried them through or is his conduct impulsive?
- Does his conduct show leadership or does it show that he is led around by others?
- Is his conduct in response to external stimuli rational and appropriate, regardless of whether it is socially acceptable?
- Does he respond coherently, rationally, and on point to oral or written questions or do his responses wander from subject to subject?
- Can the person hide facts or lie effectively in his own or others' interests?

- Putting aside any heinousness or gruesomeness surrounding the capital offense, did the commission of that offense require forethought, planning, and complex execution of purpose? (*Ex Parte Briseño*, 2004; pp. 8–9)

As has been noted by numerous clinicians and academics, even a casual review of the *Briseño* factors reveals that they are steeped in stereotype and have no grounding in the clinical consensus definitions of intellectual disability (see Polloway, 2015). And, prior to *Moore*, Texas courts had rejected many (very) strong claims of intellectual disability—even some where there was no expert challenging the defense expert's intellectual disability diagnosis (see *Petetan v. State*, 2017). Nonetheless, the Supreme Court had refused to hear numerous challenges to the *Briseño* factors' legitimacy. That changed in *Moore*.

The Supreme Court majority, in an opinion authored by Justice Ruth Bader Ginsburg, emphatically repudiated the CCA's analysis. On the question of intellectual functioning, the Court, relying on its decision two terms before in *Hall v. Florida*, held that, because "the lower end of Moore's score range [fell] at or below 70, the CCA had to move on to consider Moore's adaptive functioning" (*Moore v. Texas*, 2017; p. 1049). The Court made clear that lower courts are required "to continue the inquiry and consider other evidence of intellectual disability where an individual's IQ score, adjusted for the test's standard error, falls within the clinically established range for intellectual-functioning deficits" (*Moore v. Texas*, 2017; p. 1050). In the High Court's view, the CCA erred in finding that Moore's IQ scores precluded a finding of intellectual disability.

The Court then turned to the second prong and concluded that the CCA's analysis on the adaptive functioning prong "also deviated from prevailing clinical standards," as well as from the "older clinical standards that the court claimed to apply" (*Moore v. Texas*, 2017; p. 1050). Although the clinical standards have not changed significantly over the last 50 years (see Tassé, Luckasson, & Schalock, 2016), there has been some small variation in the definition of intellectual disability in the different editions of the DSM and in the definition promulgated by the American Association on Intellectual and Developmental Disabilities. A primary defect in the state trial court's analysis was its focus on Moore's adaptive strengths (e.g., that he lived on the streets, mowed lawns and played pool for money), which the CCA concluded overcame the evidence of Moore's adaptive deficits (*Moore v. Texas*, 2017; p. 1050). The Supreme Court noted, however, that this was a deviation from clinical consensus because the "medical community focuses the adaptive functioning inquiry on adaptive deficits" (*Moore v. Texas*, 2017; p. 1050). Additionally, the Court found that the CCA's focus on Moore's improved adaptive behavior in prison was inappropriate because clinicians agree that it is an inappropriate forum in which to assess adaptive deficits due to the fact that it is a "controlled setting" (*Moore v. Texas*, 2017; p. 1050). Also found wanting by the Supreme Court was the CCA's bases for finding that Moore's adaptive deficits were not related to his low intellectual functioning. Relying on the *DSM-5* and the brief filed by the American Psychological Association, the Court rejected the CCA's conclusion that Moore's adaptive functioning deficits were best attributed to a personality disorder. The Court noted that mental health professionals recognize that "many intellectually disabled people also have other mental or physical impairments," and thus the "existence of a personality disorder or mental health issue, in short, is 'not evidence that a person does not also have intellectual disability'" (*Moore v. Texas*, 2017; p. 1051). In a similar vein, the Court rejected the CCA's misguided notion that Moore's history of childhood abuse and poverty somehow negated a finding that there was any link between his low intellectual functioning and adaptive deficits, noting that Moore's traumatic experiences were actually risk factors for intellectual disability as opposed to reasons to reject that claim (*Moore v. Texas*, 2017).

Finally, the Court focused its sight on the previously discussed *Briseño* factors, finding that they were rooted not in clinical consensus but in lay stereotypes of what persons with intellectual disability can (and cannot) do. The Court recognized that, "by design and operation," the *Briseño* factors created a constitutionally intolerable risk that persons with intellectual disability would be executed (*Moore v. Texas*, 2017; p. 1052). The Court also noted the evidentiary factors were an outlier in two respects: First, only one other state had adopted them, and second, even in Texas they were used only in death penalty cases and not in any other intellectual disability context (*Moore v. Texas*, 2017).

In conclusion, the Supreme Court reaffirmed *Hall*'s admonition that while states have "some flexibility" in enforcing *Atkins'* mandate, they do not have "unfettered discretion" to effectively gut the Court's categorical ban (*Moore v. Texas*, 2017; p. 1053). The medical community's current standards are a critical constraint on state deviation from clinical consensus definitions of intellectual disability. The state trial court used current standards (e.g., the most recent version of the DSM) and found Moore to be a person with intellectual disability. The CCA, however, did not, and the Court summarized the state court's error as follows: In rejecting "medical guidance and clinging to the standard it laid out in *Briseño*, including the wholly non-clinical *Briseño* factors, the CCA failed adequately to inform itself of the 'medical community's diagnostic framework'" (*Moore v. Texas*,

2017; p. 1053). The High Court vacated the CCA's decision and sent the case to the state courts for further consideration in light of its opinion.

Three justices dissented (Chief Justice John Roberts and Justices Clarence Thomas and Samuel Alito) believing that—on balance—the CCA's methodology on Prong 1 of the intellectual disability inquiry was not necessarily inconsistent with *Hall* (*Moore v. Texas*, 2017). As the dissenting justices viewed the case, the majority's decision was not compelled by *Hall* but rather was an expansion of it that was not compelled by national consensus (*Moore v. Texas*, 2017). However, it is important to note that even the dissenters acknowledged that the seven *Briseño* evidentiary factors were "an unacceptable method of enforcing the guarantee of Atkins" and were thus "incompatible with the Eighth Amendment" (*Moore v. Texas*, 2017; p. 1060).

Conclusion

In the remaining chapters of this book, we will explore in more detail the legal, practical, and clinical implications of the Supreme Court's decisions creating—and refining—the categorical exclusion from capital punishment for persons with intellectual disability. Obviously, we applaud the Court for recognizing and holding that persons with intellectual disability should not—and may not—be executed. The disability is profound, and the pre-*Atkins* legal regime of allowing juries in individual cases to decide whether a person with intellectual disability was so impaired that his or her life should be spared was unsatisfactory. In fact, as the Court noted, evidence of intellectual disability could—and did—"backfire" as prosecutors would argue that since it was a condition that could not be "fixed," it established that the individual was likely to be dangerous in the future (despite the complete lack of empirical evidence that persons with intellectual disability are more dangerous than persons without the disability; *Atkins v. Virginia*, 2002; see pp. 304 & 321).[9] Thus, a categorical exclusion was necessary.

That being said, the Court did—hopefully unwittingly—give recalcitrant states ammunition to attempt to circumvent its constitutional mandate. In both *Atkins* and *Bies*, the Court used language suggesting that state definitions of intellectual disability would be sufficient as long as they "generally conformed" to clinical definitions (*Atkins v. Virginia*, 2002; p. 308). This, in combination with the pronouncements that (1) the Court was leaving to the states the "task of developing appropriate ways to enforce the constitutional restriction upon [their] execution of sentences" and (2) *Atkins* did not establish either "procedural or substantive guides" for making the determination, has led to tremendous variation in state practices and devi-ation from accepted clinical consensus. *Hall* rectified one aspect of that deviation by requiring decision makers to take into account the standard error of measurement inherent in any IQ test. *Moore* rejected Texas's idio-syncratic *Briseño* factors and also cautioned courts not to (1) let evidence of adaptive strengths overshadow adaptive deficits, (2) weigh prison behav-ior as indicative of adaptive potential, or (3) let other comorbid conditions be attributed as the "cause" of adaptive functioning deficits (as opposed to the person's intellectual functioning). It remains to be seen whether state courts will heed the Court's admonitions. As will be discussed elsewhere in this volume, a number of active death penalty jurisdictions, in addition to Florida and Texas, have embraced definitions of intellectual disability and procedures for determining intellectual disability that have resulted in the execution of individuals who clearly should have been protected by the Eighth Amendment categorical bar.

Two examples, one procedural and one substantive, will suffice for pres-ent purposes. Georgia, which ironically was one the first states in the country to enact a bar to the execution of persons with intellectual dis-ability, requires a capital defendant to prove that he is intellectually dis-abled "beyond a reasonable doubt" (O.C.J.A., 2010). Virtually all other jurisdictions require only proof by a preponderance of the evidence.[10] Given the ease with which the prosecution can raise the possibility, however remote, that the defendant is malingering, Georgia juries routinely reject capital defendant's claims of intellectual disability (O'Grady, 2014). In fact, since *Atkins* was decided more than a decade ago, there has not been a sin-gle Georgia jury verdict finding a defendant "guilty but mentally retarded" (*Pittman v. State*, GA, 1998). The Georgia Supreme Court and the federal courts have shrugged off legal challenges to the beyond-a-reasonable-doubt standard, relying upon the language in *Atkins* and *Bies* previously detailed (see *Head v. Hill*, 2003; *Hill v. Humphrey*, 2011).

As for substantive deviations from accepted clinical consensus, the most significant one remaining is the lower courts' failure to consider (fully or at all) aging and obsolete norms for IQ tests. It is well documented that overall performance on IQ testing instruments goes up over time. The pre-cise reasons for this phenomenon, sometimes referred to as the "Flynn effect" (for the academic James Flynn who first documented the test score rise), are debated, but no one disputes that it happens (see Blume, John-son, & Seeds, 2009; Young, 2012).[11] Thus the longer a particular IQ test is in existence, average scores (and thus the mean) crept upward. The aver-age rate of the rise was approximately 3 points per decade. To compensate for the increased scores, IQ tests are periodically "re-normed" to adjust the mean score on the IQ bell curve to 100 (a more detailed discussion of IQ scores is found in Chapter 5). In the capital case context, this can be (and in some cases has been) literally a matter of life and death. A death row inmate, for example, that was administered an IQ test after it had been in existence for 5–10 years could obtain a score that was artificially "inflated" due to the use of the test's aging norms. Clinical consensus suggests that this needs to be taken into account, and, if necessary, scores should be adjusted downward so as not to overstate an individual's intelligence (Blume et al., 2009; Schalock et al., 2007). While many courts have followed the science and made the necessary adjustments, a (not insignificant) number refuse to do so (see *Hooks v. Workman*, 2012; *Thomas v. Allen*, 2010; *Walker v. True*, 2005; *Wiley v. Epps*, 2010).[12] Thus persons who fall within the clinical consensus understanding of intellectual disability have been executed and continue to be at risk of being executed.

Darryl Atkins Redux

Finally, we close this chapter by returning to Daryl Atkins. Following the Supreme Court's decision in his case, the Virginia courts held a hearing to determine whether Atkins was—in fact—a person with intellectual disability (*Atkins v. Commonwealth*, 2006). After days of testimony by competing experts—one of whom is a coauthor of this book—a Virginia jury concluded that he had not proved by a "preponderance of the evidence"—the Virginia legal standard—that he was such an individual (*Atkins v. Commonwealth*, 2006; p. 93). Atkins appealed, and the Virginia Supreme Court reversed the jury's judgment because one of the state's experts was not qualified to opine on the issue of intellectual disability as a matter of Virginia law and because the trial judge told the jury that Atkins had previously been sentenced to death (*Atkins v. Commonwealth*, 2006; p. 93). The court sent the case back for a new trial on the issue. That trial never happened. Before it could take place, evidence came to light that during preparation sessions before the first trial, prosecutors turned a tape recorder off, "coached" Jones (Atkins' codefendant) to modify his version of events in a way that was consistent with the prosecution's theory that Atkins was the actual shooter, and then turned the tape recorder back on and finished the interview. Despite clear Supreme Court precedent requiring the prosecution to disclose this "manicuring" of Jones' testimony, the prosecution had never disclosed this information to Atkins or his lawyers (see *Brady v. Maryland*, 1963; p. 83).[13] Given that there was no longer any credible evidence that Atkins was the "trigger-man," which as noted previously was a necessary prerequisite to a death sentence in Virginia, the trial judge commuted Atkins' sentence to life imprisonment, and the Virginia Supreme Court refused to hear the prosecution's appeal. Thus, Atkins' life was ultimately spared but not as a result of landmark Supreme Court decision that bears his name.[14]

Notes

1. At times, throughout this chapter (and to a lesser degree elsewhere in this book), we will use the term "mental retardation" or "people with mental retardation" or "mentally retarded" because that is the term used both by the Supreme Court in *Atkins v. Virginia* and by many state and federal courts in cases where a capital defendant claims that he is not eligible for the death penalty pursuant to the Supreme Court's decision in *Atkins*. We do this to avoid confusion, not because we are unaware that it is outdated and that the current and more appropriate term is "intellectual disability."

2. The Court actually first granted certiorari in *McCarver v. North Carolina*, a North Carolina case that also asked the Court to revisit *Penry* and to declare that executing persons with mental retardation violated the Eighth Amendment. 532 U.S 975 (2001). Pursuant to long-standing Supreme Court practice, Atkins' case was "held" by the Court while it decided the North Carolina case. However, the Court replaced *McCarver* with *Atkins v. Virginia* after North Carolina passed a statute barring the execution of persons with mental retardation, thus making the *McCarver* case moot. N.C. Gen Stat. Ann. §15A-2005 (West 2015).

3. *Id.* (quoting *Trop v. Dulles*, 356 U.S. 86, 100–01, 311–12 (1958)).

4. *Id.* (quoting *Harmelin v. Michigan*, 501 U.S. 957, 312 (1991)).

5. Several other Supreme Court decisions discuss *Atkins* in some detail but in different contexts, i.e., ineffective assistance of counsel for failing to present evidence of low intellectual functioning, e.g., *Wood v. Allen*, 558 U.S. 290 (2010), or how evidence of low intellectual functioning could be considered by the sentence in an idiosyncratic Texas capital sentencing scheme, e.g., *Tennard v. Tretke*, 524 U.S. 274 (2004). Because neither case deals directly with *Atkins'* core principle that people with intellectual disability may not be sentenced to death or executed, we have decided not to discuss them in this book.

6. In the interest of full disclosure, one of the authors of this book (Blume) represented Mr. Bies in the Supreme Court proceedings.

7. As is discussed in more detail elsewhere in this volume (e.g., Chapter 5), significantly subaverage intellectual functioning generally means that the person has an IQ of 70, which is two standard deviations below the mean IQ of 100.

8. The state court judge's decision was affirmed by the Louisiana State Court on direct appeal. 737 So. 2d. 660 (La. 2012). A federal district court judge concluded the state court decision was an unreasonable determination of the facts, granted funds for investigators and experts, and conducted a multiday evidentiary hearing, at the conclusion of which he found Brumfield to be a person with

intellectual disability and vacated his sentence. 854 F.Supp.2d 366 (La. 2012). The United States Court of Appeals for the Fifth Circuit reversed this decision and reinstated Brumfield's claim. 744 F. 3d 918 (5th Cir. 2014). The Supreme Court then granted certiorari (i.e., voted to hear the case) and reversed the decision of the Fifth Circuit. 135 S. Ct. 2269 (2015).

9. "As Penry demonstrated, moreover, reliance on mental retardation as a mitigating factor can be a two-edged sword that may enhance the likelihood that the aggravating factor of future dangerousness will be found by the jury" *Atkins v. Virginia*, 2002).

10. See infra n. 54. "[T]he Supreme Court held that placing the burden on the defendant to prove by clear and convincing evidence that he was incompetent to stand trial was unconstitutional." . . . [T]he defendant's right not to be executed if mentally retarded outweighs the state's interests as a matter of federal constitutional law."

11. See *Young* (2012): "[A]lthough a heated debate surrounds the question of what causes the Flynn effect's IQ gains, this causality debate does not affect the Flynn effect's accepted existence" (pp. 643–644).

12. The different treatment aging norms receive is found in the following cases: *Walker v. True* (4th Cir. 2005) ("[O]n remand the district court should consider the persuasiveness of [Petitioner's] Flynn effect evidence"); *Thomas v. Allen* (11th Cir. 2010) (noting that, at an evidentiary hearing: "all the experts acknowledged that the Flynn effect is a statistically-proven phenomenon"); *Hooks v. Workman* (10th Cir. 2012) ("*Atkins* does not mandate an adjustment for the Flynn effect"); and, *Wiley v. Epps* (5th Cir. 2010) (refusing to consider the impact of the Flynn effect on petitioner's claim of mental disability because the argument was not raised previously).

13. More specifically, in constitutional criminal procedure terms, the judge found that the prosecution had withheld exculpatory, favorable information in violation of the Due Process Clause of the Fourteenth Amendment. See *Brady v. Maryland*, 373 U.S. 83 (1963).

14. An interesting and related aside is the final disposition of Johnny Paul Penry's case. Penry, readers may recall, was the death row inmate at the center of the Supreme Court's first foray into intellectual disability and capital punishment in *Penry v. Lynaugh*, 492 U.S. 302 (1989). While the Court rejected Penry's contention that there was a categorical bar to executing persons with intellectual disability, it did vacate his death sentence due to a jury instruction error. Penry was again sentenced to death, and that sentence was (again) vacated due to a similar defect in the jury instructions. *Penry v. Johnson*, 532 U.S. 782 (2001). As fate would have it, the Supreme Court decided *Atkins* while Penry's third capital sentencing trial was under way. Rather than declare a mistrial, the trial judge pressed on, attempting to create a mechanism for the jury to decide whether Penry was a person with intellectual disability. Penry was again sentenced to death. This time, the Texas Court of Criminal Appeals concluded that the trial judge's *Atkins* "fix" was constitutionally inadequate. *Penry v. State*, 178 S.W. 3d 782 (Tx. Crim. App. 2005).

Faced with the prospect of a fourth sentencing proceeding, the prosecution agreed to drop its quest for the death penalty but only if Penry would stipulate that he was not—in fact—a person with intellectual disability. While Penry's lawyers found the request "galling" given the strong evidence of intellectual disability, they entered into the agreement in order to bring the litigation to a close and save Penry's life. Mike Tolson, "Deal keeps death row inmate Penry imprisoned for life." http://www.chron.com/news/houston-texas/article/Deal-keeps-death-row -inmate-Penry-imprisoned-for-1578006.php

References

American Psychiatric Association (APA). (2000). *Diagnostic and Statistical Manual of Mental Disorders* (4th Edition, text revision). Washington, DC: Author.

Atkins v. Commonwealth, 631 S.E. 2d 93 (VA, 2006).

Atkins v. Virginia, 536 U.S. 304, 308, 310–311, 315–322, 353–354, atn. 5 (2002).

Bies v. Sheldon, 775 F. 3d 386 (6th Cir., 2014).

Blume, J. H., Johnson, S., & Seeds, C. W. (2009). Of Atkins and men: Deviations from clinical definitions of mental retardation in death penalty cases. *Cornell Journal of Law and Public Policy*, 18, 689–733.

Bobby v. Bies, 556 U.S. 825, 829, 831, 836 (2009).

Brady v. Maryland, 373 U.S. 83 (1963).

Brumfield v. Cain, 135 S. Ct. 2269, 2277–2279 (2015).

Cherry v. State, 959 So. 2d. 702 (FL, 2007).

Ex Parte Briseño, 135 S.W. 3d 1, 6, 8–9 (TX Court of Criminal Appeals, 2004).

Hall v. Florida, 134 S Ct. 1986 (2014).

Hall v. State, 201 So. 3rd 628 (FL, 2016).

Head v. Hill, 587 S. 2d 613, 621–22 (FL Dist. Ct. App., 2003).

Hill v. Humphrey, 662 F.3d 1335, 1339 (11th Cir., 2011).

Hooks v. Workman, 689 F.3d 1148, 1170 (10th Cir., 2012).

Keyes, D., Edwards, W., & Perske, R. (2002). People with mental retardation are dying—legally: At least 44 have been executed. *Mental Retardation*, 40, 243–244.

List of Defendants with Mental Retardation Executed in the United States (n.d.). [nonperiodic web document]. http://www.deathpenaltyinfo.org/list-def endants-mental-retardation-executed-united-states?did=1858

Luckasson, R., Coulter, D. L., Polloway, E. A., Reiss, S., Schalock, R. L., Snell, M. E., Spitalnik, D. M., & Stark, J. A. (1992). *Mental Retardation: Definition, Classification, and Systems of Supports* (9th Edition). Washington, DC: American Association on Mental Retardation.

McCarver v. North Carolina, 532 U.S. 975 (2001).

Moore v. Texas, 137 S. Ct. 1039, 1045, 1047, 1049, 1050–1053, 1060–1061 (2017).

NC General Statutes Annotated, §15A-2005 (West, 2015).

O.C.G.A., § 17-7-131(c)(3) and (j) (2010).

O'Grady, V. M. (2014). Beyond a reasonable doubt: The constitutionality of Georgia's burden of proof in executing the mentally retarded, *Georgia Law Review, 48,* 1189–1223.

Olive, M.E. (2014). The Daryl Atkins story. *William & Mary Bill of Rights Journal, 23*(2), 363–381.

Penry v. Johnson, 532 U.S. 782 (2001).

Penry v. Lynaugh, 492 U.S. 302 (1989).

Penry v. State, 178 S.W. 3d 782 (Tx. Crim. App. 2005).

People v. Smithey, 978 P.2d 1171, 1222 (CA, 1999)

Petetan v. State, No. AP-77,038, 2017 WL 915530 (Tex. Ct. Crim. App. Mar. 8, 2017).

Pittman v. State, 269 Ga. 419 (GA, 1998).

Polloway, E.A. (2015). *American Association on Intellectual and Developmental Disabilities, the Death Penalty and Intellectual Disability.* Washington, DC: American Association on Intellectual and Developmental Disabilities.

Rogers v. State, 698 N.E. 2d 1772, 1775–1776 (IN. 1998).

Schalock, R. L., Buntinx, W. H. E., Borthwick-Duffy, S., Luckasson, R., Snell, M. E., Tassé, M. J., & Wehmeyer, M. L. (2007). *User's Guide: Mental Retardation: Definition, Classification, and Systems of Supports, 10th Edition. Applications for Clinicians, Educators, Disability Program Managers, and Policy Makers.* Washington, DC: American Association on Intellectual and Developmental Disabilities.

Schirro v. Smith, 546 U.S. 6 (2005).

Tassé, M. J., Luckasson, R., & Schalock, R. L. (2016). The relation between intellectual functioning and adaptive behavior in the diagnosis of intellectual disability. *Intellectual Developmental Disabilities, 54,* 381–390.

Tennard v. Tretke, 524 U.S. 274 (2004).

Texas Health and Safety Code, § 591.003(12).

Thomas v. Allen, 607 F.3d 749, 757 (11th Cir., 2010).

VA Code Annotated, § 18.2–31 (West, 2016).

Walker v. True, 399 F.3d 315, 323 (4th Cir., 2005).

Wiley v. Epps, 625 F.3d 199, 210 (5th Cir., 2010).

Wood v. Allen, 558 U.S. 290 (2010).

Young, G. W. (2012). A more intelligent and just Atkins: Adjusting for the Flynn Effect in capital determinations of mental retardation or intellectual disability. *Vanderbilt Law Review, 65,* 615–664.

CHAPTER FOUR

Atkins on the Ground: Post-*Atkins* Lower Court Decisions[*]

As discussed in the last chapter, the Supreme Court ruled in *Atkins* that people with intellectual disability could not be executed or sentenced to death. As is true with many landmark decisions, the Supreme Court's creation of the new categorical bar to capital punishment created new obligations on death penalty jurisdictions and also left a number of open questions. While we addressed several of those issues (and the Supreme Court's responses) in Chapter 3, in this chapter, we will discuss what has transpired in the lower courts since *Atkins* was decided. We will do this both quantitatively and qualitatively. After a review of procedures and an overview of filing and success rates and a similar analysis of why (and how) cases win and lose, we will discuss in this and other chapters some of the implications of what has taken place in the lower state and federal courts for clinical and legal practitioners.

---

[*] Portions of this chapter have been adapted from J. H. Blume, S. L. Johnson, P. Marcus, and E. C. Paavola, E. C. (2014). "A Tale of Two (and Possibly Three) *Atkins*: Intellectual Disability and Capital Punishment Twelve Years After the Supreme Court's Creation of a Categorical Bar." *William & Mary Bill of Rights Journal*, 23, 393–414.

Procedures for Deciding *Atkins* Claims

Prior to *Atkins*, some states had created their own state law exemptions from capital punishment for persons with intellectual disability and thus already had procedures in place to address claims by death-sentenced inmates and people charged with capital crimes who they thought fell within the protected class. But the remaining death penalty jurisdictions were faced with the requirement of creating them. Some did this by legislative enactment (statutes passed by state legislature) (Blume, Johnson, Marcus, & Paavola, 2014); in other states, where no legislation was proposed or passed, the task fell to courts, with the state's highest court setting out procedures in the context of litigation in a particular case (Blume et al., 2014).

In the wake of *Atkins*, two general categories of cases quickly emerged. The first involved people who were already on death row at the time *Atkins* was decided and who, after the Court's decision, challenged their death sentence on the basis that they had intellectual disability and thus could not be executed. While we will do our best to stay out of the procedural weeds, most of these individuals were permitted to file postconviction petitions in state courts asserting that their death sentences violated the Eighth Amendment because of their intellectual disability.[1] The postconviction *Atkins* contentions were—for the most part—decided in the first instance by a state court judge, and then, if there was an appeal, reviewed by state appellate judges (see *Franklin v. Maynard*, S.C. 2003). The person asserting intellectual disability was required to do so (again for the most part) by a preponderance of the evidence, which requires showing that it is more likely than not that he has intellectual disability (*Franklin v. Maynard*, 2003).[2] If the court(s) concluded that the death row inmate was a person with intellectual disability, then the death sentence was modified to life imprisonment. Ultimately, if the inmate was unsuccessful, the cases could be and generally were reviewed by federal courts in what are known as federal habeas corpus proceedings.[3] We will turn to the results of those cases in short order.

Additionally, however, there were new cases involving people charged with capital crimes whose trials commenced after the *Atkins* decision. There was more state court variation for assertions of intellectual disability in the new case procedural posture. In most states, it was determined that the issue should be decided by a judge in a pretrial hearing. If the judge determined that the defendant had intellectual disability, then the death penalty was removed as a sentencing option. Generally, both the prosecution and the defense were given the right to appeal an "adverse" decision.

A small handful of states (e.g., Oklahoma and Texas), however, opted to have the jury decide the intellectual disability issue at the same time it determined whether the defendant should be sentenced to death or life imprisonment (Blume, Johnson, & Seeds, 2009a). A smaller set still (e.g., South Carolina) allowed for the issue to be put to the jury if the judge decided the issue of intellectual disability adversely to the capital defendant (*Franklin v. Maynard*, 2003). As we will discuss later in this chapter, the judge/jury issue turned out to have more significant consequences than anyone would have predicted.

Filing and Success Rates

Initially, there was a great deal of uncertainty as to how many people would seek the benefit of the Court's new rule. The uncertainty was not, as is often the case, a question of retroactivity (i.e., whether the decision would apply to cases that had already been adjudicated on appeal). *Atkins* was clearly a case that had retroactive effect. Rather, it was a matter of speculating how many of the people on death row or facing capital charges would seek its safe harbor. In his dissenting opinion in *Atkins*, the late Justice Antonin Scalia maintained that the Court's new categorical bar exempting people with intellectual disability from execution would promote frivolous litigation (*Atkins v. Virginia*, 2002). In keeping with his general disdain for death row inmates (and their lawyers), he predicted that courts would be overwhelmed with spurious claims of intellectual disability (*Atkins v. Virginia*, 2002).[4] He stated:

> One need only read the definitions of mental retardation . . . to realize that the symptoms of this condition can readily be feigned. And whereas the capital defendant who feigns insanity risks commitment to a mental institution until he can be cured (and then tried and executed), the capital defendant who feigns mental retardation risks nothing at all. (*Atkins v. Virginia*, 2002; p. 353)

Justice Scalia, as it turns out, was quite wrong. To date, less than 10% of people whose lives could potentially be spared by a determination of intellectual disability have raised such claims (Blume et al., 2014). There were 3,557 persons on death row at the time *Atkins* was decided in 2002. From 2002 through the end of 2015, another 1,383 were sentenced to death, providing a total death row population of 4,940 inmates during the relevant time period. The filing rate was calculated using 4,940 as the relevant denominator. The actual number, however, is larger (and likely substantially so) than that. Blume and colleagues (2014) did not include cases in which the prosecution sought the death penalty but instead were resolved by plea bargain, acquittal, conviction of a non-capital lesser included offense, or a life sentence imposed by jury or judge. This rate has also been relatively constant over time (e.g., the filing rate from 2002 through 2009 was also approximately 7%). Whether this number is a fixed steady state is unknowable (although it seems to be), but it is fair to say that almost 15 years after the Court's creation of the Eighth Amendment categorical bar, the objective, empirical evidence refutes Justice Scalia's prediction. He wildly misspoke in forecasting that hordes of death row inmates would attempt to game the system and delay their (deserved) execution by asserting intellectual disability (see *Atkins v. Virginia*, 2002 at 353). And the filing rates are (more or less) in line with estimated rates of incarcerated people with intellectual disability (Davis, 2009). According to Davis (2009), while only 2–3% of people in the general population have intellectual disability, it is generally estimated that between 4–10% of incarcerated individuals have intellectual disability.

The empirical evidence also refutes concerns about frivolous litigation. As noted, not only did a relatively small number of death-sentenced inmates and capital defendants claim to be people with intellectual disability, those who did prevailed in a significant number of cases. The overall "success" rate (i.e., from 2002 through the end of 2016) was approximately 37% (Blume et al., 2014; p. 397). Thus, in more than one-third of the cases, the individual *Atkins* claimant was found to be a person with intellectual disability and therefore not eligible for the death penalty. That is substantially higher than the rate at which death-sentenced inmates prevail on other frequently raised claims including allegations of ineffective assistance of counsel (see Alper, 2013), prosecutorial misconduct (see Weiner & Reiter-Palm, 2004), competence to stand trial or be executed (Blume, Johnson, & Ensler, 2013), and other claims of legal error (see Gelman, Liebman, West, & Kiss, 2004). Furthermore, that number is almost certainly artificially low because there are a number of cases where prosecutors agreed to forego a death sentence in the face of strong evidence that the defendant/death row inmate was a person with intellectual disability. It is also artificially low because, as has been and will be discussed, some "high volume" capital punishment jurisdictions have embraced procedural and substantive rules that inevitably lead to false negatives (i.e., people losing despite having objectively meritorious intellectual disability claims). Thus, we assert with some confidence that the number of frivolous intellectual disability assertions has been rare. Taking into account filing and success rates, *Atkins* has not generated (relatively speaking) a substantial amount of litigation, much less frivolous litigation.

It is worth mentioning some significant variation in success rates throughout the relevant time period. From 2002 to 2008, the known success rate was approximately 40% (Blume et al., 2014). That number was accurate at the time, as the unreported and unpublished decisions had not yet been obtained and analyzed. Using that same matrix, however, the success rate in the years from 2009 to 2015 declined to 26%. Using the same method of analysis (but including all known unpublished decisions), there was still a significant change in success rates. From 2002 to 2008, the overall success rate was 63%, and from 2009 to 2015 the rate at which people asserting intellectual disability succeeded declined to 43% (Blume et al., 2014).[5]

Why? One must be cautious in attempting to answer this question with certainty, although there are several likely explanations for the more recent decline in success rates. First, there is a difference in the "data sets." At the time Atkins was decided, there were people on death row or awaiting trial whose intellectual disability no one disputed (or seriously disputed; Streib, 2003). The only matter of contention was whether there were any legal impediments to their execution (Streib, 2003). Thus, when the Supreme Court created an Eighth Amendment categorical bar, many of these individuals who were clearly ineligible for execution were removed from death row by agreement or after hearings where the evidence was quite lopsided and the result inevitable (e.g., Inmate Removed from Death Row, 2012). Given this reality, higher success rates in the years immediately following Atkins was quite predictable. Second, in the post-Atkins–era trial cases, strong cases of intellectual disability are less likely to be actually litigated. Undisputed or very strong evidence of a capital defendant's intellectual disability should, in a rational world, lead to either withdrawal of the death notice or a negotiated settlement (i.e., plea bargain). And the available information, while difficult to gather systematically, supports that commonsense proposition. There are more than 60 documented cases that have "settled" due to evidence of intellectual disability. There are almost certainly a (not insignificant) number of other cases that we are not aware of.

The third and fourth reasons that likely explain the decline of the success rate over time are potentially more nefarious and worthy of more detailed discussion later in this and other chapters of this book. After *Atkins*, some states modified their definitions of intellectual disability or erected procedural obstacles intended to make it more difficult for people with intellectual disability to prevail. The two most pronounced examples, mentioned previously, are Florida and Texas. The Sunshine State employed a strict IQ cutoff precluding a finding of intellectual disability if the person had an IQ over 70 (*Cherry v. State*, 2002). The Lonestar State created out of nonclinical whole cloth the so-called *Briseño factors*, which make it extraordinarily difficult to prove deficits in adaptive functioning (see Blume et al., 2009a). Although, as discussed in Chapter 3, the Supreme Court found that Florida's IQ cutoff and Texas's *Briseño* factors frustrated the Eighth Amendment right, it created in *Atkins* (*Hall v. Florida*, 2014), other substantive and procedural impediments (e.g., Georgia's beyond-a-reasonable-doubt" standard) remain for now at least intact. The final reason that could explain the more recent downward trend is that lawyers representing the state (district attorneys and attorneys general) have become more "sophisticated" in their litigation strategies and have also been able to develop a cadre of "experts" willing to depart from clinical consensus in opining that capital defendants do not have intellectual disability. The words "sophisticated" and "experts" are in quotation marks advisedly because, as will be discussed subsequently, analysis of the decided cases reveals an increased use of stereotypes and other irrelevant considerations (e.g., behavior in prison) to defeat strong claims that a capital defendant or death row inmate is a person with intellectual disability (Blume et al., 2014).

Winning and Losing Cases by Prong

Despite the high overall rates at which people claiming intellectual disability prevail, there is much to be learned from a more robust examination of the lower court cases. Why do some individuals lose, and, for that matter, why do others (often with very similar or in some cases weaker proof of intellectual disability than some losing cases) win? This analysis should give lawyers, clinicians, and other interested readers a richer understanding of how *Atkins* is working at the ground level.

First, both to recap and to set the table for further discussion, a death row inmate or capital defendant asserting exemption from capital punishment under *Atkins* must establish that he meets all three of the intellectual disability criterion: significantly subaverage intellectual functioning (i.e., an IQ of approximately 70; Prong 1); accompanied by significant deficits in adaptive functioning (Prong 2); and manifestation during the developmental period (i.e., generally prior to the age of 18; Prong 3). The failure to establish any one of the three prongs defeats the claim.

Of the cases that lose, a slight majority of unsuccessful *Atkins* claimants (51%) lost on all three prongs (Blume et al., 2014). In these instances, the reviewing court concluded that the claim failed because the individual did not make a sufficient showing that he (or *much* less often she)[6] met any of the three prongs of the relevant state's definition for intellectual disability. The analysis in many of the cases that lose on all three prongs is often quite superficial on one or more of the prongs, primarily age of onset, but nevertheless courts often do find (when the claim loses) that none of the intellectual disability criteria are satisfied.

That being said, approximately a quarter (26%) of all unsuccessful cases lost on Prong 1 only. In those cases, the reviewing court specifically found that the claim failed because (and only because) the individual asserting intellectual disability had not demonstrated that he had significantly sub-average intellectual functioning. In most of these cases, the decision of the court contained little or no specific discussion of the evidence relevant to the other two prongs of the intellectual disability criteria. This stands in contrast to the smaller number of cases that failed on Prong 2 alone. Approximately 12% of the total number of unsuccessful cases were found lacking only because the individuals had not proven deficits in adaptive functioning. Even when they did, however, the decisions typically contained a more robust discussion of the evidence relevant to the other two prongs—particularly the individual's intellectual functioning. Approximately three-quarters of the Prong 2–only losses included a discussion of the evidence on Prong 1, with many in fact including findings that Prong 1 was satisfied.[7] Finally, very few cases, approximately 2%, lost solely on the basis that the person claiming intellectual disability could not demonstrate onset during the developmental period (Prong 3).[8] This is not surprising, as one would expect it to be the rare case where a person persuaded the reviewing court that he had both significantly subaverage intellectual functioning and deficits in adaptive functioning, but there was some etiology for the compromised intellectual functioning and adaptive behavior other than intellectual disability. In theory it could happen, for example, as a result of some very serious brain injury occurring after the end of the developmental period, but that would be atypical. The interested reader should see Mulroy (2013) for a good discussion of the difficulties with the 18-year-old threshold. Interestingly, the percentage of losing cases by prong has remained fairly consistent over time; there has been no significant shift in percentages of losses by prong from the time *Atkins* was decided to the publication of this book (Blume et al., 2014).

Significantly Subaverage Intellectual Functioning: A Closer Look at IQ Scores

We will now look more deeply at the Prong 1 cases. Interestingly, there has been a change in average IQ scores and in how the courts handle those scores in both winning and losing cases over time. For cases that lost on Prong 1 only, the total average IQ score was 78. Almost all of the claimants (94%) who lost on Prong 1 had an average IQ score over 70, and a majority (78%) had an average IQ score over 75.[9] Eighty percent of claimants who lost on Prong 1 had at least one IQ score over 75, and virtually all (96%) had at least one IQ score over 70.

By contrast, the average IQ score for successful cases was 69. This figure increased from an average score of 66 in prevailing cases decided from 2002 to 2008 to an average of 69 in successful cases decided between 2009 and 2015, indicating a slightly increased likelihood of success with somewhat higher IQ scores as *Atkins* litigation has progressed in the lower courts over the past 12 years. As discussed, this is explainable due to the difference in case sets in the two time periods given that, at the time *Atkins* was decided, there were a number of people on death row who undisputedly had intellectual disability (and thus one would expect lower average IQs).

Thus, some observers might look at this data and conclude that courts are generally getting it right when it comes to assessing whether an individual has significantly subaverage intellectual functioning. In some cases that is undoubtedly true. But a closer examination of the cases reveals several troubling trends and a set of cases in which the intellectual functioning issue was not nearly as cut-and-dried as the court rejecting the claim believed. A number of intellectual disability claimants in this group lost when—objectively speaking (in our view)—they should have prevailed. This generally occurs for one of three basic reasons: (1) The cases were adjudicated in states that utilized a strict IQ cutoff of 70 or a rebuttable presumption against a finding of intellectual disability if the person had an IQ score over 70 (see e.g., *Parrish v. Commonwealth*, 2008; *Cribbs v. State*, 2009); (2) the court failed to account for clinically accepted concepts such as the standard error of measurement (SEM) (see *Hall v. Florida*, 2014), practice effects,[10] or aging norms[11] (sometimes referred to as the "Flynn effect"; see *Thomas v. Allen*, 2010); and (3) the court credited scores derived from clinically unacceptable methods, such as relying on undocumented IQ scores, short form and screening tests, making adjustments for ethnicity and "cultural factors," and other types of scientifically invalid estimates.[12]

Phillip Elmore, an Ohio death row inmate whose *Atkins* claim was rejected by the state courts, is (in our view) someone who, applying clinically sound criteria, should have prevailed.[13] In postconviction, Elmore offered an affidavit from an expert who opined that Elmore's IQ score was 72 but that a full diagnosis could not be made without an opportunity to assess Elmore's adaptive behavior.[14] The state court denied Elmore that opportunity, instead granting the State's motion for summary judgment because an IQ score over 70 creates a rebuttable presumption under Ohio law that a defendant does not have intellectual disability.[15] The court concluded:

> Dr. Rheinscheld does not dispute that appellant's IQ is above 70; rather he relies on the five-point margin of error which was not adopted by the Supreme Court in *Lott*. Without this five-point margin of error, appellant would not meet the first prong of the Atkins-Lott test. Accordingly, Dr. Rheinscheld's affidavit adds nothing new to the record and is based on an assumption that, while it may be valid in the field of psychology, is not a valid factor in assessing [intellectual disability] for an *Atkins-Lott* claim.[16]

While the injustice that happened to Elmore may be (but has not yet been) rectified post *Hall v. Florida*, many other deviations from accepted clinical understandings of Prong 1 are replete in judicial decisions.

For example, the United States Court of Appeals for the Fifth Circuit found Texas death row inmate Virgilio Maldonado not to be a person with intellectual disability after the State's expert used an unqualified translator to administer the English version of the WAIS and made upward adjustments to the obtained IQ score based on "cultural and educational factors" because Maldonado is Hispanic (*Maldonado v. Thaler*, 2010). Hispanic *Atkins'* claimants—in fact—are almost always unsuccessful regardless of the evidence. Their lack of success is often due to the prosecution's ability to find experts who will engage in the kind of clinically unsound upward adjustment of IQ scores that took place in Maldonado's case (see e.g., *Lizcano v. State*, 2010). Similar upward adjustments to IQ scores have been made by prosecution experts in cases involving African American defendants on the basis that the low scores are reflective not of low intellectual functioning but of cultural deprivation (see e.g. *Brown v. State*, 2016).[17]

Whether an *Atkins* claimant prevails on Prong 1 depends in most cases—not surprisingly—on the actual IQ scores themselves. That being said, it is not impossible for claimants with relatively high IQ scores to succeed on an *Atkins* claim. More than one-third of the reported decisions finding intellectual disability involved individuals with at least one IQ score over 75, and 22% involved one or more IQ scores over 80 (Blume et al., 2014). One of the most significant differences between successful and unsuccessful claims on Prong 1 was whether the adjudicating court was willing to accept the clinical consensus commonsense proposition that only a reliable, individually administered, full-scale IQ score should be considered in assessing intellectual functioning. Many losing cases involved purportedly high IQ scores that courts accepted at face value when clinical standards would not necessarily have considered them to be a valid measure of intellectual functioning. At times, courts have relied on IQ scores when there was no information regarding the test that produced the score, who administered the test, or how it was administered. Courts have also used scores from screening tests, short form tests, and nonstandardized tests to reject otherwise strong evidence of subaverage intellectual functioning.[18] On the other side of the ledger, when judges give effect to accepted clinical standards, including, as noted previously, the SEM, practice effect and Flynn effect, the success rate is much higher.[19] For similar reasons, claimants with high "outlier" IQ scores fared much better when courts were willing to evaluate the totality and quality of the available evidence relevant to the individual's intellectual functioning. This is in sharp contrast with judges who mistakenly treated single IQ scores as creating various presumptions or strict cutoff limitations.[20]

Deficits in Adaptive Functioning

Cases that lost on the adaptive behavior prong also present a complex picture. As previously noted, approximately 12% of the losing claimants in the reported decisions lost on Prong 2 alone. Although most of these cases do not contain a specific finding that the claimant satisfied Prong 1, many of these opinions did report the claimant's IQ scores. These scores typically were in the range needed to demonstrate significantly subaverage intellectual functioning of approximately 70 on an appropriate test.[21] Cases that lost on Prong 2 generally lost based on one or more of the following factors: (1) the individual's prison behavior,[22] (2) the alleged facts of the crime (see e.g., *Walker v. Kelly*, 2010),[23] (3) attributing deficits in adaptive functioning to something other than low intellectual functioning, (4) ethnicity/race, and (5) stereotypes of what people with intellectual disability can (and cannot) do (*Walker v. Kelly*, 2010 at 326).[24]

In Prong 2 losses, courts increasingly rely upon prison behavior in finding that a death row inmate or capital defendant is not a person with intellectual disability. Virtually all losses on Prong 2 from 2008 until the publication of this book discussed some aspect of the claimant's prison behavior as support for the court's conclusion that the claimant failed to demonstrate deficits in adaptive behavior sufficient to satisfy Prong 2. Courts have concluded that (1) a positive adjustment to prison life, including the ability to follow prison rules; (2) employment in prison; (3) officer testimony that the defendant was a "normal" inmate, seemed to be of average intelligence, could communicate effectively, or was "polite" and well-groomed; (4) testimony that the prisoner was seen with books or magazines;

(5) the ability to order items from the prison commissary; and (6) prison gang affiliation, all justified findings that an intellectual disability claim failed.[25] Courts have made such findings despite the fact that the clinical literature in the field, as will be discussed in Chapter 6, specifically advises against relying on this type of prison conduct (see, e.g., *United States v. Smith,* 2011).[26] And the reasons for this admonition are quite obvious. How an individual adjusts to the intensely structured environment of death row is—for the most part—irrelevant to whether the person can function in the "free world."[27] People on death row operate in a universe where choices are extremely limited, even for such basic matters as when to get up and go to bed, what to eat, when to shower or change clothes, and other life basics. Also, any "employment" available to a death row inmate would be of the type that could be performed by a person with intellectual disability. The same would be true with being recruited into a gang given the gullibility of many people with intellectual disability (see, e.g., Snell et al., 2009).[28] And, it almost goes without saying, the opinion of a correctional officer that an individual was "normal" is the thinnest of reeds upon which to decide whether a person should live or die (*United States v. Smith,* 2011).[29] The Supreme Court may have sufficiently discouraged courts from relying on prison behavior in its recent decision in *Moore v. Texas* (2017); only time will tell.

The facts of the crime, including whether they demonstrate planning or deception, are often used as reasons to deny an *Atkins* claim on Prong 2—particularly in Texas where the previously discussed *Briseño* factors require the court to consider this criterion as an indicator relevant to a decision on intellectual disability (see e.g., *Matamoros v. Thaler,* 2010; *Chester v. Quarterman,* 2008; *Hodges v. State,* 2010; *State v. Dunn,* 2010). We do not dispute that there are situations where the "sophistication" of the crime could be beyond the means of a person with intellectual disability. However, most of the reported decisions relying on this consideration to reject a claim of intellectual disability do not fall in that category. For example, in *Ex Parte Moore,* the Texas Court of Criminal Appeals believed that the fact that Moore attempted to conceal his appearance during the offence by wearing a wig and sunglasses was inconsistent with an individual who had deficits in adaptive functioning.[30]

Attributing deficits in adaptive behavior to another cause/etiology is another creeping negative trend in cases that fail on Prong 2. A recent case from Arkansas involved a judicial finding that the deficits in adaptive behavior could have been caused by other conditions such as ADHD or conduct disorder (*Jackson v. Norris,* 2016). Other cases have seen adaptive behavior deficits attributed to schizophrenia, antisocial personality disorder, and drug abuse rather than intellectual disability (Blume et al., 2009a). These cases, for the most part, create a false dichotomy and ignore the clinical reality that intellectual disability often does not exist in a vacuum. Many people with intellectual disability have other mental impairments, and, in such cases, attempting to parse etiology is not only often a fool's errand but is also discouraged by clinical consensus (Blume et al., 2009a). Recent cases have also seen courts willing to attribute (and thus discount) what defense experts have identified as deficits in adaptive behavior as normal considering the individual's culture or ethnicity.

Finally, stereotypes and general misunderstandings about what people with intellectual disability can achieve are likely the most significant factors affecting Prong 2 losses. Although people with intellectual disability are "often able to perform basic life functions and tasks, such as holding jobs, driving cars, and supporting their families" (*Wiley v. Epps*, 2010; *DSM-IV-TR*; APA, 2000; pp. 151, 46, 43),[31] many courts have relied on these factors and other stereotypes to deny *Atkins* claims (see, e.g., *United States v. Williams*, 2014). Among other reasons, courts have found that the claimant did not have deficits in adaptive behavior sufficient to satisfy Prong 2 because he (1) could read, write, and perform some rudimentary math; (2) had friends; (3) was able to maintain his personal hygiene; (4) drove a car on occasion; (5) was appropriately groomed and possessed a driver's license; (6) was a hard and reliable worker; and (6) maintained relationships with women (see *Walker v. Kelly*, 2010; *Dufour v. State*, 2011; *State v. Campbell*, 2008; *Branch v. State*, 2007; *Lizcano v. Texas*, 2010). None of these skills or abilities are necessarily inconsistent with intellectual disability. And focusing on the things a person with intellectual disability can do often ignores the clinical maxims that strengths coexist with weaknesses and deficits and that the focus of Prong 2 is on deficits. An excellent example of the failure to recognize these important considerations can be found in the Mississippi Supreme Court's decision in *Wiley v. State* (2004) where the court made the following blanket statements in the course of rejecting strong proof of intellectual disability:

> [R]etarded people do not operate heavy machinery, retarded people do not drive tractors, retarded people do not hold jobs for much longer than a year at a time. . . . retarded people do not get driver's licenses, buy cars and drive cars.

On both Prongs 1 and 2, prosecutorial accusations of malingering are ubiquitous. It is true, of course, that a death row inmate, in theory, has an incentive to attempt to cheat the executioner by being found to be a person with intellectual disability. Given the lack of formalized, reliable assessments designed to determine whether a person is attempting to fake symptoms of intellectual disability (see *Allen v. Wilson*, 2012; *United States v. Smith*, 2011), the best method for assessing malingering is looking for consistency (or conversely, inconsistency) in both deficits in intellectual functioning and adaptive behavior over time.[32] But given the ease with which the specter of malingering is raised, even people with strong evidence of deficits in adaptive behavior and/or intellectual functioning have lost due to accusations of malingering (see, e.g., *State v. Grell*, 2006).[33] These generally come in the form of a prosecution expert's subjective feeling or perception based on experience, or an opinion based on other evidence in the case, which may or may not be reliable, such as the defendant's self-reported social history information (see, e.g., *United States v. Umana*, 2010; *Doss v. State*, 2009). Ramiro Hernandez-Llanas was executed by the State of Texas despite presenting an overwhelming case of intellectual disability. The State's expert (who did not personally evaluate the defendant and who was unfamiliar with the three prongs of the intellectual disability definition) discounted Hernandez-Llanas's multiple IQ scores in the intellectual disability range on the basis that he understood that good scores on the tests would result in his execution being expedited (*Hernandez v. Stephens*, 2013).

Manifestation During the Developmental Period

As for losses on Prong 3 (onset during the developmental period), very few people raising claims of intellectual disability lose on Prong 3 alone; in fact, we were only able to identify four cases appropriately classified as a loss on Prong 3 only. Ohio death row inmate Michael Stallings presented evidence of two IQ scores of 76, one obtained at age 16 and another post-crime (*Stallings v. Bagley*, 2008). Stallings's expert testified that both of these scores were inflated due to the out-of-date testing instruments used (2008 at 881). Based on these scores and the score of an adaptive behavior scale administered while Stallings was in prison, his expert concluded that he satisfied the first two prongs of intellectual disability (*Stallings v. Bagley*, 2008). The expert waivered, however, on the third prong because Stallings was never specifically evaluated for intellectual disability prior to age 18 (*Stallings v. Bagley*, 2008). A second expert, who was originally retained by the State, agreed with Stallings's expert and ultimately opined that it was more likely than not that Stallings satisfied all three prongs of Ohio's definition of intellectual disability (*Stallings v. Bagley*, 2008). The state court rejected the expert testimony, however, finding that Stallings failed to rebut Ohio's presumption that he does not have intellectual disability because he had an IQ score above 70 (*Stallings v. Bagley*, 2008). Although Stallings had proven both Prongs 1 and 2, the court concluded that he had not proven that it was more likely than not that his condition began prior to age 18 as required by the criteria for Prong 3.

It is the rare case, however, where Prong 3 is determinative of an intellectual disability claim, although several cases have exhibited confusion about whether intellectual disability needs to be diagnosed during the developmental period. A state trial court rejected Sonny Boy Oats' intellectual disability claim on the basis that he had not been diagnosed as having intellectual disability prior to the age of 18. The Florida Supreme Court, reversed however, correctly holding that the lower court improperly conflated "manifested" with "diagnosed" (*Oats v. State*, 2015).

Variation

Aggregated filing and success rates conceal great variation. Both the identity of the decision maker—judge or jury—and the state in which the claim is brought powerfully influence the likelihood that an *Atkins* claim will succeed.

Variation by Decision Maker

As previously noted, Atkins "le[ft] to the State[s] the task of developing appropriate ways to enforce the constitutional restriction upon [their] execution of sentences" (*Atkins v. Virginia*, 2002).[34] Consequently, each state had to make a variety of decisions concerning the implementation of the *Atkins* ban, including the identity of the decision maker, the timing of the eligibility determination, and the allocation of the burden of proof (see, e.g., *Franklin v. Maynard*, 2003). For pre-*Atkins* cases—cases where a death sentence had already been imposed when *Atkins* was decided—all states elected to have a judge make the determination (*Franklin v. Maynard*, 2003).

Given the cost of impaneling a jury, as well as the greater likelihood of reversible error inherent in a jury proceeding, this unanimous choice was not surprising. In the post-*Atkins* cases, one would expect that efficiency considerations would still have weighed against jury determinations; a judicial determination of intellectual disability would have obviated the need for impaneling a jury or at least permitted the impaneling of a noncapital jury—a much less costly process. Nonetheless, ten states—Alabama, Arkansas, Georgia, Louisiana, New Mexico, North Carolina, Oklahoma, Pennsylvania, Texas, and Virginia—chose to allocate the determination of intellectual disability in the post-*Atkins* cases to juries (see Ala. Code § 13A-5-45(a), 1975; Ark. Code Ann. § 5-4-618(d)(2) (B)(i), 1993; N.C. Gen. Stat. Ann. § 15A-2005(e), 2001; Pa. R. Crim. P. 844(B); Va. Code. Ann. § 19.2-264, 2003; *Rogers v. State*, 2007; *State v. Flores*, 2004; *Williams v. State*, 2008). In addition, California permits the defendant to elect a judge or jury (Cal. Penal Code § 1376(b)(1), 2003). South Carolina provides for an initial judicial determination and, in the event of a finding of no intellectual disability, permits the defendant to submit the issue to the jury as well (*Franklin v. Maynard*, 2003).

If the state legislatures that chose jury determinations did so believing that juries would be more reluctant to find intellectual disability, it appears that they guessed right. From 2002 to 2016, there have been 23 jury determinations of intellectual disability, and in 22 of those cases, or 96%, the jury determined that the defendant did not have intellectual disability (Blume et al., 2014). The contrast between this rate and the overall success rate is striking. Although it is possible that intellectual disability claims presented to juries vary in some systematic way from those presented to judges, there is no reason to believe that is the case.[35] Any way the matter is analyzed, juries seem to be vastly harsher in their evaluation of intellectual disability claims than are judges.

This is an interesting fact because it stands in contrast to other comparisons of judge and jury decision making that have found that juries tend toward greater leniency (see, e.g., Hans, 2007). Prior empirical studies find great judge–juror agreement in both civil and criminal trials and that when disagreement does occur in criminal cases, juries are likely to be more lenient (see Eisenberg et al., 2005; Hans, 2007; Hans, 2012; Hans, Hannaford-Agor, Mott, & Munsterman, 2003; Vidmar & Hans, 2007). Sentencing in capital cases follows the pattern of greater jury lenience, but the disparity is much more pronounced (see Judicial Override in Alabama, 2008; Radelet, 2011).

Perhaps juries are more lenient than judges in ordinary guilt and sentencing determinations but harsher in determinations of intellectual disability because—in the context of a horrible crime—judges are more able to set aside their feelings and correctly apply a legal standard than jurors, who could be more inclined to decide whether the individual claiming to have intellectual disability "deserves" the death penalty and then retrofit the intellectual disability determination in accord with their sentencing outcome preference. Another factor may be the timing of the decision; juries determine intellectual disability after hearing all the evidence in aggravation, including victim impact evidence, as compared to judges, who generally make pretrial rulings of intellectual disability and consequently have been exposed to fewer emotional, retributive triggers (see *Franklin v. Maynard*, 2003). Regardless of the reason, it is clear that jurors are much more reluctant to find intellectual disability than are judges.

Variation by State

There is substantial state variation in success rates for intellectual disability claims. In North and South Carolina, for example, the overall success rates are 80% or higher; in Alabama on the other hand, by state, it is less than 15% (Blume et al., 2009b). This disparity "corresponds with the availability of funding for post-conviction litigation," which is minimal in Alabama and (generally) at least adequate in North and South Carolina (Blume et al., 2009b; p. 629). The restrictiveness of the applicable definition of intellectual disability was also analyzed. Texas, as has been discussed, until recently utilized the *Briseño* factors, making it almost impossible for a death sentenced inmate to prevail on Prong 2. Alabama (unlike North Carolina) applied pre-*Hall* a strict IQ cutoff and still assesses adaptive behavior deficits by focusing on what the claimant can do rather than focusing, as those clinical definitions require, on the individual's limitations (Blume et al., 2009b).

Table 4.1 reflects all of the win–loss data as of the end of 2016.[36]

Of course, some of the jurisdictions have so few cases that the success rate is not meaningful; Oregon's and Idaho's 0% success rate cannot profitably be compared to anything, given that the percentage is derived from one case in each state. On the other hand, 29 cases have been litigated in Florida, and through 2016, the claimants lost in all but three of those cases, with the wins all being post-*Hall*.[37] The success rates in Alabama (5 out of 39), Georgia (1 out of 12), Kentucky (2 out of 10), Tennessee (0 out of 10), Texas (16 out of 64), and Virginia (0 out of 8) are also strikingly low. In contrast, the North and South Carolina rates (84 and 83% respectively) are strikingly high.

Thus, in sum, there is significant jurisdictional variation in success rates that aligns for the most part with procedural and substantive differences in the state system. Rates are lower in states with substantive deviations from clinical definitions. Florida and Alabama are in that category, as both of them (prior to *Hall*) adhered to an IQ cutoff (*Hall v. Florida*, 2014; *Morris v. State*, 2010).

Table 4.1   Success Rate by State

State	Claims Decided on Merits	Merit Wins	Merit Losses	Success Rate
Alabama	39	5	34	13%
Arizona	12	6	6	50%
Arkansas	4	1	3	25%
California	12	7	5	58%
Colorado	3	3	0	100%
Florida	29	3	26	10%
Georgia	12	1	11	8%
Idaho	1	0	1	0%
Illinois	0	0	0	0%
Indiana	6	3	3	50%
Kentucky	10	2	8	20%
Louisiana	15	7	8	47%
Mississippi	18	9	9	50%
Missouri	6	3	3	50%
Nebraska	1	0	1	0%
Nevada	3	2	1	67%
New Jersey	1	0	1	0%
New Mexico	0	0	0	0%
New York	0	0	0	0%
North Carolina	37	31	6	84%
Ohio	22	6	16	27%
Oklahoma	10	3	7	30%
Oregon	1	0	1	0%
Pennsylvania	19	14	5	74%
South Carolina	6	5	1	83%
Tennessee	10	0	10	0%
Texas	64	16	48	25%
Utah	2	1	1	50%
Virginia	8	0	8	0%
Federal DP	13	5	8	38%
Military	1	0	1	0%

Texas also deviated greatly (pre-*Moore*), having adopted its own idiosyncratic approach to adaptive behavior (*Ex parte Briseño*, 2004).[38] And Georgia, too, is an oddity, as it requires proof of intellectual disability beyond a reasonable doubt (*Head v. Hill*, 2003).

Having now examined the *Atkins* decision itself, as well as the legal landscape prior to and after *Atkins*, we will shift our focus in the next several chapters to appropriately understanding issues related to the determination—clinically—of whether an individual has intellectual disability.

Notes

1. We say "most" because some states (e.g., Virginia) did not allow death row inmates to challenge their death sentences in state court if they had already completed the state collateral appeals process at the time of the *Atkins* decision.

2. Some states (e.g., Arizona) did require that the death-sentenced inmate establish intellectual disability by clear and convincing evidence.

3. We say "for the most part" because there is some variation in state law in whether a state appellate court would first "screen" the death-sentenced inmate's allegation to see if he had made out a prima facie case (i.e., whether there was a sufficient factual basis for the case to go forward; *Chase v. State* (2004). But a detailed explanation of state collateral review law is beyond the scope of this book (and frankly not that interesting to all but the most idiosyncratic reader).

4. Justice Scalia was joined by the Chief Justice and Justice Clarence Thomas.

5. The same basic pattern is observed regardless of whether the direct appeal losses are included (50% versus 36%) or if all losses are excluded (80% versus 54%), as well as if only reported decisions are analyzed (42% versus 26%, excluding direct appeal losses) (30% versus 21%, including all losses) (66% versus 35%, excluding direct appeal and postconviction losses).

6. There are only a handful of cases where female death row inmates or capital defendants sought the protection of *Atkins*' categorical rule. This is not surprising given that only 2% of death row inmates are women.

7. For instance, in *Wood v. Allen* (11th Cir. 2008), *cert. denied*, 525 U.S. 1042 (1998), the reviewing court found that because Prong 2 had not been satisfied—"Wood did not have significant or substantial deficits in his adaptive functioning"—there was no need to make a determination as to Prong 1. Having said that, however, the court also noted that two mental health professionals "evaluated Wood together and concluded Wood['s] . . . full-scale IQ was 64 and his true IQ was between 61 and 69." *Id.*; see also *Rodgers v. State*, 948 So. 2d 655, 667 (Fla. 2006) ("As to the first prong—intellectual functioning—the trial court found that Rodgers fell within the mild mental retardation range.").

8. In 3% of the reported losing decisions, we were unable to determine whether the claimant lost on Prong 1, 2, 3 or on all three prongs.

9. By "average IQ score," we mean that in each reported loss on Prong 1, the average of all raw IQ scores reported in the decision exceeds 70 for 94% of claimants who lost on Prong 1, and the average raw IQ score exceeds 75 for 71% of that same pool of claimants. While this calculation produces informative and interesting information about general trends from a large pool of cases, we are not suggesting that an "average IQ score" is an individual person's "true IQ." Nor do we think that calculating an individual's average IQ score is necessarily an appropriate method for making a clinical assessment of whether a person has an intellectual disability. But courts frequently do it, and it can provide an informative data point.

10. "Practice effect" refers to gains in IQ scores on tests of intelligence that result from a person being retested on the same or similar test within a relatively short period of time—generally within one year. "For this reason, established clinical practice is to avoid administering the same intelligence test within the same year to the same individual because it will often lead to an overestimate of the examinee's true intelligence" (Schalock et al., 2010); see also Kaufman (1994).

11. "Failure to adjust IQ scores in the light of IQ gains over time turns eligibility for execution into a lottery—a matter of luck about what test a school psychologist happened to administer" (Flynn, 2006; pp. 174–175). "[V]irtually all nations in the developed world show an upward trend in performance on IQ tests from and after the date they are developed or 'normed'" (*United States v. Davis*, 611 F. Supp. 2d 472, 485 (D. Md. 2009). Accordingly:

> the population generally will achieve higher scores on IQ tests proportional to the amount of time between when the test was normed and when it was taken. . . . Standardized measures of IQ are normalized ("normed") on a given population such that the average, or mean, score is 100. . . . [O]ver time, the test norms become outdated, such that the average score is no longer 100, but something higher. . . . Corrections for the Flynn effect adjust scores to account for the amount of time between when the test was originally normed and when it was administered to an individual. This allows for fair comparisons between scores obtained at different times.

12. *Henderson v. Director*, No. 1:06-CV-507, 2013 WL 4811223, at *9 (E.D. Tex. Sept. 6, 2013) (stating that a State's expert testified that the highest IQ score is the most reliable because "'you can't fake knowing the answer'"); *Anderson v. State*, 163 S.W.3d 333, 355–56 (Ark. 2004) (relying on a ten-question questionnaire that provides an estimated IQ score, as well as expert testimony extrapolating an estimated IQ range from scores on the Wide Range Achievement Test (WRAT), which is not a test designed to measure IQ); *State v. Were*, 890 N.E.2d 263, 293 (Ohio 2008) (rejecting an *Atkins* claim where the defendant offered an IQ score of 69 because of expert testimony that the test scores should be adjusted due to "cultural bias" that tends to depress the IQ scores of minorities); *Lizcano v. State*, No. AP-75879, 2010 WL 1817772, at *11 (Tex. Crim. App. May 5, 2010) (stating that the State's expert adjusted IQ scores upward because "Hispanic test subjects historically score 7.5 points lower on IQ tests than Caucasian subjects" due to "culture and influence" rather than cognitive deficiency).

13. *State v. Elmore*, No. 2005-CA-32, 2005 WL 2981797, at *7–9 (Ohio Ct. App. Nov. 3, 2005).

14. *Id.* at *7.

15. *Id.* at *8–9.

16. *Id.* at *9 (emphasis added).

17. See, e.g., *Brown v. State*, 982 So. 2d 565 (Ala, 20016) (the Court credited a prosecution expert who testified that the defendant's IQ scores were "artificially" deflated because he was black).

18. See, e.g., *Esparaza v. Thaler*, 408 F. App'x 787, 795 (5th Cir. 2010) (relying, in part, on IQ scores of 86 and 88 listed on Esparaza's penitentiary packets where no other information was given), *cert. denied*, 131 S. Ct. 2446 (2011); *Cribbs v. State*, No. W2006-01381-CCA-R3-PD, 2009 WL 1905454, at *16 (Tenn. Crim. App. July 1, 2009) (focusing on a score of 82 from the Ammons Picture Vocabulary test); *Ex parte Hearn*, 310 S.W.3d 424, 429 n.13 (Tex. Crim. App. 2010) (using an IQ score of 82 from a short-form test).

19. See, e.g., *Holladay v. Allen*, 555 F.3d 1346, 1357–58 (11th Cir. 2009); *Walker v. True*, 399 F.3d 315, 323 (4th Cir. 2005); *United States v. Smith*, 790 F. Supp. 2d 482, 491 (E.D. La. 2011); *United States v. Lewis*, No. 1:08 CR 404, 2010 WL 5418901, at *8, 11–12 (N.D. Ohio Dec. 23, 2010); *Wiley v. Epps*, 668 F. Supp. 2d 848, 893–96 (N.D. Miss. 2009); *Thomas v. Allen*, 614 F. Supp. 2d 1257, 1281, 1291 (N.D. Ala. 2009); *United States v. Davis*, 611 F. Supp. 2d 472, 475, 477 (D. Md. 2009); *Green v. Johnson*, No. CIVA 2:05CV340, 2006 WL 3746138, at *43–45 (E.D. Va. Dec. 15, 2006) (recognizing the Flynn effect, but rejecting the SEM and the practice effect); *Commonwealth v. Williams*, 61 A.3d 979, 982–83 (Pa. 2013).

20. See, e.g., *Wiley v. Epps*, 625 F.3d 199, 215 (5th Cir. 2010); *Thomas v. Allen*, 607 F.3d 749, 757 (11th Cir. 2010); *Smith*, 790 F. Supp. 2d at 495–96; *Hughes v. Epps*, 694 F. Supp. 2d 533, 544 (N.D. Miss. 2010); *Williams*, 61 A.3d at 982–83.

21. See, e.g., *Chester v. Thaler*, 666 F.3d 340, 355 (5th Cir. 2011); *Wood v. Allen*, 542 F.3d 1281, 1286 (11th Cir. 2008), *cert. denied*, 525 U.S. 1042 (1998); *Ladd v. Thaler*, No. 1:03cv239, 2013 WL 593927, at *8 (E.D. Tex. Feb. 15, 2013); *Ex parte Smith*, No. 1080973, 2010 WL 4148528, at *3 (Ala. Oct. 22, 2010); *Lane v. State*, No. CR-10-1343, 2013 WL 5966905, at *6 (Ala. Crim. App. Nov. 8, 2013); *Lee v. State*, 898 So. 2d 790, 809–10 (Ala. Crim. App. 2003); *Dufour v. State*, 69 So. 3d 235, 244–45 (Fla. 2011); *Rodgers v. State*, 948 So. 2d 655, 667 (Fla. 2006); *Rodriguez v. State*, 919 So. 2d 1252, 1265 (Fla. 2005); *State v. Dunn*, 41 So. 3d 454, 462–63 (La. 2010); *State v. Campbell*, 983 So. 2d 810, 825 (La. 2008); *Doss v. State*, 19 So. 3d 690, 710 (Miss. 2009); *State v. Hill*, 894 N.E.2d 108, 121 (Ohio Ct. App. 2008); *State v. Pruitt*, 415 S.W.3d 180, 199 (Tenn. 2013).

22. See, e.g., cases cited *infra* note 65.

23. See, e.g., *Walker v. Kelly*, 593 F.3d 319, 324–25 (4th Cir. 2010), *cert. denied*, 560 U.S. 921 (2010).

24. See, e.g., *id.* at 326 (noting the defendant's "ability to ingratiate himself to women and establish intimate relationships with them in a relatively short period of time as evidence of social skills").

25. See, e.g., *Walker*, 593 F.3d at 325–27; *Umana*, 2010 WL 1052271, at *5–6; *Webster v. United States*, No. Civ.A. 4:00-CV-1646-, 2003 WL 23109787, at *13 (N.D. Tex. Sept. 30, 2003); *State v. Hill*, 894 N.E.2d 108, 124–25 (Ohio Ct. App. 2008); *Ex parte Briseño*, 135 S.W.3d 1, 18 (Tex. Crim. App. 2004).

26. See, e.g., *United States v. Smith*, 790 F. Supp. 2d 482, 517 (E.D. La. 2011) ("[T]he authors of the ABAS-II [a standardized measure of adaptive functioning] strongly recommend against using correctional officers as respondents . . . [because] adaptive behavior is supposed to be assessed in a 'real community' where the person has to make his own choices, as opposed to a structured prison setting, where much of the inmate's daily life is scheduled by the institutional staff."). As stated in *United States v. Hardy*, 762 F. Supp. 2d 849, 899 (E.D. La. 2010), "An institutional environment of any kind necessarily provides 'hidden supports' whereby the inmates . . . are told when to get up, when to eat, when to bathe, and their movements are highly restricted."

27. See *supra* note 66.

28. See, e.g., Martha E. Snell et al., *Characteristics and Needs of People with Intellectual Disability Who Have Higher IQs*, 47 Intell. & Developmental Disabilities 220, 226 (2009). http://www.aaiddjournals.org/doi/pdf/10.1352/1934-9556-47.3 .220 (describing the impact that gullibility has on individuals with intellectual disabilities)

29. *Smith*, 790 F. Supp. 2d at 518 ("Prison guards can hardly be expected to be able to [determine adaptive functioning]. Furthermore, as was noted in Hardy, 'prison officers' observations are limited to an extremely unusual set of circumstances, and are likely to be filtered through their experience with other prisoners, many of whom may also suffer from intellectual limitations.' A further shortcoming relating to the use of prison personnel as respondents is the bias they might have, as law enforcement officers, against a criminal." [quoting *Hardy*, 762 F. Supp. 2d at 900)].

30. *Ex Parte Moore*, 470 S.W. 3d 481 (Tx. Crim. App. 2015); compare *State v. Vela*, 777 N.W.2d 266 (Neb. 2010) (finding that the defendant failed on Prong 2 because of his job and relationships) with *United States v. Jiménez-Bencevi*, 934 F. Supp. 2d 360 (D.P.R. 2013) (finding that the defendant failed on Prong 2 because of the sophistication of the crime).

31. *Wiley v. Epps*, 625 F.3d 199, 203, 204 (5th Cir. 2010); see also DSM-IV-TR, *supra* note 7, at 151 (stating that people with mental retardation may "be able to live independently" and "[d]ocumented successful outcomes of individuals with appropriate supports contrasts sharply with incorrect stereotypes that these individuals never have friends, jobs, spouses, or children"); *id.* at 46 ("There are no specific physical features associated with Mental Retardation"); *id.* at 43 (people with mild mental retardation "can acquire academic skills up to approximately the sixth-grade level[,]" . . . "have minimal impairment in sensorimotor areas, . . . often are not distinguishable from children without Mental Retardation until a later age[,]" and "usually achieve . . . vocational skills" and even successfully live independently).

32. *Allen*, 2012 WL 2577492, at *7; Tarver v. Thomas, No. 07-00294-CG-B, 2012 WL 4461710 (S.D. Ala. Sept. 24, 2012); *Smith*, 790 F. Supp. 2d at 535.

33. See *State v. Grell* (2006) stating one reason for heightened standard of review for mental retardation, by clear and convincing evidence, is because of the legislature's fear of malingering.

34. *Atkins v. Virginia*, 536 U.S. 304, 317 (2002) (alterations in original) (quoting *Ford v. Wainwright*, 477 U.S. 399, 405, 416–17 (1986)).

35. Perhaps, however, a comparison of the success rate in jury cases in the more recent period—post-2008—is more appropriate than a comparison to the overall rate for all *Atkins* cases, given that most jury determinations occurred in that stretch. Moreover, as previously discussed, one *would* expect that success rates between pre- and post-*Atkins* cases would differ because some of the pre-*Atkins* cases are ones that were so strong they would have been settled had they been decided after *Atkins*—and the set of judge cases (unlike the set of jury cases) include some of those "would-have-settled" cases. But even if jury cases are compared to all post-2008 cases, a huge discrepancy in success rates remains: 26% versus 4%. A comparison to overall success rates during the later period can also be criticized. Because overall success rates reflect both the initial decision maker's determination and subsequent reversals, it could be argued that the overall success rate overstates the willingness of judges to find intellectual disability. Yet a comparison limited to initial decisions is also an "apples and oranges" comparison because our review shows that jury decisions are amazingly invincible on appeal and judge decisions are not; we have only encountered two jury determinations of no intellectual disability that have been reversed on appeal. See *Lambert v. State*, 126 P.3d 6646 (Okla. Crim. App. 2005); *Pickens v. State*, 126 P.3d 612 (Okla. Crim. App. 2005).

36. This table reflects the current status of all cases by state, regardless of what stage of litigation the case is now in. Overall success rates would rise in most states if we counted only the cases that are final as "losses." As discussed in the Introduction, any method of determining success rates has its disadvantages, but for the purpose of examining variation by state, we thought it was most instructive to include the largest set of cases possible.

37. As discussed earlier, in 2014, the Supreme Court reversed Hall's death sentence, improving Florida's success rate to 1 in 24.

38. Instructing a focus upon factors related to the crime and perceptions of the defendant by laypersons.

References

Alabama Code § 13A-5-45(a) (1975).

Allen v. Wilson, No. 1:01 cv-1658-JDT-TAB, 2012 WL 2577492, at *7 (S.D. Ind. July 3, 2012).

Alper, T. (2013). Toward a right to litigate ineffective assistance of counsel. *Washington & Lee Law Review, 70*(2), 839–882.

American Psychiatric Association. (2000). *Diagnostic and Statistical Manual of Mental Disorders* (4th Edition, text revision). Washington, DC: Author.

Arkansas Code Annotated § 5-4-618(d)(2) (B)(i) (1993).

Atkins v. Virginia, 536 U.S. 304, 337, 353–54 (2002).

Blume, J. H., Johnson, S. L., & Ensler, K. E. (2013). Killing the oblivious: An empirical study of competency to be executed litigation. *UMKC Law Review, 82*(2), 335–358.

Blume, J. H., Johnson, S. L., Marcus, P., & Paavola, E. (2014). A tale of two (and possibly three) *Atkins*: Intellectual disability and capital punishment twelve years after the Supreme Court's creation of a categorical bar. *William & Mary Bill of Rights Journal, 22*, 393–414.

Blume, J. H., Johnson, S. L., & Seeds, C. W. (2009a). Of *Atkins* and men: Deviations from clinical definitions of mental retardation in death penalty cases. *Cornell Journal of Law and Public Policy, 18*, 689–733.

Blume, J. H., Johnson, S. J., & Seeds, C. (2009b). An Empirical Look at *Atkins v. Virginia* and its Application in Capital Cases. *Tennessee Law Review, 76*, 625–639.

Branch v. State, 961 So. 2d 659 (Miss., 2007).

Brown v. State, 982 So. 2d 565 (Ala., 20016).

Cal. Penal Code § 1376(b)(1) (West, 2003).

Chase v. State, 873 So. 2d 1013 (Miss. 2004).

Cherry v. State, 959 So. 2d 702, 712–13 (Fla., 2007).

Chester v. Quarterman, No. 505cv29, 2008 WL 1924245 (E.D. Tex. Apr. 29, 2008).

Davis, L.A. (2009). People with Intellectual Disabilities in the Criminal Justice System: Victims and Suspects: The Arc [nonperiodic web document]. http://www.thearc.org/document.doc?id=3664

Doss v. State, 19 So. 3d 690 (Miss., 2009).

Dufour v. State, 69 So. 3d 235 (Fla., 2011).

Eisenberg, T., Hannaford-Agor, P. L., Hans, V. P., Waters, N. L., Munsterman, G. T., Schwab, S. J., & Wells, M. T. (2005). Judge–jury agreement in criminal cases: A partial replication of Kalven & Zeisel's *The American Jury. Journal of Empirical Legal Studies, 2*(1), 171–206.

Franklin v. Maynard, 588 S.E. 2d 604 (S.C., 2003).

Gelman, A., Liebman, J. S., West, V., & Kiss, A. (2004). A broken system: The persistent patterns of reversals of death sentences in the United States, *Journal of Empirical Legal Studies, 1*(2), 209–261.

Hall v. Florida, 134 S. Ct. 1986, 1995 (2014).

Hans, V. P. (2007). Judges, juries, and scientific evidence. *Journal of Law and Policy, 16*, 19–46.

Hans, V. P., Hannaford-Agor, P. L., Mott, N. L., & Munsterman, G. T. (2003). The hung jury: The American jury's insights and contemporary understanding. *Criminal Law Bulletin, 39*, 33–50.

Head v. Hill, 587 S.E.2d 613 (2005).

Hernandez v. Stephens, 537 Fed. Appx. 531 (5th Cir., 2013).

Hodges v. State, 55 So. 3d 515, 526 (Fla., 2010).

Inmate Removed from Death Row (2012). *ABC-11 Eyewitness News* (Feb. 2, 2012, 8:41 a.m.) [nonperiodic web document] http://abc11.com/archive/8528653

Jackson v. Norris, 2016 WL 1740419 (E.D. Ark., 2016).

Judicial Override in Alabama, Equal Justice Initiative (2008) [nonperiodic web document] http://www.eji.org/files/03.19.08%20Judicial%20Override%20 Fact%20Sheet_0.pdf

Kaufman, A. S. (1994). Practice effects. In R. J. Sternberg (Ed.), *Encyclopedia of Human Intelligence*, Vol. 2 (pp. 828–833). New York: MacMillan.

Lizcano v. State, 2010 WL 1817772 (Tex. Crim. App. 2010).

Lizcano v. Texas, ___ U.S. ___, 136 S.Ct. 584 (2015).

Maldonado v. Thaler, 625 F. 3d 222 (237–238 (5th Cir. 2010).

Matamoros v. Thaler, No. H-07-2613, 2010 WL 1404368 (S.D. Tex. Mar. 31, 2010).

Moore v. Texas, 137 S. Ct. 1039, 1045, 1047, 1049, 1050–1053, 1060–1061 (2017).

Morris v. State, 60 So. 3d 326 (Ala. Crim. App., 2010).

Mulroy, S. J. (2013). Execution by accident: Evidentiary and constitutional problems with the "childhood onset" requirement in Atkins claims. *Vermont Law Review*, 37, 591–651.

N.C. Gen. Stat. Ann. § 15A-2005(e) (2001).

Oats v. State, 2015 WL 9169766 (FL, 2015).

Parrish v. Commonwealth, 272 S.W.3d 161, 168 (KY, 2008)

Pa. R. Crim. P. 844(B).

Radelet, M. (2011). Overriding jury sentencing recommendations in Florida capital cases: An update and possible half-requiem. *Michigan State Law Review*, 2011, 793–857.

Rogers v. State, 653 S.E.2d 31 (Ga., 2007).

Schalock, R. L., Buntinx, W. H. E., Borthwick-Duffy, S., Bradley, V., Craig, E. M., Coulter, D. L., Gomez, S. C., Lachapelle, Y., Luckasson, R. A., Reeve, A., Shogren, K. A., Snell, M. E., Spreat, S., Tassé, M. J., Thompson, J. R., Verdugo, M. A., Wehmeyer, M. L., & Yeager, M. H. (2010). *Intellectual Disability: Definition, Classification, and System of Supports* (11th Edition). Washington, DC: American Association on Intellectual and Developmental Disabilities.

Snell, M. E., Luckasson, R., Borthwick-Duffy, S., Bradley, V., Buntinx, W. H. E. Craig, E. P, Gomez, S. C., Lachapelle, Y., Reeve, A., Schalock, R. L., Shogren, K. A., Spreat, S., Tassé, M. J., Thompson, J. R., Verdugo, M. A., Wehmeyer, M. L., & Yeager, M. H. (2009). Characteristics and needs of people with intellectual disability who have higher IQs. *Intellectual and Developmental Disabilities*, 47, 220–233.

Stallings v. Bagley, 561 F. Supp. 2d 821, 881 (N.D. Ohio, 2008).

State v. Campbell, 983 So. 2d 810 (La., 2008).

State v. Dunn, 41 So. 3d 454, 458–59 (La., 2010).

State v. Flores, 93 P.3d 1264 (N.M., 2004).

State v. Grell, 135 P.3d 696 (Ariz., 2006).

Streib, V. L. (2003). Adolescence, mental retardation, and the death penalty: The siren call of *Atkins v. Virginia. New Mexico Law Review, 33*, 183–206.

Thomas v. Allen, 607 F.3d 749, 753 (11th Cir., 2010).

United States v. Davis, 611 F. Supp. 2d 472, 485 (D. Md., 2009).

United States v. Smith, 790 F. Supp. 2d 482, 517 (E.D. La., 2011).

United States v. Williams, Criminal No. 06-00079 JMS-KSC, 2014 WL 869217 (D. Haw. Mar. 6, 2014).

United States v. Umana, No. 3:08cr134, 2010 WL 1052271 (W.D.N.C. Mar. 19, 2010).

Va. Code. Ann, § 19.2-264 (2003).

Vidmar, N., & Hans, V. P. (2007). *American Juries: The Verdict.* New York: Prometheus Books.

Walker v. Kelly, 598 F.3d 167 (4th Cir. 2010).

Weiner, R. L. & Reiter-Palmon, R. (2004). *Prosecutorial Misconduct in Death Penalty Cases: The U.S. Supreme Court rules that the state may not suppress evidence that is material to guilt or punishment.* Psychology Faculty Publications. Paper 63. http://digitalcommons.unomaha.edu/psychfacpub/63

Wiley v. Epps, 625 F.3d 199, 203, 204 (5th Cir., 2010)

Wiley v. State, 890 So. 2d 892 (Miss., 2004).

Williams v. State, 270 S.W.3d 112 (Tx. Court of Crim. App., 2008).

CHAPTER FIVE

Assessing Intellectual Functioning

Prong 1 of the diagnostic criteria for intellectual disability in state statutes and national treatises is significant deficits in intellectual functioning (American Psychiatric Association (APA), 2013; DeMatteo, Marczyk, & Pich, 2007; Duvall & Morris, 2006; Schalock et al., 2010; Wood, Packman, Howell, & Bongar, 2014). As covered in Chapter 1, we see that *Atkins v. Virginia* refused to set forth a national standard for defining intellectual disability, rather leaving it up to individual states to define and operationalize how the diagnosis should be made. Although all states' statutes defining intellectual disability seem to agree on the three necessary prongs (deficits in intellectual functioning, deficits in adaptive behavior, and age of onset), they do not all agree on the operationalization of these three elements of the diagnosis (see Duvall & Morris, 2006; Demateo et al., 2007; Amos, 2011; Wood, Packman, Howell, & Bongar, 2014). In this chapter, we will review how "intelligence" is generally defined and how experts in forensic and *Atkins* cases should conduct their assessment of intellectual functioning for the purposes of making a determination of intellectual disability.

The study of human intelligence is certainly among the most intensely researched phenomena in the field of psychology. Wasserman (2012) attributes the first attempts at systematically studying intelligence and the brain to the field of phrenology in the early 1800s. The pioneering work of Francis Galton on the measurement of individual differences in sensory and motor reaction times in the late 1880s is often credited for advancing the scientific study of human intelligence (Greenwood, 2015; McGrew,

2015). It was nonetheless the groundbreaking work of Frenchmen Alfred Binet and his associate Theodore Simon in the creation of the first norm-referenced standardized test of intelligence (Wasserman, 2012). The Binet–Simon scale was quickly translated into English by Henry H. Goddard and disseminated in the United States as the Stanford–Binet scale (now in its fifth edition) (Roid, 2003).

Probably the best known and most widely accepted theory of intelligence is the general intelligence theory ("g") put forth by Spearman (1904). The Cattell–Horn–Carroll (CHC) theoretical model of intelligence is probably the most widely used today (Flanagan & Kaufman, 2004). The CHC model includes two forms of intelligence: Fluid intelligence (Gf) and Crystalized intelligence (Gc). Fluid intelligence generally involves abilities that involve reasoning, problem solving, or tapping cognitive abilities that are not encountered in school or everyday life (e.g., recognizing patterns, abstract reasoning, responding to novel situations). Crystallized intelligence involves using knowledge, experience, and acquired understanding (often learned in school) and includes vocabulary and general knowledge. Despite these two well established theories of intelligence and more than a century of scientific work in the area of intelligence, there is still no unanimity on a theory or definition of human intelligence (Conway & Kovacs, 2015; Goldstein, 2015). Although there may not be a unified theory of intelligence or definition of intelligence that all intelligence researchers have unanimously endorsed, both the AAIDD's *Terminology and Classification Manual* (Schalock et al., 2010) and the *DSM-5* (APA, 2013) have adopted this consensus definition of intelligence published by Gottfredson (1997):

> Intelligence is a very general mental capability that, among other things, involves the ability to reason, plan, solve problems, think abstractly, comprehend complex ideas, learn quickly and learn from experience. It is not merely book learning, a narrow academic skill, or test-taking smarts. Rather, it reflects a broader and deeper capability for comprehending our surroundings—"catching on," "making sense"' of things, or "figuring out" what to do. (p. 13)

Assessing Intellectual Functioning

Despite the debate regarding what is the prevailing theory of human intelligence, using individually administered standardized tests of intelligence that have a comprehensive set of tasks and subtests with adequate national norms remains the recommended means of determining Prong 1 of the diagnostic criteria for intellectual disability (APA, 2013; Schalock et al., 2010). The use of the full-scale IQ score remains the best way to represent the construct of general intellectual functioning for the purpose of making a diagnosis of intellectual disability (McGrew, 2015; Schalock et al., 2010). *Significant deficit* in intellectual functioning is operationally defined as a standard score that is approximately two standard deviations below the population mean, with consideration of all sources of measurement error (APA, 2013; Schalock et al., 2010). We will discuss measurement error, but first we should define some of the key terms used.

Defining Terms

We will define these psychometric terms before moving any further. *Intelligence quotients* (IQ) are a form of standard score commonly used by tests of intellectual functioning. A person's *standard score* on a test is calculated by transforming the individual's obtained raw score on Test A (e.g., the sum of the number of correct responses on a test) using the population's known mean and standard deviation on Test A, which transforms the individual's test performance onto a common metric allowing us to compare his or her score to anyone else tested with Test A. Standard scores are possible only for tests where, if administered to the entire population, the distribution of all test scores on said test would be normally distributed (see Figure 1.1 in Chapter 1). A percentile score is one form of a standard score that permits the interpretation of a person's performance in relation to a reference group. Although not a requirement, in the case of many psychological tests the scale for standard scores is set to have a mean or average score of 100 and a standard deviation of 15. Thus, a test performance that results in a standard score of 70 is said to be "significantly" below average or approximately two standard deviations below the population mean. A *standard deviation* is a unit of measure that indicates the distance from the average. During the standardization phase of the development of a standardized test, the test and its items are administered to a large and representative sample of the reference group of interest or population. This is generally referred to as the standardization sample or *norming group*. From this norming group, the test developers compute the population's mean score and standard deviation on the test. The mean score and standard deviation are essential to transforming subsequently obtained raw scores (i.e., the sum of the number of correct items) on said test to a standard scale score (e.g., intelligence quotient, or IQ).

Tests of Intelligence

We do not have sufficient space in this chapter to review in depth all the available tests of intelligence that are adequately constructed, standardized, and normed for the purpose of evaluating intellectual functioning when making a determination of intellectual disability. When making a determination of intellectual disability, including in *Atkins* hearings, these relevant stipulations offered by AAIDD (Schalock et al., 2010) and *DSM-5* (APA, 2013) should guide the clinical judgment of all mental health experts in their selection of an appropriate test:

- Individually administered
- Comprehensive measure of intellectual functioning (e.g., verbal comprehension, perceptual reasoning, quantitative reasoning, working memory, abstract thinking, and cognitive efficiency)
- Strong psychometric properties (including established reliability and validity)
- Recent national norms that are representative of the U.S. census

Short forms, scales that yield an abbreviated IQ score, group-administered tests, and tests that rely on only a subset of tasks or yield only a subset of scores for a narrow band of intellectual abilities are not appropriate for use in informing whether or not a person has intellectual disability (Schalock et al., 2012). These tests have a purpose—and in fact, are quite useful for screening purposes—but have limited validity for providing a definitive score for the purposes of ruling in or ruling out intellectual disability. The use of appropriate standardized tests of intelligence, in and of itself, may not be sufficient. Clinicians assessing the person's intellectual functioning must rely on their clinical judgment throughout the process of conducting their psychological evaluation, including selecting the appropriate, culturally sensitive standardized measure of intellectual functioning, administering it competently, assessing the examinee's effort, and scoring and interpreting the examinee's performance.

The Wechsler Adult Intelligence Scale (4th Edition) (Wechsler, 2008) and Stanford-Binet (5th Edition) intelligence scales are considered by many experts as the gold standard for the assessment of intellectual functioning for the purpose of making an intellectual disability determination, especially in death penalty cases. These are certainly two of the most widely used, but attorneys and ID experts will come across other standardized tests of intelligence that are also considered comprehensive, multiability tests of intelligence. Some of the available instruments that might have been previously administered or might be considered when assessing a person's intellectual functioning for the purpose of making a determination of intellectual disability include Cognitive Assessment System, 2nd Edition (CAS2) (Naglieri, Das, & Goldstein, 2014), Kaufman Assessment Battery for Children, 2nd Edition (KABC-II) (Kaufman & Kaufman, 2004), Stanford-Binet Intelligence Scales, Fifth Edition (SB5) (Roid, 2003),

Wechsler Intelligence Scale for Children, 5th Edition (WISC-V) (Wechsler, 2014), Wechsler Adult Intelligence Scale, 4th Edition (WAIS-IV) (Wechsler, 2008), and Woodcock–Johnson, Fourth Edition Tests of Cognitive Abilities (WJ-IV COG) (Shrank, McGrew, & Mather, 2014). It is possible that we have omitted a test that can be argued as an equally robust, comprehensive and multiability test of intelligence and could have been included in this list of tests. Hence, this list should not be considered exhaustive.

Specifically excluded from this list are short forms or abbreviated tests of intelligence (such as Kaufman Brief Intelligence Test, Wide Range Intelligence Test, Wechsler Abbreviated Scale of Intelligence, Slosson Intelligence Test, and other similar screening tests). Also to be avoided in *Atkins* cases are other narrow-band tests, such as Test of Nonverbal Intelligence, Comprehensive Test of Nonverbal Intelligence, Peabody Picture Vocabulary Test, and the like. As with the short form, abbreviated tests, narrow-band tests, and group-administered tests (e.g., beta tests) should also be used and reviewed with great caution, and their results should be given substantially less weight than the preceding comprehensive, multiability tests of intelligence.

Clinicians will rely upon their clinical judgment and consider several factors when selecting the appropriate standardized assessment test to use, including which tests of intelligence have been previously administered and when, as well as the examinee's chronological age, English-language proficiency, cultural background, and motor ability/limitations. Clinicians will also want to closely review previously administered test protocols for any observable administration errors, verify the tabulation of raw scores and transformation to standard scores, and examine any recording of the administration, if available, for administration errors. Again, clinical judgment plays a key role in reviewing and interpreting the results obtained on standardized tests of intelligence (APA, 2013), including taking into consideration the many sources of measurement error associated with the standardized test used. We will briefly review the definition of measurement error and some of its more common types.

Measurement Error

Measurement error, simply put, is any variance in obtained scores that is attributable to sources other than the individual's true ability on the trait measured by the test. The obtained score (e.g., full-scale IQ score or composite adaptive behavior score) from any standardized test is the test's approximate measure of the person's true ability on the construct or trait assessed by said test. All standardized tests have measurement error embedded in the obtained scores that they yield. It is critical to interpret all obtained scores, even from the most robust and reliable standardized tests, while considering that test's reliability and all potential sources of measurement error. Relevant to the determination of intellectual disability, both the AAIDD *Manual* (Schalock et al., 2010) and the *DSM-5* (APA, 2013) recommend the use of clinical judgment and consideration of all sources of measurement error when interpreting results from standardized tests. Three potential sources of measurement error are standard error of measurement, age of the test's norms, and practice effects.

Standard Error of Measurement

The Supreme Court of the United States in *Hall v. Florida* ruled that states must consider the test's standard error of measurement when interpreting obtained IQ scores in cases where the defendant is making an intellectual disability claim (*Hall v. Florida*, 2014). In fact, the justices reiterated in their decision the importance to consider IQ test scores not as a fixed number but as a range of scores (*Hall v. Florida*, 2014; p. 10).

The standard error of measurement (SEM) is a direct measure of the test's reliability and is computed by administering the test to a large and representative sample of the population to be assessed on the test and computing the test's reliability coefficient, which can then be translated into an average error of measurement for the population (American Educational Research Association (AERA), 2014). Generally, the SEM is computed and then used to create confidence intervals around the obtained standard scores (e.g., 95% certainty). A confidence interval of 95% represents a statistical certainty that, based on the knowledge of this test's reliability coefficient, there is a 95% chance that the person's true score falls within a confidence interval that is +/−2 times the test's SEM. Thus, a professional reporting on an assessed individual's "obtained" full-scale IQ score of 70 on IQ Test A and knowing that Test A has a SEM of 2.5 around its full-scale IQ score, he would report that there is a 95% certainty that the assessed person's "true" full-scale IQ score falls within the range of 65–75 (i.e., 2×2.5= +/−5 points). Using a confidence interval of 95% is recommended practice when interpreting IQ scores for the purposes of making an intellectual disability determination (Schalock et al., 2010).

Aging Test Norms or Flynn Effect

James Flynn established unequivocally that the U.S. population's mean IQ score has been increasing. In fact, historical IQ data going as far back as 1930s indicate that this upward trend has been in existence for more than 60 years, and there appears to be no end in sight (Flynn 1984, 2006; Flynn & Weiss, 2007). This increase in IQ scores is not limited to only U.S. populations but has been shown to be true in all industrialized countries that have population data on standardized IQ tests (Flynn, 1987). This phenomenon was coined the "Flynn effect" by Hernstein and Murray (1994) and refers to the increase in IQ scores over time (i.e., about 3 full-scale IQ points per decade).

For example, when interpreting an individual's obtained full-scale IQ score on standardized test of intelligence x, which was normed 10 years prior to the date of administration, it would be expected to provide an unadjusted IQ score that would be inflated by approximately 3 points. This is so because we are using "old norms" (i.e., collected on a comparative/normative sample from 10 years ago) and does not factor in the established fact that the comparative sample's mean IQ has been increasing at a rate of 0.3 points per year, hence 10 years $\times$ 0.3 = 3.0 IQ points. Therefore, the Flynn effect raises potential challenges in the interpretation of IQ scores obtained on tests that have aging norms.

It is financially untenable for test publishers to revise and restandardize tests every two or three years. However, as Kaufman (2009) pointed out, the importance of the Flynn effect has jolted test publishers out of their complacency and forced them to be more accountable and to revise and restandardize tests more frequently.

Once challenged by some experts as a "red herring" raised by defense experts to explain high IQ scores, we now find entire chapters in test manuals such as WISC-V (Grégoire, Daniel, Llorente, & Weiss, 2016) and WAIS-IV (Zhou, Grégoire, & Zhu, 2010) about the Flynn effect. In fact, a special issue of the *Journal of Psychoeducational Assessment* devoted to the discussion of the Flynn effect invited three authors to address the issues, not of whether or not the Flynn effect exists because that debate seems to have been settled but rather whether we should be adjusting obtained IQ scores based on the age of the test's norms (see Kaufman & Weiss, 2010). Hence, it can be safely said that the Flynn effect is real (Weiss, 2010). We will briefly describe the Flynn effect and why it matters in *Atkins* hearings.

It can be argued that there is a majority opinion among scientists and psychometric experts that there is a necessity in death penalty cases to make adjustments to obtained IQ scores when these scores were obtained on tests with old norms (see Kaufman, 2010). Kaufman aptly concluded that adjustments should be made in *Atkins* hearings: "The point is that a person tested on an outdated test will earn spuriously high scores as each year goes by, and that amount of spuriousness amounts to about 3 [IQ] points per decade for Americans" (p. 503). Young (2012) has argued that *not* correcting for the Flynn effect across U.S. jurisdictions has led to the inconsistent application of the protections provided under *Atkins v. Virginia*.

We will briefly address three common arguments raised against the use of the Flynn effect when interpreting IQ test results and explain why these arguments are not valid.

Flynn Effect and Its Relevance to Interpreting Test Results

Hagan and his colleagues (2008) have argued that such adjustments should not be made in *Atkins* hearings because they are not made in everyday clinical practice. Cunningham and Tassé (2010) argued that adjusting individual scores based on the obsolescence of the test's norms is justified in *Atkins* hearings because simply, when life is in the balance, it's different. Clinicians should take into account all known sources of error variance to inform their clinical opinion when interpreting IQ test results. The truth of the matter is that the stakes in everyday clinical practice pale in comparison to those in *Atkins* hearings. Grégoire and colleagues agreed that high stakes cases are different than everyday IQ testing cases for the purpose of obtaining classroom accommodations: "In our opinion, when using an older test before the new version is available, a generalized estimate of FE [Flynn effect] based on .30 points per year is reasonable practice in high stakes legal cases" (Grégoire et al., 2016; p. 203). Reynolds and his colleagues (2010) summed up the clinical practice issue very well when they concluded: "If the [Flynn effect] is real, the failure to apply the Flynn correction as we have described it is tantamount to malpractice. No one's life should depend on when an IQ test was normed" (p. 480).

Flynn Effect and the Interpretation of Individual Scores

Hagan and his colleagues (2010) have argued that the adjustments based on the Flynn effect cannot be made because these are observed measurement characteristics made at a population level and cannot be assumed transferable at an individual score level. Although this might appear like a reasonable argument to a layperson, it is somewhat absurd from a psychometrics standpoint. Most of our psychometrics, or science of testing, concepts are based on the premise that one obtains large population statistics and then applies them to individual scores and performances. A couple of key examples include norming of tests and standard error of measurement, which are two crucial elements in all individual standardized testing.

Norming is the process during test development, revision, and standardization where the test publisher administers the test to large groups of people from the desired population to be tested and obtains information on how these different age groups score on each individual item and then subsets of items. This process of accumulating population information on the test items then allows the test developer to create normative tables and transform eventual obtained individual scores on subsets of items and transform them to what is called a "standardized score" by applying the reference norming group's mean and standard deviation to the assessed person's individual score and transforming their raw score to a standard score. Thus, data and statistics obtained from a large population group that almost certainly does not include the assessed individual are used to interpret the assessed individual's performance on that test.

Standard error of measurement (SEM) is mathematically derived from the test's reliability coefficient. Test reliability is defined as the consistency of scores obtained on a test across multiple administrations, assuming the person's ability level remained unchanged (AERA, 2014). For the sake of simplicity, it suffices to say that a test's reliability and related standard error of measure are computed using the data obtained by administering said test to a large population (i.e., standardization sample). Hence, the SEM is derived from data obtained from a large group administration, and it is then subsequently applied to make a correction to individual test scores to inform the interpretation of that individual's performance on the test. In other words, we apply group statistics to individual scores all the time in testing.

Flynn Effect in People with Low IQs

Although much of Flynn's research was done on IQ test scores from the general population, several researchers have documented that the rise in IQ scores extends to the lower end of the normal curve and impacts persons in the "significant deficit" range (i.e., minus 2 standard deviations below the population mean). Ceci and his colleagues have reported data from school evaluations of children referred for disability evaluations in relation to the Flynn effect (Ceci & Kanaya, 2010; Ceci, Scullin, & Kanaya, 2003; Kanaya & Ceci, 2012). These authors reported that the number of children identified with intellectual disability increased almost threefold when assessed on the newer/more recently normed WISC-III than in previous years when children's evaluations relied on the older version and more outdated norms of the WISC-R. Not only does the obsolescence of the test norms extend downward to low IQ ranges, many agree that its impact may be even greater than 3.0 points per decade (Flynn, 2010; Habets, Jeandarme, Uzieblo, Oei, & Bogaerts, 2015; Reynolds, Niland, Wright, & Rosenn, 2010; Weiss, 2010; Zhou, Zhu, & Weiss, 2010).

Both *AAIDD* (Schalock et al., 2010) and the *DSM-5* (APA, 2013) state clearly that in cases where a test with aging norms is used as part of a diagnosis of intellectual disability, this potential source of error must be considered by the clinician when interpreting the results. Of the three articles specifically addressing the question of adjusting IQ scores to account for the Flynn effect in *Atkins* cases, two of them agreed (see Fletcher, Stuebing, & Hughes, 2010 and Reynolds et al., 2010), as did one of the special issue editors (Kaufman, 2010), who was swayed by their arguments.

Practice Effects

Practice effects refer to gains in IQ scores on tests of intelligence that result from a person being retested on the same instrument. Kaufman (1995) noted that practice effects can occur when the same individual is retested on a similar instrument. Both the AAIDD *Terminology and Classification Manual* (Schalock et al., 2010) and the *DSM-5* (APA, 2013) emphasize the importance of accounting for artificially increased IQ scores during the readministration of the same IQ test to the same individual within a short period of time. The *WISC-V Technical and Interpretive Manual* (Wechsler, 2014) presents test–retest data showing an increase in IQ scores when the WISC-V is readministered to the same group of children within a time interval ranging from 1 week to 12 weeks. The average increase in FSIQ from time 1 to time 2 was 6 points (Wechsler, 2014; p. 65). This artificial increase of approximately 6 points on the obtained FSIQ is due to the readministration of the same IQ test to the same individual within a short period of time and is known as the "practice effect." The practice effect on the FSIQ can be as high as 15 points (see Kaufman, 1995).

Thus, best practice recommends avoiding administering the test of intelligence to the same individual within a 12-month period to avoid potential practice effects artificially inflating the obtained scores. Also, when reviewing test results from assessments that were administered close in time, whether the results are from the same or a similar type of test to the same individual, one should use caution and clinical judgment in evaluating the accuracy and reliability of the scores obtained on these test administrations.

Measurement Error can Result in an Under- or Overestimation of True Ability

A common misconception about test performance held by some laypeople is that you cannot possibly obtain a score that is higher than your true ability. Hence, all scores that are lower had to have been malingered, and the highest score must be the true estimate of the person's score. This fallacy fails to take into consideration that there is administrator error for one and, second, that measurement error extends below and above the person's true score. Thus, someone who has a true IQ score of 69 could conceivably obtain a higher IQ score. Therefore, it is possible to obtain a test performance score that is higher than one's actual ability, not because of feigning (although feigning must always be carefully ruled out) but rather because a score can be inflated due to errors in test administration, scoring, practice effects, and the different types of measurement error.

Assessing Non-Native English Speakers and Foreign Nationals

The U.S. demographics are changing and becoming more racially, ethnically, and linguistically diverse. As of July 2014, the U.S. Hispanic population was estimated at 55 million (i.e., 17% of U.S. population), making people of Hispanic origin the nation's largest ethnic or racial minority (U.S. Census Bureau, 2014). Of the estimated 38 million U.S. residents 5 years and older who reported speaking Spanish in the home, 58% also reported speaking English "very well" (U.S. Census Bureau, 2014).

There are a number of considerations to take into account when assessing the intellectual functioning of a non-native U.S. English speaker or a foreign national. An important recommendation regarding language in testing is that the assessed person's language proficiency be evaluated and all assessments be administered in the language in which he or she is proficient (Benuto, 2013). The use of interpreters is not best practice and should be done only as a last resort and only if an appropriately standardized and normed version of an intelligence test does not exist.

Several factors need to be considered when selecting and interpreting the results from an appropriate standardized test of intelligence for a non-English-speaking examinee. Thaler and Jones-Forrester (2013) listed the following considerations: (1) generalizability and limitations of the test's normative sample in relation to assessed individual, (2) language proficiency, (3) examinee's and examiner's sociocultural and ethnic backgrounds and impact on rapport during testing, and (4) level of acculturation of examinee. A decision that needs to be made is whether to use a Spanish-language test of intelligence with U.S. norms or a Spanish-language test of intelligence with foreign norms (e.g., Spain or Mexico). The latter may be appropriate in cases of foreign nationals (e.g., Spaniards or Mexicans respectively), but for most foreign nationals, it may be a moot issue (e.g., Guatemalan, Cuban, Peruvian, etc.) because there may not exist a Spanish-language standardized test of intelligence that was normed in the individual's country of origin. The use of non-English language tests of intelligence and foreign established norms would be an appropriate choice for a foreign national if such tests were available. The United States is particularly rich when it comes to the availability of quality standardized and norm-referenced tests. Finding similarly robust standardized measures for examinees who were born and raised in a foreign country may not always be this easy.

Based on Thaler and Jones-Forrester's (2013) review, there are four Spanish-language tests of intelligence available for use: (1) Bateria III Woodcock-Munoz (Mexican, Spanish, and Central American norms), (2) WAIS-III (Mexican norms), (3) WAIS-III (Spanish norms), and (4) WAIS-III (Puerto Rican norms). These scales have all been translated to Spanish using professional translators and have developed separate norms from the U.S. norms.

Olley (2012) recommended the use of the Bateria III Woodcock-Munoz because of its psychometric properties and its benefit of having norms that are inclusive of U.S. natives, as well as Spanish speakers from Mexico, Costa Rica, Panama, Argentina, Columbia, Spain, Puerto Rico, and the United States. The Bateria III has reportedly good reliability and validity, and although some of the normative sample cells are small, overall it appears to be a good Spanish language test of intelligence (Thomsen, Gallup, & Llorente, 2008).

Suen and Greenspan (2009) were excoriatingly critical of the WAIS-III with Mexican norms. These authors raised several distinct flaws with the instrument, including (1) a very large standard error of measurement, (2) a large number of psychometric and technical errors found in the user's manual, and (3) problems with the normative sample itself and resulting standard scores. Suen and Greenspan's (2009) concerns were such that they called for the test publisher to withdraw the WAIS-III (Mexican norms) from the market. When using the WAIS-III (with Mexican norms) or interpreting results from this or any other non-English language test that was normed either in the United States or abroad, it is strongly encouraged to use caution, and the clinician should use clinical judgment in placing the appropriate amount of weight on these results in light of these issues.

The Spanish WAIS-III publisher claims it can be used with Spanish speakers from the United States and Latin America (TEA Ediciones, 2001). Choca, Krueger, Gabriel, Corral, & Garside (2009) reviewed the Spanish WAIS-III and concluded it was fine to use with adults between the ages of 16–34 years but tended to overestimate full-scale IQ scores for adults aged 35 and older compared to U.S. norms. These authors proposed a method of adjusting obtained scores on older individuals to bring them in closer alignment with U.S. norms. Choca and his colleagues concluded that the inflation of IQ scores produced on this Spanish version of the WAIS-III, if unadjusted, would lead to inaccurate assessment of older adults (35 years and older) when the test is used in the United States.

The WAIS-III Spanish version that was normed exclusively on Puerto Rican Americans is called the Escala de inteligencia de Wechsler para adultos—Tercera Edicion (EIWA-III) and is the second revision of the EIWA. The original EIWA was fraught with methodological and psychometric problems (Maldonado & Geisinger, 2004). There are currently no available independent published studies of the scale's psychometric properties, and it should be used with caution. Thaler and Jones-Forrester (2010) questioned the usefulness and validity of the EIWA-III on a Spanish-speaking population other than Puerto Ricans.

All fluent English speakers should be assessed on one of the aforementioned English language comprehensive multiability tests of intelligence that have been standardized and normed on a large and representative sample of the American population. A long time ago, there was some valid concern with the race/ethnicity bias in standardized tests of intelligence. Since then, there has in fact been more than a century of research to study the issue regarding why African Americans, as a group, score consistently differently than their Euro-American counterparts. Although the reasons for these differences have been debated with no unanimously agreed-upon consensus, it can be unequivocally affirmed that these group differences are real but are not attributable to bias in the tests and that the differences in test scores reflect true differences, not in particular bits of cultural knowledge but in more general and abstract abilities (Brody, 1992). In other words, today's comprehensive multiability test of intelligence (i.e., see examples of these tests listed earlier in this chapter) have undergone robust development and standardization parameters and rigorous psychometric testing to ensure that these modern tests are free of gender, race, and ethnic bias (Gottfredson & Saklofske, 2009).

Test Scores and Race/Ethnic or Socioeconomic Influence

Some experts have developed home-brewed correction formulae devised to make adjustments to obtained IQ scores to correct for the assessed person's impoverished upbringing, race or ethnicity, which is equated to a "handicap" on the IQ test score. This is inappropriate and incorrect. There is absolutely no scientific or psychometric evidence to support such practice (see the preceding discussion regarding lack of race/ethnicity bias in tests). In fact, one psychologist who engaged in such practice was severely sanctioned by the Texas State Board of Examiners of Psychologists and as a consequence was fined and restricted from practicing in criminal cases involving the determination of intellectual disability (Grissom, 2011).

Effort Testing Versus Malingering

Justice Scalia's nightmare scenario was that everyone on death row or sentenced to the death penalty would feign having intellectual disability (*Atkins v. Virginia*, 2002). Of course, feigning intellectual disability is not as easy as just failing an IQ test. This seems to have been borne out in the analyses of *Atkins* claims to date, where these rates are comparable to the estimated prevalence rates of inmates with ID (Blume, Johnson, Marcus, & Paavola, 2014; see Chapter 4 of this volume).

Malingering is defined in the *DSM-5* as "the intentional production of false or grossly exaggerated physical or psychological symptoms, motivated by external incentives" (APA, 2013; p. 726). Some have correctly argued that what we are concerned with in Atkins cases is more in line with effort testing than actual malingering, evaluating that the assessed person is putting forth their best effort on the test of intellectual functioning and thus producing an output that is indicative of their true capacity. It is perhaps because of this distinction that there has been confusion and inconsistent results regarding the utility of commonly used standardized measures of "malingering" (e.g., feigning the presence of psychiatric symptoms) and their validity in detecting when a person might be feigning low cognitive ability, when what we are most interested in assessing in this latter group is feigning low cognitive ability (i.e., possibly for the purpose of being diagnosed with intellectual disability). Probably of greater relevance for Atkins cases is identifying the optimal method to assessing effort and performance on tests of intellectual ability.

The Minnesota Multi-Phasic Inventory (MMPI) has been shown to be a poor proxy for malingering or effort testing in individuals with intellectual disability and should be avoided (Frumkin, 2006; Keyes, 2004). Some research has been done on standardized assessment tools used in forensic evaluations to detect malingering or poor effort (e.g., Test of Memory Malingering (TOMM), Rey 15-Item Memory Test, Rey Dot Counting Test, Validity Indicator Profile (VIP), Structured Interview of Reported Symptoms (SIRS), and results have been mixed. Most of the standardized tests used to assess malingering have not been standardized or normed on persons with an intellectual disability (Macvaugh & Cunningham, 2009).

Hurley and Deal (2006) reported significant limitations in the use of some of the measures they evaluated with people who had intellectual disability. It should also be noted that although the SIRS was developed as a measure of malingering of mental illness, most of the preceding measures of malingering were not specially developed to assess for malingering of "intellectual disability." In fact, a couple of these measures (e.g., TOMM, Rey 15-Item Memory Test) were specifically developed to assess feigning of memory problems, which has little to do with intellectual disability. Hurley and Deal (2006), using a group of 39 adults with mild intellectual disability, sought to assess the validity (i.e., whether the test measures what it says it measures) of the following measures used to assess for malingering or effort: TOMM (Tombaugh, 1996), Rey 15-Item Memory Test, Rey Dot Counting Test, and SIRS (Rogers, Bagby & Dickens, 1992). They reported that three of four of these tests had unacceptably high rates of false positives (i.e., results incorrectly indicated that the person was malingering or intentionally performing lower than their true ability), including the TOMM, Rey 15-Item Memory Test, and SIRS. Hurley and Deal (2006) thus concluded that the only valid measure of these four instruments was the Rey Dot Counting Test, which is a measure of effort by presenting increasingly difficult tasks with the expectation to observe a specific pattern of right/wrong responses linked to the established difficulty level of the tasks.

Graue et al. (2007) tested the false positive rates of the TOMM on a sample of 26 adults who had mild intellectual disability, as well as a demographically matched sample of controls who were either asked to malinger low IQ ($n = 25$) or complete the tests honestly ($n = 10$). They assessed several different measures of malingering mental illness symptoms to assess their effectiveness at identifying poor effort, including Miller Forensic Assessment of Symptoms Test (MFAST) (Miller, 2001) and Structured Inventory of Malingered Symptomatology (SIMS) (Widows & Smith, 2005), both tests used for measuring malingering of mental illness symptoms. Graue and her colleagues also tested three measures that purport to assess for malingering of cognitive deficits: Digit Memory Test (DMT) (Guilmette, Hart, Guiliano, & Leininger, 1994), Test of Memory Malingering (TOMM) (Tombaugh, 1997), and the Letter Memory Test (LMT) (Orey, Cragar, & Berry, 2000). Lastly, they also administered the Wechsler Adult Intelligence Scale, 3rd Edition (WAIS-III) (Wechsler, 1997) to all their participants and evaluated the effectiveness of some proposed profile analyses, never tested before on people with ID, at detecting poor effort and feigning of brain injury: Mittenburg Discriminant Function (Mittenburg et al., 2001), Vocabulary-Digit Span subtest scaled scores (Iverson & Tulsky, 2003), Reliable Digit Span (Greiffenstein, Baker, & Gola, 1994), and the Age-Corrected Digit Span Scaled Scores (Babikian, Boone, Lu, & Arnold, 2006).

Graue and her colleagues (2007) reported obtaining unacceptably high rates of false positives with both measures of malingering mental illness (MFAST and SIMS) and all WAIS-III profile analyses (Vocabulary-Digit Span, Reliable Digit Span, and Age-Corrected Digit Span) that they tested. Graue and colleagues (2007) also reported high rates of false positives when using the DMT, TOMM, and LMT, but these rates improved to an acceptable range with the use of different cut-scores. They proposed some substantially different alternate cut-scores for the DMT (<80% instead of <90%), TOMM (<60% correct instead of <90% correct), and LMT (<70% instead of <93%) when assessing individuals with intellectual disability. Graue and her colleagues (2007) reported acceptable levels of accuracy when using these proposed cut-scores for these three instruments. These findings and their proposed modified cut-scores need replication and to be independently validated for sensitivity and specificity to identify poor effort on cognitive measures in adults with ID.

Shandera et al. (2010) replicated the Graue and colleagues (2007) study using a sample of 24 adults with ID and a sample of 35 demographically matched participants who were randomly assigned to two groups: $n=10$ instructed to respond honestly on all assessments and $n=25$ instructed to malinger on all assessments. Although the Shandera and colleagues study used an entirely different sample of participants, this study cannot be truly considered an independent replication because the two research teams had three overlapping researchers on both teams/publications (i.e., Graue, Berry, and Clark). Using a criterion of acceptance of 90% accuracy, Shandera and her colleagues found similar results to Graue and associates (2007), indicating unacceptably high rates of false positives on all measures of malingering and effort testing, with the exception of the TOMM. When they substituted the test's suggested cut-scores and used the proposed alternate cut-scores from Gaue and colleagues (2007), both the TOMM and the DMT performed well, with acceptable success rates of identification of poor effort (Shandera et al., 2010).

Lastly, Love, Glassmire, Zanolini, and Wolf (2014) reported slightly different findings in a separate and independent sample of 21 inpatient forensic adults with mild to moderate intellectual disability. These authors compared three different tests TOMM, Rey 15-Item Memory Test, and Rey Word Recognition Test (Lezak, 1995) to assess the validity of these measures with persons with intellectual disability. Love and colleagues (2014) concluded that the TOMM yielded valid rates of effort in their sample of 21 individuals using the proposed cut-score of <45, reporting a false positive rate of less than 5% on both trials. The Rey Word Recognition Test also produced rates of identification that had acceptable levels of false positive. The results of the Love and associates (2014) may be the first evaluation of the effectiveness of the Rey Word Recognition Test with adults with intellectual disability and would hence need replication before making conclusions regarding its merits. Much like Hurley and Deal (2006), the Rey 15-Item Memory Test did not perform well with this population of adults with ID in the Love and colleagues (2014) study.

Malingering and poor effort are real concerns, and every clinician conducting an intellectual disability determination in the context of an *Atkins* hearing must be vigilant of indicators of poor effort and/or malingering (Chafetz, 2011; Frumkin, 2006). Assessing effort in *Atkins* cases should likely use a multimodal approach that will generally include a clinical interview, a review of relevant collateral information that includes patterns of performance on prior assessments, and standardized testing of effort when possible (Scott & McDermott, 2013). The very nature of the condition of intellectual disability and its diagnostic criteria require the presence of significant deficits in intellectual functioning and adaptive behavior before the age of 18. Thus, the best protection against malingering is probably the availability of a record of years of poor test performance permitting one to assess examinee effort by analyzing the consistency in test performance over time. Comparing test scores across multiple administrations, over years, and even across different standardized tests, may provide the most robust evidence of effort and performance.

It should also be noted that the experts and attorneys involved in the criminal justice system with individuals who may have an intellectual disability should perhaps be equally vigilant of the assessed person faking "good." Masking one's deficits is rather common among adults with intellectual disability (Edgerton, 1967, 1993). Olley (2012) reported that even individuals being evaluated in an *Atkins*-type claim, who have everything to gain by malingering, often exaggerate their accomplishments in an effort to avoid being labeled as having ID. The level of stigma associated with intellectual disability cannot be understated.

Facts of the Crime

Perhaps nothing is more absurd than cherrypicking discrete facts of the crime to try and feed into misconceptions and misunderstandings of judges and jurors. AAIDD (Schalock et al., 2010) has categorically stated that the facts of the crime should not be used as evidence of intellectual ability or adaptive skills. The sophistication of a crime may well be more of a correlate with the intellectual capacity than the adaptive functioning of a perpetrator; generally speaking, however, we might reserve these generalizations to crimes where the perpetrator's clever planning and sophistication are such that it has been virtually impossible for law enforcement to solve the crime. Facts related to wearing a mask, using a borrowed name, having bought a weapon to commit the crime are sometimes used in *Atkins* cases to assert higher-order intelligence and cited as counterexamples to results obtained on one or more comprehensive tests of intelligence.

It does happen from time to time, when elements of a crime are used to illustrate planning skills or problem-solving skills because the crime was premeditated or the person lied to someone to avoid being caught. For example, it was argued that a defendant did not have intellectual disability because he had to fill out a form to obtain the murder weapon (*Nicholson v. Branker*, 2010), or in another case it was similarly argued that the defendant did not have intellectual disability because he got rid of his weapon after the murder (*Lane v. State*, 2013). It is useful to know that there may be any number of other elements of the crime that speak volumes to the individual's lack of intelligence.

Behaviors and skills involved in telling a lie, planning, engaging in basic problem solving, remembering things, and basic academic skills are not beyond the ability level of the vast majority of adults with intellectual disability. Most adults with intellectual disability can achieve reading, arithmetic, and writing skills equivalent to a 5th- or 6th-grade level (Jacobson & Mulick, 1996). It might also help to frame many of these abilities in the mind of the layperson by thinking that an adult with intellectual disability who has mild deficits in intellectual and adaptive functioning (e.g., IQ of 55–70) as comparable to the functioning level of a typical 12-year-old child. Sadly, most 12-year-old children lie, hide, plot, and deceive to get out of trouble.

Summary

In summary, conducting and interpreting an assessment of an individual's intellectual abilities for the purpose of making a determination of intellectual disability in an *Atkins* hearing requires the consideration of a number of important factors, starting with clinical judgment. Despite having more than 100 years of experience in developing and fine-tuning standardized tests of intelligence, none are perfect. There remain a number of potential sources of error, including administrator error and error associated with the test itself. Ultimately, even when assessed with the greatest rigor possible, a person's obtained IQ score should not be considered as a single digit but rather within a range of scores. Assessment of effort during standardized testing sessions with adults with intellectual disability is an important aspect of any *Atkins* case. There are a number of standardized assessment instruments that portend to assess effort on cognitive measures, but the empirical results regarding their effectiveness with this population are rather disappointing. The TOMM seems to be one measure that may provide some valid information regarding effort testing in adults with ID. Nonetheless, the assessment of malingering or effort in *Atkins* cases remains a complex procedure that would best be accomplished using a multimodal approach that includes a clinical interview, a review of relevant clinical information and prior psychological evaluations, and standardized testing of effort when possible.

References

American Educational Research Association (AERA), American Psychological Association, & National Council on Measurement in Education. (2014). *Standards for educational and psychological testing* (5th Edition). Washington, DC: Authors.

American Psychiatric Association (APA). (2013). *Diagnostic and Statistical Manual of Mental Disorders* (5th Edition). Arlington, VA: American Psychiatric Publishing.

Amos, B. (2011). *Atkins v. Virginia*: Analyzing the correct standard and examination practices to use when determining mental retardation. *The Journal of Gender, Race, & Justice, 14*, 469–496.

Babikian, T., Boone, K. B., Lu, P., & Arnold, G. (2006). Sensitivity and specificity of various digit span scores in the detection of suspect effort. *The Clinical Neuropsychologist, 20*(1), 145–159.Benuto, L. T. (2013). Guide to psychological assessment with Hispanics: An introduction (pp. 1–14). In L. T. Benuto (Ed.), *Guide to Psychological Assessment with Hispanics*. New York: Springer.

Blume, J. H., Johnson, S. L., Marcus, P., & Paavola, E. (2014). A tale of two (and possibly three) *Atkins*: intellectual disability and capital punishment twelve years after the Supreme Court's creation of a categorical bar. *William & Mary Bill of Rights Journal, 23*, 393–414.

Brody, N. (1992). *Intelligence* (2nd Edition). San Diego: Academic Press.

Ceci, S. J., & Kanaya, T. (2010). "Apples and oranges are both round": Furthering the discussion on the Flynn effect. *Journal of Psychoeducational Assessment, 28*, 441–447.

Ceci, S. J., Scullin, M., & Kanaya, T. (2003). The difficulty of basing death penalty eligibility on IQ cutoff scores for mental retardation. *Ethics & Behavior, 13*, 11–17.

Chafetz, M. (2011). Reducing the probability of false positives in malingering detection of social security disability claimants. *The Clinical Neuropsychologist, 25*, 1239–1252.

Choca, J. P., Krueger, K. R., Gabriel, G., Corral, S., & Garside, D. (2009). Demographic adjustments for the Spanish version of the WAIS-III. *Archives of Clinical Neuropsychology, 24*(6), 619–629.

Conway, A. R., & Kovacs, K. (2015). New and emerging models of human intelligence. *Wiley Interdisciplinary Reviews: Cognitive Science, 6*(5), 419–426.

Cunningham, M. D., & Tassé, M. J. (2010). Looking to science rather than convention in adjusting IQ scores when death is at issue. *Professional Psychology: Research and Practice, 41*, 413–419.

DeMatteo, D., Marczyk, G., & Pich, M. (2007). A national survey of state legislation defining mental retardation: Implications for policy and practice after *Atkins. Behavioral Sciences & the Law, 25*, 781–802.

Duvall, J. C., & Morris, R. J. (2006). Assessing mental retardation in death penalty cases: Critical issues for psychology and psychological practice. *Professional Psychology: Research and Practice, 37*, 658–665.

Edgerton, R. B. (1967). *The Cloak of Competence.* Berkeley: University of California Press.

Edgerton, R. B. (1993). *The Cloak of Competence* (revised and updated). Berkeley: University of California Press.

Flanagan, D. P., & Kaufman, A. S. (2004). *Essentials of WISC-IV Assessment.* New York: John Wiley & Sons.

Fletcher, J. M., Stuebing, K. K., & Hughes, L. C. (2010). IQ scores should be corrected for the Flynn effect in high-stakes decisions. *Journal of Psychoeducational Assessment, 28*, 469–473.

Flynn, J. R. (1984). The mean IQ of Americans: Massive gains 1932 to 1978. *Psychological Bulletin, 95*, 29–51.

Flynn, J. R. (1987). Massive IQ gains in 14 nations: What IQ tests really measure. *Psychological Bulletin, 101*, 171–191.

Flynn, J. R. (2006). Tethering the elephant: Capital cases, IQ, and the Flynn effect. *Psychology, Public Policy, and Law, 12*, 170–189.

Flynn, J. R. (2010). Problems with IQ gains: The huge vocabulary gap. *Journal of Psychoeducational Assessment, 28*, 412–433.

Flynn, J. R., & Weiss, L. G. (2007). American IQ gains from 1932 to 2002: The WISC subtests and educational progress. *International Journal of Testing, 7*, 209–224.

Frumkin, I. B. (2006). Challenging expert testimony on intelligence and mental retardation. *The Journal of Psychiatry & Law, 34*, 51–71.

Goldstein, S. (2015). The evolution of intelligence (pp. 3–7). In S. Goldstein, D. Panciotta, and J. A. Naglieri (Eds.), *Handbook of Intelligence: Evolutionary Theory, Historical Perspective, and Current Concepts.* New York: Springer.

Gottfredson, L. (1997). Mainstream science on intelligence: An editorial with 52 signatories, history, and bibliography. *Intelligence, 24*, 13–23.

Gottfredson, L. & Saklofske, D. H. (2009). Intelligence: Foundations and issues in assessment. *Canadian Psychology, 50*, 183–195.

Guilmette, T. J., Hart, K. J., Giuliano, A. J., & Leininger, B. E. (1994). Detecting simulated memory impairment: Comparison of the Rey Fifteen-Item Test and the Hiscock forced-choice procedure. *The Clinical Neuropsychologist*, 8, 283–294.

Graue, L. O., Berry, D. T. R., Clark, J. A., Sollman, M. J., Cardi, M., Hopkins, J., & Werline, D. (2007). Identification of feigned mental retardation using the new generation of malingering detection instruments: Preliminary findings. *The Clinical Neuropsychologist*, 21, 929–942.

Greenwood, J. D. (2015). Intelligence defined: Wundt, James, Cattell, Thorndike, Goddard, and Yerkes (pp. 123–126). In S. Goldstein, D. Panciotta, and J. A. Naglieri (Eds.), *Handbook of Intelligence: Evolutionary Theory, Historical Perspective, and Current Concepts*. New York: Springer.

Grégoire, J., Daniel, M., Llorente, A. M., & Weiss. L. G. (2016). The Flynn effect and its clinical implications (pp. 187–209). In L. G. Weiss, D. H. Saklofske, J. A. Holdnack, & A. Prifitera (Eds.), *WISC-V Assessment and Interpretation: Scientist–Practitioner Perspectives*. New York: Academic Press. DOI: http://dx.doi.org/10.1016/B978-0-12-404697-9.00006-6

Greiffenstein, M. F., Baker, W. J., & Gola, T. (1994). Validation of malingered amnesia measures with a large clinical sample. *Psychological Assessment*, 6, 218.

Grissom, Brandi. (2011). Psychologist who cleared death row inmates is reprimanded. *The Texas Tribune*, April 14, 2010.

Habets, P., Jeandarme, I., Uzieblo, K., Oei, K., & Bogaerts, S. (2015). Intelligence is in the eye of the beholder: Investigating repeated IQ measurements in forensic psychiatry. *Journal of Applied Research in Intellectual Disabilities*, 28, 182–192.

Hagan, L. D., Drogin, E. Y., & Guilmette, T. J. (2008). Adjusting IQ scores for the "Flynn Effect": Consistent with the standard of practice? *Professional Psychology: Research and Practice*, 39, 619–625.

Hagan, L. D., Drogin, E. Y., & Guilmette, T. J. (2010). IQ scores should not be adjusted for the Flynn effect in capital punishment cases. *Journal of Psychoeducational Assessment*, 28, 474–476.

Hall v. Florida, 134 S. Ct. 1986 (2014).

Herrnstein, R. J., & Murray, C. (1994). *The Bell Curve. Intelligence and Class Structure in American Life*. New York: Free Press.

Hurley, K. E., & Deal, W. P. (2006). Assessment instruments measuring malingering used with individuals who have mental retardation: Potential problems and issues. *Mental Retardation*, 44, 112–119.

Iverson, G. L., & Tulsky, D. S. (2003). Detecting malingering on the WAIS-III: Unusual Digit Span performance patterns in the normal population and in clinical groups. *Archives of Clinical Neuropsychology*, 18, 1–9.

Jacobson, J. W., & Mulick, J. A. (1996). *Manual of Diagnosis and Professional Practice in Mental Retardation*. Washington, DC: American Psychological Association.

Kanaya, T., & Ceci, S. (2012). The impact of the Flynn effect on LD diagnoses in special education. *Journal of Learning Disabilities*, 45, 319–326.

Kanaya, T., Scullin, M. H., & Ceci, S. J. (2003). The Flynn effect and US policies: The impact of rising IQ scores on American society via mental retardation diagnoses. *American Psychologist*, 58, 778–790.

Kaufman, A. S. (1995). Practice effects (pp. 828–833). In R. J. Sternberg (Ed.), *Encyclopedia of Human Intelligence*. New York: Simon & Schuster Macmillan.

Kaufman, A. S. (2010). Looking through Flynn's rose-colored scientific spectacles. *Journal of Psychoeducational Assessment, 28,* 494–505.

Kaufman, A. S., & Kaufman, N. L. (2004). *Kaufman Assessment Battery for Children Manual* (2nd Edition; KABC-II). Circle Pines, MN: American Guidance Service.

Kaufman, A. S., & Weiss, L. G. (2010). Guest editors' introduction to the special issue of JPA on the Flynn effect. *Journal of Psychoeducational Assessment, 28,* 279–281.

Lane v. State, 169 So.3d 1076 (Ala. Crim. App. 2013).

Lezak, M. D. (1995). *Neuropsychological Assessment* (3rd Edition). New York: Oxford University Press.

Love, C. M., Glassmire, D. M., Zanolini, S. J., & Wolf, A. (2014). Specificity and false positive rates of the Test of Memory Malingering, Rey 15-Item Test, and Rey Word Recognition Test among forensic inpatients with intellectual disabilities. *Assessment, 21,* 618–627.

Macvaugh, G. S., & Cunningham, M. D. (2009). *Atkins v. Virginia*: Implications and recommendations for forensic practice. *Journal of Psychiatry & Law, 37,* 131–187.

Maldonado, C. Y., & Geisinger, K. F. (2004). Conversion of the Wechsler Adult Intelligence Scale into Spanish: An early test adaptation effort of considerable consequence (pp. 213–234). In R. K. Hambleton, P. F. Merenda, & C. D. Spielberger (Eds.), *Adapting Educational and Psychological Tests for Cross-Cultural Assessment*. Mahwah, NJ: Lawrence Erlbaum Associates.

McGrew, K. S. (2015). Intellectual functioning (pp. 85–112). In E. Polloway (Ed.), *The Death Penalty and Intellectual Disability*. Washington, DC: American Association on Intellectual and Developmental Disabilities.

Miller, H. A. (2001). *M-Fast: Miller Forensic Assessment of Symptoms Test*. Lutz, FL: PAR, Inc.

Mittenberg, W., Theroux, S., Aguila-Puentes, G., Bianchini, K., Greve, K., & Rayls, K. (2001). Identification of malingered head injury on the Wechsler Adult Intelligence Scale. *The Clinical Neuropsychologist, 15,* 440–445.

Naglieri, J. A., Das, J. P., & Goldstein, S. (2014). *Cognitive Assessment System* (2nd Edition; CAS2). Austin, TX: Pro-Ed.

Nicholson v. Branker, 739 F. Supp. 2d 839 (E.D.N.C. 2010).

Olley, J. G. (2012) The death penalty, the courts, and intellectual disabilities (pp. 229–240). In J. K. Luiselli (Ed.), *The Handbook of High-Risk Challenging Behaviors in People with Intellectual and Developmental Disabilities*. Baltimore: Paul H. Brookes Co.

Orey, S. A., Cragar, D. E., & Berry, D. T. (2000). The effects of two motivational manipulations on the neuropsychological performance of mildly head-injured college students. *Archives of Clinical Neuropsychology, 15,* 335–348.

Reynolds, C. R., Niland, J., Wright, J. E., & Rosenn, M. (2010). Failure to apply the Flynn correction in death penalty litigation: Standard practice of today maybe, but certainly malpractice of tomorrow. *Journal of Psychoeducational Assessment, 28*, 477–481.

Rogers, R., Bagby, R. M., & Dickens, S. E. (1992). *Structured Interview of Reported Symptoms: Professional Manual.* Odessa, FL: Psychological Assessment Resources.

Roid, G. H. (2003). *Stanford-Binet Intelligence Scales—Fifth Edition* (SB-5). Itasca, IL: Riverside Publishing.

Schalock, R. L., Buntinx, W. H. E., Borthwick-Duffy, S., Bradley, V., Craig, E. M., Coulter, D. L., Gomez, S. C., Lachapelle, Y., Luckasson, R. A., Reeve, A., Shogren, K. A., Snell, M. E., Spreat, S., Tassé, M. J., Thompson, J. R., Verdugo, M. A., Wehmeyer, M. L., & Yeager, M. H. (2010). *Intellectual Disability: Definition, Classification, and System of Supports* (11th Edition). Washington, DC: American Association on Intellectual and Developmental Disabilities.

Schalock, R. L., Luckasson, R. A., Bradley, V., Buntinx, W. H. E., Lachapelle, Y., Shogren, K. A., . . . & Wehmeyer, M. L. (2012). *Intellectual disability: Definition, classification, and system of supports (11th Edition)—User's Guide.* Washington, DC: American Association on Intellectual and Developmental Disabilities.

Schrank, F. A., McGrew, K. S., & Mather, N. (2014). *Woodcock-Johnson IV Tests of Cognitive Abilities.* Rolling Meadows, IL: Riverside Publishing.

Scott, C. L., & McDermott, B. (2013). Malingering and mental health disability evaluations (pp. 155–182). In L. H. Gold & D. L. Vanderpool (Eds.), *Clinical Guide to Mental Disability Evaluations.* New York: Springer Science+Business Media. DOI: 10.1007/978-1-4614-5447-2_6

Shandera, A. L., Berry, D. T. R., Clark, J. A., Schipper, L. J., Graue, L. O., & Harp, J. P. (2010). Detection of malingered mental retardation. *Psychological Assessment, 22*, 50–56.

Spearman, C. (1904). "General intelligence," objectively determined and measured. *The American Journal of Psychology, 15*(2), 201–292.

Suen, H. K., & Greenspan, S. (2009). Serious problems with the Mexican norms for the WAIS-III when assessing mental retardation in capital cases. *Applied neuropsychology, 16*, 214–222.

TEA Ediciones (2001). *WAIS-III, Escala de Inteligencia Wechsler para Adultos—III.* Madrid, Spain: Author.

Thaler, N. S., & Jones-Forrester, S. (2013). IQ testing and the Hispanic client. In L. T. Benuto (Ed.), *Guide to psychological assessment with Hispanics* (pp. 81–98). New York: Springer.

Thomsen, C., Gallup, L., & Llorente, A. M. (2008). Intellectual abilities: Theoretical and applied assessment considerations (pp. 55–77). In A. M. Llorente (Ed.), *Principles of Neuropsychological Assessment with Hispanics: Theoretical Foundations and Clinical Practice.* New York: Springer.

Tombaugh, T. N. (1996). *Test of Memory Malingering*. North Tonawanda, NY: Multi-Health Systems.

U.S. Census Bureau. (2014). *Annual Estimates of the Resident Population by Sex, Age, Race, and Hispanic Origin for the United States and States: April 1, 2010 to July 1, 2014. 2014 Population Estimates*. http://factfinder.census.gov/faces /tableservices/jsf/pages/productview.xhtml?src=bkmk

Wasserman, J. D. (2012). A history of intelligence assessment: The unfinished tapestry (pp. 3–55). In Dawn P. Flanagan and Patti L. Harrison (Eds.), *Contemporary Intellectual Assessment: Theories, Tests, and Issues* (3rd Edition). New York: Guilford Press.

Wechsler, D. (1997). *Wechsler Adult Intelligence Scale* (3rd Edition; WAIS-III). San Antonio, TX: Psychological Corporation.

Wechsler, D. (2008). *Wechsler Intelligence Scale for Children* (4th Edition; WISC-IV). San Antonio: Pearson.

Wechsler, D. (2014). *Wechsler Intelligence Scale for Children* (5th Edition; WISC-V): *Administration and Scoring Manual*. Bloomington, MN: Pearson Clinical Assessment.

Weiss, L. G. (2010). Considerations on the Flynn effect. *Journal of Psychoeducational Assessment, 28*, 482–493.

Widows, M. R., & Smith, G. P. (2005). *SIMS: Structured Inventory of Malingered Symptomatology*. Lutz, FL: PAR, Inc.

Wood, S. E., Packman, W., Howell S., & Bongar, B. (2014). A failure to implement: Analyzing state responses to the Supreme Court's directives in *Atkins v. Virginia* and suggestions for a national standard. *Psychiatry, Psychology and Law, 21*(1), 16–45.

Young, G. W. (2012). A more intelligent and just *Atkins*: Adjusting for the Flynn effect in capital determination of mental retardation or intellectual disability. *Vanderbilt Law Review, 65*, 616–675.

Zhou, X., Grégoire, J., & Zhu, J. (2010). The Flynn effect and the Wechsler Scales (pp. 141–166). In L. G. Weiss, D. H. Saklofske, D. L. Coalson, & S. E. Raiford (Eds.), *WAIS-IV Clinical Use and Interpretation: Scientist-Practitioner Perspectives*. San Diego: Elsevier.

Zhou, X., Zhu, J., & Weiss, L. G. (2010). Peeking inside the "black box" of the Flynn effect: Evidence from three Wechsler instruments. *Journal of Psychoeducational Assessment, 28*, 399–411.

CHAPTER SIX

Assessing Adaptive Behavior

Adaptive behavior has its roots in the field of disabilities and specifically intellectual disability. Adaptive behavior is defined as behavior that has been learned and is performed to meet society's expectations across settings, including the home, school, work, and other community-based settings in our respective culture and for one's chronological age (Schalock et al., 2010). Hence, since society's demands and expectations of any individual generally increase with the passage from infancy, to childhood, and into adulthood, it is expected that we acquire and perform a more complex array of adaptive skills as we grow older. In other words, society expects different skills from a child than we do from an adult. The American Association on Intellectual and Developmental Disabilities defined adaptive behavior as the collection of conceptual, social, and practical skills that have been learned by people to function in their everyday lives (Lucasson et al., 2002; Schalock et al., 2010). These three adaptive behavior domains have been defined as follows: (1) Conceptual skills consist of communication skills, functional academics, and self-direction; (2) social skills consist of interpersonal skills, social responsibility, following rules, self-esteem, gullibility, naiveté, and avoiding victimization; and (3) practical skills consist of basic personal care skills, such as hygiene, domestic skills, health and safety, as well as work skills.

Adaptive behavior is a required criterion of all diagnostic systems defining intellectual disability (see American Psychiatric Association (APA), 2000; Schalock et al., 2010; World Health Organization (WHO), 1992). The American Association on Intellectual and Developmental Disabilities (AAIDD) is generally considered the leading professional authority in defining "intellectual disability." The AAIDD, first established in 1876, is the oldest interdisciplinary professional association in the field of intellectual and developmental disabilities (Tassé & Grover, 2013). The AAIDD has led the field in establishing the definition and diagnostic criteria for intellectual disability for over a century. Since its first definition of intellectual disability in 1905, AAIDD has revised its definition 10 times to reflect the changes in research and understanding of this condition. The AAIDD definition of intellectual disability has historically been adopted by all federal and state governments, as well as by the American Psychiatric Association's *Diagnostic and Statistical Manual* (*DSM*) in defining intellectual disability. It wasn't, however, until the fifth edition of its diagnostic manual, that AAIDD required the assessment of adaptive behavior as a criterion for defining intellectual disability (Heber, 1959, 1961).

The American Psychiatric Association has historically adopted the AAIDD definition and diagnostic criteria of intellectual disability in its *Diagnostic and Statistical Manual of Mental Disorders*. The *DSM* first included adaptive behavior in its diagnostic criteria of intellectual disability in its second edition of the *DSM* (APA, 1968). In fact, in the *DSM-II*, the American Psychiatric Association actually refers the reader to the AAIDD 1961 definition of intellectual disability (see Heber, 1961) for the complete definition of intellectual disability (*DSM-II*, p. 14). The text in the *DSM-II* reads: "Mental retardation refers to subnormal general intellectual functioning which originates during the developmental period and is associated with impairment in either learning and social adjustment or maturation, or both" (APA, 1968, p. 14). This reads exactly the same as Heber's (1959) definition of adaptive behavior, which he described as maturation, learning, and social adjustment.

Since then, the 2002 and 2010 editions of AAIDD's *Terminology and Classification Manual* have returned to the psychometrically supported framework of three adaptive behavior domains: conceptual, social, and practical skills (see Luckasson et al., 2002; Schalock et al., 2010), originally proposed by Heber (1959).

Relationship Between Intellectual Functioning and Adaptive Functioning

One of the forefathers of intelligence testing used the concept of "adaptation" in his definition of "intelligence" (Binet & Simon, 1905). For a long time and still to this day, the two concepts are sometimes intertwined. Increasingly, however, the larger definition of intelligence is more focused on mental capabilities and capacity, whereas adaptive behavior is more focused on the actual performance of skills when needed and in response to societal demands and expectations. The definition of intelligence adopted by AAIDD (Schalock et al., 2010) comes from the existing consensus position of prominent intelligence researchers and is defined as follows:

> Intelligence is a very general mental capability that, among other things, involves the ability to reason, plan, solve problems, think abstractly, comprehend complex ideas, learn quickly and learn from experience. It is not merely book learning, a narrow academic or test-taking smarts. Rather, it reflects a broader and deeper capability for comprehending our surroundings—"catching on," "making sense" of things, or "figuring out" what to do. (Gottfredson, 1997, p. 13)

A number of studies have examined the changes in adaptive functioning among adults with developmental disabilities after deinstitutionalization (Felce, deKock, Thomas, & Saxby, 1986; Fine, Tangeman, & Woodard, 1990; Silverman, Silver, Sersen, Lubin, & Schwartz, 1986). Consistently, a meaningful, positive change in adaptive functioning has been reported after moving from a more institutional living environment to a less restrictive community setting (Lakin, Larson, & Kim, 2011). In their review of the literature that included 23 longitudinal studies between 1977 and 2010, Charlie Lakin and his colleagues reported that all but three studies documented adaptive behavior improvements when individuals moved to less restrictive community-based living arrangements. The increase in adaptive behavior was especially marked in the following skill areas: self-care, domestic skills, and social skills.

As constructs, intelligence and adaptive behavior are related but distinct from each other (Keith, Fehrmann, Harrison, & Pottebaum, 1987; McGrew & Bruininks, 1990). Thus, discrepancies in the measurement of intelligence and adaptive behavior are to be expected. Not everyone with significant limitations in intellectual functioning will have commensurately limited adaptive behavior, and, conversely, not everyone with significant limitations in adaptive behavior will have comparable significant limitations in intellectual functioning. Due to a wide range of measures for IQ and adaptive functioning, conducting research on children with developmental disabilities and interpreting the results can be challenging. However, some studies have reported a low to moderate correlation between the measures of $r=0.20–0.50$ (Harrison & Oakland, 2003; Sparrow, Balla, & Ciccheti, 2005). A much smaller number of studies (Carpentieri & Morgan, 1996) have demonstrated higher correlations, while others have demonstrated that a larger portion of the variance (35%) in adaptive functioning among adults with intellectual disability can be explained by environmental variables other than intellectual ability (21%) (Hull &

Thompson, 1980). As a way to examine the relationship between these two constructs, some studies generated tables of values needed for statistical significance between various IQs and adaptive behavior scores. They concluded that a difference of at least 10 or more standard points was needed for a statistical difference between two measures when a 95% confidence level was adopted. They concluded that it is not unreasonable to interpret the IQ-Adaptive score discrepancy as indicative of a real underlying difference between cognitive capacity and day-to-day performance. Research findings have tended to document higher correlations between these two constructs in individuals with more severe to profound deficits in intellectual functioning than for those who present with milder impairments in intellectual functioning (Childs, 1982; Sattler 2002).

DSM-5 and Relatedness Phrase

The *DSM-5* introduced the following statement that reads as follows: "To meet diagnostic criteria for intellectual disability, the deficits in adaptive functioning must be *directly* related [emphasis mine] to the intellectual impairments" (APA, 2013; p. 38). This is an innocuous statement, intended to affirm that the deficits in adaptive behavior were related to the condition of intellectual disability and not to some other mental illness (e.g., dementia, schizophrenia, etc.) or other condition (e.g., acquired head injury, brain tumor, etc.). The statement is somewhat a red herring because the implication of causality that underlies the "directly related" is pointless. One does not need to establish the precise cause or identify culprit risk factors that explain the adaptive behavior deficits, nor find the exact etiology of the intellectual functioning deficits; so long as both have their onset during the developmental period, a determination of intellectual disability should be made (Tassé, Luckasson, & Schalock, 2016).

Texas argued in *Moore v. Texas* that even if Moore would have established that he had significant deficits in intellectual functioning and adaptive behavior, he failed to establish that his adaptive behavior deficits were directly related to his impairments in intellectual functioning. As eloquently summarized in the Supreme Court of United States majority decision:

> The [Texas Court of Criminal Appeals] furthermore concluded that Moore's record of academic failure, along with the childhood abuse and suffering he endured, detracted from a determination that his intellectual and adaptive deficits were related. See 470 S. W. 3d, at 488, 526; supra, at 5, 7–8. Those traumatic experiences, however, count in the medical community

as "**risk factors**" for intellectual disability. AAIDD– 11, at 59–60 (emphasis added). Clinicians rely on such factors as cause to explore the prospect of intellectual disability further, not to counter the case for a disability determination. (*Moore v. Texas*, 2017; pp. 13–14)

Assessing Adaptive Behavior in Forensic Cases and Atkins Claims in Particular

Although the assessment of intellectual functioning has a longer history (e.g., the first standardized test was developed in 1905) than the measurement of adaptive behavior, standardized tests of adaptive behavior have progressed significantly since the first such scale was published (Vineland Social Maturity Scale, Doll, 1936). The first version of the Vineland instrument consisted of items organized into six broad domains (self-help: general, dressing, and eating; self-direction; communication; socialization; motor; and work). Reflective of the times, the 1936 Vineland scale had items measuring the person's use of the telephone. Doll (1953) defined the construct of social competence as "the functional ability of the human organism for exercising personal independence and social responsibility" (see p. 10). Doll's vision of assessing social competence (what would later be called adaptive behavior) remains ingrained in today's definition of adaptive behavior and associated standardized measures: "Our task was to measure attainment in social competence considered as habitual performance rather than as latent ability or capacity" (see Doll, 1952; p. 5). This interpretation is consistent with AAIDD's current position that the assessment of adaptive behavior focuses on the individual's typical performance and not maximal ability (see Schalock et al., 2010; Schalock et al., 2012). This is a critical distinction with the assessment of intellectual functioning, where we assess best or maximal performance.

According to Tassé et al. (2012), the critical aspects of assessing adaptive behavior for the purpose of diagnosing intellectual disability include:

- Assessing the individual's typical behavior (and not maximal performance);
- Assessing the individual's present adaptive behavior;
- Assessing the individual's adaptive behavior in relation to societal expectations for his or her age group and culture;
- Using standardized adaptive behavior scales that were normed on the general population;
- Using a convergence of information (i.e., several informants, informants from different life contexts (home, school, work, play/leisure), over time (childhood, adulthood), multiple modalities and sources (see later in the chapter);
- Using clinical judgment throughout the assessment process.

The American Association on Intellectual and Developmental Disabilities has specified:

> For the purpose of making a diagnosis or ruling out ID [intellectual disability], a comprehensive standardized measure of adaptive behavior should be used in making the determination of the individual's current adaptive behavior functioning in relation to the general population. The selected measure should provide robust standard scores across the three domains of adaptive behavior: conceptual, social, and practical adaptive behavior (Schalock et al., 2010; p. 49).

It is possible in some cases that the use of a standardized assessment instrument will not be possible. A standardized adaptive behavior scale is generally completed with the information from a respondent. Multiple adaptive behavior scales can be completed, but generally only one respondent is used to complete the entire scale, per administration procedures.

Because of space limitations, we will not review the existing standardized adaptive behavior scales that are in wide use today. Some of these instruments have been normed on a representative sample of the general population, while others have been intentionally normed on a subpopulation of persons with intellectual and developmental disabilities. The former are generally better instruments when the reason for evaluation is to assess the person's adaptive behavior to rule in or rule out a diagnosis of intellectual disability. AAIDD has encouraged clinicians to avoid certain instruments that might be appropriate for intervention planning but may not necessarily be appropriate for diagnostic purposes: "The potential user must employ adaptive behavior assessment instruments that are normed within the community environments on individuals who are of the same age grouping as the individual being evaluated" (Schalock et al., 2010; p. 51). Measures normed on persons with an intellectual disability or related developmental disability are perhaps helpful in identifying the person's ability level in relation to a target disability population and may yield nonetheless helpful programmatic adaptive behavior goals.

Hence, adaptive behavior scales are used predominantly for two purposes. The first purpose is in assessing the person's adaptive behavior for the purposes of establishing planning goals for intervention and habilitation. The other reason these standardized scales are used to assess a person's adaptive behavior is to determine whether or not there is a presence of significant deficits for the purpose of determining if the person meets criteria for a diagnosis of intellectual disability or developmental disability. Some instruments have been developed to attempt to serve both functions while other instruments focus on one aspect. The following adaptive behavior instruments are considered to be among the most suitable for use in assessing adaptive behavior for the purpose of determining intellectual disability: (1) Adaptive Behavior Assessment System, 3nd Edition (ABAS-3) (Harrison & Oakland, 2015), (2) Vineland Adaptive Behavior Scale, 2nd Edition (Vineland-II) (Sparrow, Balla, & Cicchetti, 2005), (3) Scales of Independent Behavior, Revised (SIB-R) (Bruininks, Woodcock, Weatherman, & Hill, 1996), and (4) Adaptive Behavior Diagnostic Scale (ABDS) (Pearson, Patton, & Mruzek, 2016). We also expect the American Association on Intellectual and Developmental Disabilities to release, in 2017, its newest adaptive behavior instrument called the Diagnostic Adaptive Behavior Scale (see DABS) (Tassé et al., 2016).

In Addition to Standardized Measures

The use of standardized measures of adaptive behavior should not be used in isolation. There are many instances where the use of standardized adaptive behavior scales may be insufficient or impossible. This might be because no reliable respondents are available to provide comprehensive information on the assessed person's adaptive behavior, the respondents providing the adaptive information can only provide partial information, or the evaluator cannot ensure the proper administration of the instrument per test guidelines. In these instances, alternate sources of adaptive behavior information should be referenced as complementary or alternative sources of the person's adaptive behavior.

The AAIDD (Schalock et al., 2010; Schalock et al., 2012) and Olley (2015) recommend using several of the following different sources of adaptive behavior information as part of a comprehensive adaptive behavior assessment:

- Medical records
- School records
- Employment records
- Previous psychological evaluation reports and raw data (adaptive behavior, IQ, achievement, mental health, employment, career counseling, etc.)
- Therapy or intervention reports and records (e.g., mental health, habilitation services, employment support, developmental disability services, etc.)
- Drivers and motor vehicle bureau records
- Information from state or federal offices that might have eligibility information (social security administration, state developmental disabilities department, Medicaid, etc.)

- In criminal cases: affidavits, declarations, transcripts of testimony or interviews, prison records
- Informal interviews with individuals who know the person and had the opportunity to observe the person in the community, etc.
- Interview with the defendant/assessed person

All types and sources of information should be reviewed and analyzed critically for content, relevance, and accuracy. One should also ascertain the comparison group when determining ability and limitations. For example, in some special education programs, a C grade denotes something very different in achievement level than a C grade granted in a regular education classroom (Schalock et al., 2010).

Respondents

Adaptive behavior scales are typically completed via input and observations of the assessed individual's adaptive behavior and either directly rate items on an adaptive behavior scale or provide this information via an interview with an adaptive behavior assessor who is responsible for the adaptive behavior assessment. Generally, the best respondents are typically adults who know the assessed individual well and have the most knowledge and have had opportunities to observe the assessed individual in his or her everyday functioning across settings (Tassé, 2009). Adaptive behavior respondents are most often selected among the assessed person's family (e.g., parents or guardians, grandparents, older sibling, aunts/uncles), spouse, and/or roommates. Other individuals who can also provide valuable adaptive behavior information include neighbors, teachers, coworkers, supervisors, coaches, and others who have had multiple opportunities to observe the assessed person functioning in everyday community settings such as school, work, leisure, or community. The *DSM-5* specifies similarly the potential list of knowledgeable informants to include as respondents on standardized adaptive behavior scales parents or other family members, teachers, counselors, care providers, and, when possible, the individual him- or herself (APA, 2013; see p. 37). The interviewer or person responsible for conducting the adaptive behavior assessment also has the responsibility of verifying the accuracy of the respondents and ascertaining that they are providing reliable and accurate information. The use of clinical judgment and professional experience with clinical interviews and the assessment of adaptive behavior will guide the evaluator in making these determinations (see Schalock & Luckasson, 2014).

There may be situations where no respondent is available who has knowledge of the assessed individual that is sufficiently comprehensive to be able to complete a standardized adaptive behavior scale. In these instances, the assessor will need to rely more heavily on available school, work, medical, and other relevant records, as well as on information obtained from respondents who may be providing more discrete or qualitative information in specific areas of life (e.g., school, sports, leisure, work, home, etc.). In such instances, the use of multiple respondents and sources of information (as noted previously: school records, medical history, DMV, etc.) is even more critical.

Using Correctional Officers as Adaptive Behavior Informants

Both the *DSM-5* and the AAIDD are quite clear regarding the caveats of using prison behavior as a source of data to inform the evaluator on a person's adaptive behavior. An *Atkins* evaluation may include prison behavior and a review of department of corrections records, but appropriate weight needs to be placed on these observations in light of the provenance of the behavioral observations (e.g., highly controlled and contrived environments). Observing someone's everyday behavior in a context other than the "community" is antithetical to the definition of adaptive behavior (Olley & Cox, 2008). Schalock and his colleagues (2012) clearly defined community contexts as home, community, school, and place of employment (see p. 18). Prison environment, by its very nature, is highly controlled and regimented. In comparison to life in the community, life in prison has fewer choices of daily activities and, understandably, fewer adaptive behavior opportunities (e.g., functional academics, health and safety, social interactions, home living skills, or community use).

Most standardized adaptive behavior scales permit the informant to "guess" on items/behaviors that she or he may not have had the opportunity to directly observe the assessed person perform. But standardized adaptive behavior scales have very strict guidelines regarding the maximum number of items that can be "guessed" without significantly invalidating the protocol being completed by that informant. Beyond a reasonable or expected maximum number of guesses, the examiner is generally encouraged to consider that protocol invalid or give it less weight when interpreting all sources of adaptive behavior information. There are dozens of items on standardized adaptive behavior scales that cannot possibly be observed by a correctional officer. Table 6.1 presents a list of ABAS-3 items (ABAS-3 was chosen to illustrate this point—all scales have similar

Table 6.1   ABAS-3 Sample Items

Community Use: #4. Orders own meals when eating out.

Community Use: #7. Carries enough money to make small purchases.

Community Use: #10. Asks a store clerk for help.

Community Use: #13. Uses a credit card or debit card for making purchases.

Community Use: #16. Obtains money from an ATM machine.

Functional Academics: #6. Gives the clerk necessary amount of money when buying something.

Functional Academics: #16. Check for correct change after buying something.

Functional Academics: #18. Completes written forms to apply for a job.

Functional Academics: #20. Checks for accuracy of charges on a bill.

Functional Academics: #24. Checks his monthly banking statements for accuracy.

Home living: #4. Cooks simple foods on a stove.

Home living: #7. Uses a clothes dryer.

Home living: #8. Uses a washing machine to wash clothes.

Home living: #14. Takes out trash when can is full.

Home living: #20. Pays bills on time.

Health and safety: #5. Buckles own seatbelt in car.

Health and safety: #11. Refuses gifts and rides from strangers.

Health and safety: #14. Takes own medication without supervision on days/ times required.

Health and safety: #15. Buys over-the-counter medications when needed.

Health and safety: #18. Inspects contents of refrigerator and removes spoiled foods.

behaviors/items) that would be difficult to be observed by a correctional officer.

The construct of adaptive behavior requires a series of cognitive and behavioral processes to be in place for the performance of said behavior to be fully successful and independent. Items on a standardized adaptive behavior scale are written to specifically assess a targeted skill. No assessor or informant, including a correctional officer, can translate or truncate an item stem or adaptive behavior item to fit a similar behavior or an approximation of an adaptive skill without distorting the item stem's full intent. For example, an item stem from a standardized adaptive behavior scale that asks "Compares the quality and prices of consumer goods before purchase" cannot be translated to using a prison commissary account. These are not the same.

A prison setting is defined by rules and regulations, where by definition, inmates have few opportunities to choose when and how to perform certain adaptive behaviors. The prison environment is highly structured and regimented and often dictates when and where the inmates can do things and thus removes much of the cognitive component of having to recognize on one's own when the behavior should be performed as well as the motivational aspects of choosing to perform it or not. Hence, a correctional officer has the opportunity to observe only a fraction of, and portions of, the behaviors that are needed to provide a comprehensive view sufficient to complete a standardized adaptive behavior scale. They might be able to provide some observations about distinct behaviors, but these behaviors need to be interpreted within the context of a prison setting and its structures and not a typical community setting.

In the only published study comparing the adaptive behavior ratings of correctional officers with those of another informant, the results confirm this point. Boccaccini, Kan, Rufino, Noland, Young-Lundquist, and Canales (2016) compared the ratings on the ABAS-II among 56 probationers and correctional officers who reportedly knew them well. This study reported findings of poor informant agreement between the individual and the correctional officers, with the correctional officers reporting consistently and significantly lower adaptive behavior ratings, highlighting the concerns regarding the validity of using correctional officers as adaptive behavior informants.

Critical Issues with AB Assessment in Death Penalty Cases

Correcting for Sociocultural Factors

Both AAIDD and *DSM-5* stipulate that the intellectual disability evaluation must take into consideration the assessed person's sociocultural background. This is generally interpreted as using one's clinical judgment in interpreting what accommodations are needed in interpreting specific items or behaviors that might receive less weight given the person's ethnic/racial background. For example, Asian cultures have different expectations regarding certain discrete social skills behaviors such as "making eye contact"; the use of utensils at meal times may be different from culture to culture; the performance of certain domestic skills may have different gender expectations in some cultures. These are cultural considerations that the expert should consider in placing weight and consideration in areas that may have different established community expectations based on one's cultural background. This does not mean that scores are modified or items skipped. We agree with AAIDD's caution against any score corrections that are not part of established clinical practice, science, or test procedures that attempt to correct adaptive behavior scores on standardized scales for any cultural or socioeconomic factors (see Schalock et al., 2010; p. 53). The AAIDD caution specifically mentions avoiding the corrections proposed by Denkowski and Denkowski (2008) because their proposed corrections had no basis in science or practice. In fact, George Denkowski was professionally reprimanded and fined and had his practice restricted by the Texas State Board of Examiners of Psychologists because of his use of cultural and socioeconomic adjustments he made to assess individuals' obtained scores on standardized tests (see Grissom, 2011).

When assessing a foreign national's adaptive behavior, it may be difficult to find an appropriately translated, standardized, and normed adaptive behavior scale for people born and raised outside of the United States. In some situations, it may be appropriate to use an American standardized and normed adaptive behavior scale, and in other instances it may be more appropriate to find a scale standardized and normed in the person's country of origin, if available. In many instances involving a foreign national, it may difficult to find and use an appropriate standardized adaptive behavior scale, in which case a thorough adaptive behavior evaluation will have to rely on qualitative clinical interviews. The expert should use her or his clinical judgment to make that determination and be prepared to defend her or his decision. It may be helpful to hire a mental health expert who speaks the native language of the foreign national to conduct these adaptive behavior interviews. If not, the mental health expert may need to rely on an excellent translator to assist with these behavior interviews.

The expert may in all likelihood need to travel to the person's country of origin to interview family members and other significant others (e.g., family members, teachers, friends, employers/coworkers, etc.) to obtain a complete adaptive behavior profile of the individual. Visiting the foreign national's country of origin may also provide valuable information regarding issues related to age of onset and possible risk factors associated with the onset of intellectual disability. It will be essential for mental health experts to educate themselves regarding the foreign national's country of origin, including cultural standards and expectations in which the individual was raised, community/societal expectations across age groups, gender differences, and ethnic group differences. This sociocultural information will be essential to inform the clinician regarding what is typical and what might be impaired adaptive behavior. Often these assessments of adaptive behavior will be more reliant on qualitative assessment, interviews, and review of foreign records to inform the clinician's opinion regarding the foreign national's adaptive behavior. These cases pose their own set of challenges to the assessor.

Comorbid Conditions

Adaptive behavior deficits obtained from a comprehensive evaluation may erroneously be discarded on the premise of false reasoning. First, adaptive behavior deficits can and do coexist with mental illness and other behavioral disorders. The presence of other mental illnesses or behavior health problems do not dismiss or explain away deficits in adaptive behavior, nor do they negate a diagnosis of intellectual disability. Again, in the Brumfield case described in Chapter 3, the judge wrongly concluded that Brumfield's adaptive behavior deficits could be explained by a diagnosis of "antisocial personality" disorder.[1] It is not uncommon for people diagnosed with antisocial personality disorder to present with adaptive behavior deficits (Rush, Major-Sanabria, & Corcoran, 2008). The *DSM-5* (APA, 2013) is categorical, as it has been in previous iterations of its diagnostic manual; there are *no* exclusionary conditions to a diagnosis of intellectual disability. That means, regardless of the presence of any other coexisting behavioral or mental illness (such as antisocial personality disorder, to mention one), a diagnosis of intellectual disability should be made if the individual meets all three diagnostic prongs of intellectual disability, regardless of etiology or comorbid conditions. Holland and his colleagues (2002) in fact reported that comorbidity of intellectual disability and antisocial behavior or disorder are quite common in the criminal justice population. As it pertains to a diagnosis of antisocial personality disorder explaining the deficits of adaptive behavior and precluding a diagnosis of intellectual disability, firstly, they can coexist. Secondly, a diagnosis of intellectual disability originates before the age of 18 years (see APA, 2013; Schalock et al., 2010), but the diagnosis of antisocial personality disorder is not made until after the age of 18 years (*DSM-5*; APA, 2013). Again, there is no exclusionary criterion between intellectual disability and antisocial personality disorder. They can and do coexist.

People with intellectual disability can acquire a mental illness, substance abuse disorder, or other secondary health conditions. In fact, people with intellectual disability are 3–4 times more vulnerable than people in the general population to present with a comorbid mental or behavioral disorder (Cooper, Smiley, Morrison, Williamson, & Allan, 2007; Fletcher, Barnhill, & Cooper, 2016; Reiss, 1994; Rojahn & Tassé, 1996). Substance abuse by people with intellectual disability is not as common overall but is more prevalent in adults with intellectual disability intersecting with the criminal justice system (Chapman & Wu, 2012; McGillivray & Moore, 2001). For adults with an intellectual disability, a substance abuse problem increases the likelihood of criminal behavior and arrests for criminal activities (Holland et al., 2002). Sadly, many adults with intellectual disability make poor choices and end up using and abusing alcohol and drugs. To use the presence of a substance abuse disorder as a reason to rule out or explain the presence of deficits in adaptive behavior or intellectual disability is clearly tautological. These conditions can and do co-occur, especially in a forensic population. Generally speaking, when individuals stop using alcohol and drugs, they will not be cured of their intellectual disability.

Adaptive Behavior Assessment Is Objective

There is a clear distinction to be made between information that is provided by a subject and subjective information. Yes, adaptive behavior assessment relies on the reporting of observed adaptive behavior, but this is done in a rigorous, standardized, and objective manner. When respondents are asked about the assessed person's adaptive behavior, they are asked about behaviors that they have directly observed. They are not asked to estimate or imagine if he or she could do such a behavior. In fact, if they do guess on more than two items in one domain, that informant's information will be viewed as much less reliable than one that has no guessing. Having a standardized set of items, administered in a systematic fashion and scored in a prescribed manner that then yields results that are compared and converted statistically to a normative scale, yields objective results. In fact, standardized adaptive behavior scales yield standardized results that are presented on the same normative metric as IQ scores, where an average score = 100 and the population deviation score = 15 (Harrison & Oakland, 2015; Sparrow, Balla, & Cicchetti, 2005).

Typical Performance

Adaptive behavior assessment is focused on what persons typically do and the degree to which they perform that behavior independently, without aide or support (Schalock et al., 2010; Tassé, 2009). Adaptive behavior scales provide clear guidance that respondents (i.e., persons providing information regarding their observation of the individual being assessed on the adaptive behavior scale) are being asked about the person's typical performance of these behaviors or skills, versus their (respondents') estimate of the person's ability. Hence, the independent performance of a discrete adaptive behavior captures the person's knowledge or prior learning of the behavior, recognition that the behavior needs to occur (e.g., "Finds the bathroom in a public place"), their willingness or motivation to perform said behavior (e.g., "Chooses not to say mean or embarrassing things"), and the degree of prompting or assistance the individual needs to perform the adaptive behavior (e.g., "Performs behavior when needed and without reminders or help").

Adaptive behavior scales measure a complex array of cognitive and behavioral aspects of adaptive functioning and, in so doing, are aimed at measuring not what do the persons know or whether they know how to do it but rather whether they do it. For example, an item in the Home-Living Scale on the ABAS-3 asks: "Folds clean clothes." The assessed behavior is not "can . . ." or "does he know how . . ." but rather whether the person folds clean clothes without prompts or help. This is an important difference in the assessment of adaptive behavior. If a person has learned a behavior and possesses a skill but chooses not to perform that behavior when needed or expected, he or she does not get full credit for that adaptive behavior. For the purposes of assessing adaptive behavior to make a determination of intellectual disability, we assess "what does this person typically do?" If we were conducting an assessment of adaptive behavior for the purpose of intervention planning, we would likely follow up our initial assessment with a series of follow-up queries to determine whether the person does not perform the behavior due to a lack of knowledge, skill, or willingness. Of course, it takes the combination of many items where the skill/behavior is lacking to yield a standard score that is significantly subaverage. In contrast to adaptive behavior, the assessment of intellectual functioning seeks to capture the person's fullest potential and capacity, further illustrating that these are two distinct constructs of human functioning, both necessary to make a determination of intellectual disability.

Street Survival Skills Questionnaire (Linkenhoker & McCarron, 1993)

We feel compelled to mention here the Street Survival Skills Questionnaire (SSSQ). Although this is an obsolete and outdated test that does not even warrant mentioning, we will mention it because some "experts" choose to continue using this test. The SSSQ is a very narrow-band test that assesses direct knowledge and fails to capture typical adaptive behavior. Although exclusively focused on elements of practical adaptive skills, the range of skills assessed on the SSSQ is restricted and does not include important elements of social adaptive behavior, conceptual adaptive behavior, and even practical adaptive behavior (Denkowski & Denkowski, 2008). As the SSSQ authors (Linkenhoker & McCarron, 1993) clearly stipulated in their user's manual, the SSSQ was developed and standardized exclusively on a population with ID. The SSSQ does not provide standard scores in reference to the general population (i.e., with and without intellectual disability). There is absolutely no justifiable reason to use the SSSQ to assess adaptive behavior in death penalty cases or any other situation requiring the assessment of adaptive behavior for the purpose of making a determination of intellectual disability. The SSSQ is not an appropriate measure to be used to assess adaptive behavior in death penalty cases or any situation where the determination of intellectual disability is in question (Denkowski & Denkowski, 2008; Everington & Olley, 2008; Macvaugh & Cunningham, 2009).

Facts of the Crime and Maladaptive Behavior

In some *Atkins* hearing, there may be a desire to analyze the facts of the crime as an indication of the perpetrator's adaptive skills. However, how a crime was committed is probably more dependent on a person's cognitive abilities than his or her adaptive functioning. It should also be pointed out that AAIDD (Schalock et al., 2010) clearly cautions against using criminal behavior and the facts of a crime as an indication of adaptive behavior. Disobeying rules, committing a crime, break the law are in fact all examples of deficits in adaptive behavior. One might even argue that these are maladaptive or problem behaviors, which are an entirely different and distinct construct separate and independent of adaptive behavior (Schalock et al., 2010; Tassé, 2009).

By its very definition, criminal activity may be interpreted as deficits in adaptive behavior because adaptive behavior is defined as performing the skills that we learn to meet society's expectations of us and our same-age peers (APA, 2013; Schalock et al., 2010). Many standardized adaptive behavior scales have specific items that assess safety and rule-following behavior. The Vineland Adaptive Behavior Scale has, for example, several socialization domain items that relate to following rules and avoiding situations that might be dangerous (e.g., "Chooses to avoid dangerous or risky activities"; "Stops or stays away from relationships or situations that are hurtful or dangerous"; "Is aware of potential danger and uses caution when encountering risky situations"). In fact, being gullible, naïve, risk unaware, and easily duped into regrettable criminal or problem behavior is a common adaptive skill deficit of adults with "mild intellectual disability" (Greenspan, Loughlin, & Black, 2001; Greenspan, Switzky, & Woods, 2011). Hence, implying that the sophistication of one's criminal activity can be used as an indicator of one's adaptive behavior could not be more absurd and wrongheaded. Again, adults with intellectual disability are quite capable, despite significantly subaverage intellectual functioning, to lie and deceive when those behaviors suit a purpose (i.e., to get out of trouble). The sophistication of one's criminal behavior might correlate with one's intellect, but, then again, the use of a well administered standardized intelligence test will be a much more accurate and valid assessment of the person's intellectual functioning. As cautioned in Schalock et al. (2010), the assessment of adaptive behavior is much more than a mere measure of street smarts.

As discussed in Chapter 5, facts of the crime are probably better indicators of the individual's intellectual ability than her or his adaptive behavior. Criminal behavior is arguably more akin to maladaptive (or lack of adaptive) behavior than any sort of barometer of savant adaptive skills.

Malingering by Proxy

Malingering is defined as the intentional presentation of false or exaggerated physical or psychological symptoms that is motivated by the person's intent on gaining some external incentive such as avoiding work, obtaining financial compensation, evading criminal prosecution, or some other tangible gain or benefit (APA, 2013). When a respondent or third party lies or exaggerates someone else's symptoms or minimizes that person's abilities, such as in the case of reporting on a person's adaptive behavior, Tassé (2009) called this "malingering by proxy." This is a real concern when assessing adaptive behavior in a death penalty context because the informants may have an intent to make the assessed individual appear less capable than is the case in order to avert the death penalty (Bonnie & Gustafson, 2007; Hagan, Drogin, & Guilmette, 2016).

Doane and Salekin (2009) reported data indicating that some standardized adaptive behavior scales may be vulnerable to this sort of malingering by proxy. They reported that some scales of the ABAS-II were more vulnerable than scales on other tests (e.g., SIB-R) to respondents intentionally manipulating the outcome of the evaluation. This further iterates the importance that the professional expert conducting the adaptive behavior assessment be vigilant and use her or his clinical judgment and constantly assess the reliability of all informants and information obtained. This can be done by checking for inconsistencies across items, probing by asking informants to give examples of what they have observed, corroborating the information across multiple informants, and cross-referencing the informants' information across available records and other sources of information. An informant who is found to be unreliable should result in the expert reducing her or his reliance or weight placed upon that informant's information.

Briseño Factors

Although a moot issue since the publication of the Supreme Court of the United States decision in *Moore v. Texas* (2017), we present a discussion of the *Briseño* factors because they illustrate how states can err when left to their own devices. We were conflicted on where to discuss the *Briseño* factors. Should they be presented in Chapter 1 where we discuss misconceptions and stereotypes, or discuss them in Chapter 6 when we discuss adaptive behavior? We agree with Macvaugh and Cunningham (2009) that the *Briseño* factors were largely steeped in lay stereotypes and drew no foundation from the clinical or professional standards of ID and that perhaps their discussion better belongs in the misconceptions and "myth-stakes" section, but we concluded here is where most readers might look for a discussion of the *Briseño* factors.

The *Briseño* factors came out of a decision from the Texas Court of Appeals (*Ex parte Briseño*, 2004) involving the *Atkins* claim of Jose Briseño. The *Briseño* factors propose a seven-question litmus test that is intended to frame the quantification of Prong 2, significant deficits in adaptive behavior. If these seven conditions are not met, then the defendant/petitioner does not meet Prong 2 for a diagnosis of intellectual disability (see Greenspan (2015) for a more detailed discussion:

1. Did those who knew the person best during the developmental stage—his family, friends, teachers, employers, authorities—think he was mentally retarded at that time, and, if so, act in accordance with that determination?
2. Has the person formulated plans and carried them through or is his conduct impulsive?
3. Does his conduct show leadership or does it show that he is led around by others?
4. Is his conduct in response to external stimuli rational and appropriate, regardless of whether it is socially acceptable?

5. Does he respond coherently, rationally, and on point to oral or written questions or do his responses wander from subject to subject?

6. Can the person hide facts or lie effectively in his own or others' interests?

7. Putting aside any heinousness or gruesomeness surrounding the capital offense, did the commission of that offense require forethought, planning, and complex execution of purpose? (*Ex parte Briseño*, 2004; p. 8)

The Texas Court of Appeals relied on the fictional character of Lennie Small in John Steinbeck's novella *Of Mice and Men* to illustrate that having intellectual disability was not sufficient to be exempt from the death penalty but rather that the person had to be sufficiently "retarded" to be deserving of this protection. The problem with this assertion is (1) the Supreme Court of the United States (*Atkins v. Virginia*, 2002) ruled that having a diagnosis of intellectual disability is in and of itself sufficient to be exempt from capital punishment, and (2) Lennie Small is a fictional character who does not exist in real life. We argue that when the Supreme Court of the United States said, "Not all people who claim to be mentally retarded will be so impaired as to fall within the range of mentally retarded offenders about whom there is a national consensus" (*Atkins v. Virginia*, 2002; p. 317), the Court was referring to the national consensus as set forth by the scientific and professional expert community in the field of ID and that is why they pointed to the AAIDD and *DSM* manuals for guidance in defining ID. If you meet diagnostic criteria for intellectual disability under these two national treatises, you have intellectual disability as defined by a national consensus.

In closing, having intellectual disability is not like having a cold. You either have intellectual disability or you don't. You don't have a "touch of ID." If one draws another medical analogy, having intellectual disability might be akin to having cancer. No one takes real solace in knowing they have or a loved one has been diagnosed with a nonaggressive form of cancer. Cancer is cancer! Intellectual disability is a disabling condition no matter the severity level.

Moore v. Texas

The State of Texas argued in *Moore v. Texas* that they had a right to establish how the state would determine who has intellectual disability and, specifically, that this definition could include the *Briseño* factors. It should be noted that Texas used their state definition that consists of a three-prong definition including significant deficits in intellectual functioning, significant deficits in adaptive behavior, and the onset of these deficits during the developmental period. However, in death penalty cases, they also added the supplemental criterion of the *Briseño* factors.

In a 5–3 decision, the Supreme Court of the United States ruled in favor of Bobby James Moore and vacated the Texas ruling denying Moore's claim of intellectual disability and remanded the case. In an amazing turn of events, however, the three dissenting justices sided with the majority in rejecting the state's use of the *Briseño* factors. The Court unanimously rejected the use of the *Briseño* factors on the grounds that these factors were largely inspired from stereotypes, misconceptions, and misinformed beliefs of what people with intellectual disability can and cannot do and that the *Briseño* factors are not part of any established clinical/medical definition of intellectual disability. In fact, Texas does not use these *Briseño* factors in making determinations of intellectual disability except in death penalty matters. The Court also stated in its ruling that, although states retain the right to establish how they determine who has intellectual disability, how states define intellectual disability should conform with established clinical/medical consensus (*Moore v. Texas*, 2017).

Measurement Error

Just as standardized tests of intellectual functioning yield scores that should be interpreted with clinical judgment and consideration for all sources of measurement error, so do the results of adaptive behavior scales. The observed scores should be interpreted within the accepted recommended practice (see Schalock et al., 2010) of 95% confidence interval of +/–2×the test's standard error of measurement. Unlike with performance on tests of intelligence, current research on adaptive behavior assessment results do not indicate a rise in obtained scores or significant inflation in results due to obsolescence of adaptive behavior test norms. Because of the nature of adaptive behavior assessment, practice effects are a nonissue. The Supreme Court of the United States in *Hall v. Florida* (2014) reminded states of the importance to consider measurement error when interpreting results from standardized scales and that intellectual disability is not a number.

Retrospective Assessment

The diagnosis of intellectual disability implicitly requires two conditions related to the adaptive behavior criterion: (1) Adaptive functioning (i.e., conceptual, social, practical skills) is defined as behavior that is learned and typically performed to *meet society's expectations/demands* for individuals of that person's chronological age and cultural group and (2) the assessment of the individual's *present adaptive functioning*. These two conditions, however, are often at odds when assessing adaptive behavior in criminal cases where the individual's "present" adaptive functioning can only be assessed against life in prison (Tassé, 2009). It is in these situations that an expert will need to conduct a retrospective evaluation of the individual's adaptive functioning to a time period when he lived in the community (i.e., prior to incarceration). Using retrospective assessment has been endorsed by AAIDD (Schalock et al., 2010; Schalock et al., 2012).

Again, adaptive behavior is defined as conceptual, social, and practical skills that are learned and performed to meet community standards of personal independence and social responsibility, in comparison to same-age peers and of similar sociocultural background (APA, 2013; Schalock et al., 2010). The assessment of a person's adaptive behavior is done with a combination of standardized adaptive behavior scales, clinical evaluations, and interviews of significant others, as well as a thorough review of all available records. The historical records can inform the expert's clinical judgment regarding Prong 3 (i.e., age of onset during the developmental period), but often a retrospective method of conducting adaptive behavior interviews can provide two valuable pieces of information: the assessed person's adaptive functioning level prior to incarceration (i.e., while still living in the community) and an assessment of the person's adaptive functioning prior to age 18.

Using a retrospective assessment to make a determination of intellectual disability relies heavily upon informants' memory of the assessed individual's functioning and their ability to accurately recall this information. See Chapter 7, where we discuss in more detail how to proceed with a retrospective assessment.

Summary

Adaptive behavior assessment is just as important as the assessment of intellectual functioning in making a determination of intellectual disability (*Moore v. Texas*, 2017). Adaptive behavior is conceptualized as the skills and behaviors we learn and perform that are driven by our society's expectations of us, and these expectations will be indexed on the person's chronological age (Schalock et al., 2010). A comprehensive assessment of a person's adaptive behavior should include a multifaceted approach that includes, when possible, objective information obtained from a standardized assessment involving multiple sources and respondents, as well as a review of all available records and reports over the course of the person's life in the community.

Note

1. The state court judge's decision was affirmed by the Louisiana State Court on direct appeal. 737 So. 2d. 660 (La. 2012). A federal district court judge concluded the state court decision was an unreasonable determination of the facts, granted funds for investigators and experts, and conducted a multiday evidentiary hearing, at the conclusion of which he found Brumfield to be a person with intellectual disability and vacated his sentence. 854 F.Supp.2d 366 (La. 2012). The United States Court of Appeals for the Fifth Circuit reversed this decision and reinstated Brumfield's claim. 744 F.3d 918 (5th Cir. 2014). The Supreme Court then granted certiorari (i.e., voted to hear the case) and reversed the decision of the Fifth Circuit. 135 S.Ct. 2269 (2015).

References

American Psychiatric Association (APA). (1968). *Diagnostic and Statistical Manual of Mental Disorders* (2nd Edition). Washington, DC: Author.

American Psychiatric Association (APA). (2000). *Diagnostic and Statistical Manual of Mental Disorders* (4th Edition, text revised). Washington, DC: Author.

American Psychiatric Association (APA). (2013). *Diagnostic and Statistical Manual of Mental Disorders* (5th Edition). Arlington, VA: American Psychiatric Publishing.

Binet, A., & Simon, T. (1905). Méthodes nouvelles pour le diagnostic du niveau intellectuel des anormaux. *L'Année Psychologique, 11*, 191–244.

Boccaccini, M. T., Kan, L. Y., Rufino, K. A., Noland, R. M., Young-Lundquist, B. A., & Canales, E. (2016). Correspondence between correctional staff and offender ratings of adaptive behavior. *Psychological Assessment, 28*, 1608–1615.

Bonnie, R. J., & Gustafson, K. (2007). The challenges of implementing *Atkins v. Virginia*: How legislatures and courts can promote accurate assessments and adjudications of mental retardation in death penalty cases. *University of Richmond Law Review, 41*, 810–860.

Bruininks, R. H., Woodcock, R., Weatherman, R. F., & Hill, B. K. (1996). *Scales of Independent Behavior—Revised (SIB-R)*. Itasca, IL: Riverside Publishing.

Carpentieri, S., & Morgan, S. B. (1996). Adaptive and intellectual functioning in autistic and nonautistic retarded children. *Journal of Autism and Developmental Disorders, 26*, 611–620.

Chapman, S. L. C., & Wu, L. T. (2012). Substance abuse among individuals with intellectual disabilities. *Research in developmental disabilities, 33*(4), 1147–1156.

Childs, R. E. (1982). A study of the adaptive behavior of retarded children and the resultant effects of this use in the diagnosis of mental retardation. *Education and Training of the Mentally Retarded, 17,* 109–113.

Cooper, S. A., Smiley, E., Morrison, J., Williamson, A., & Allan, L. (2007). Mental ill-health in adults with intellectual disabilities: Prevalence and associated factors. *The British Journal of Psychiatry, 190*(1), 27–35.

Denkowski, G. C., & Denkowski, K. M. (2008). Misuse of the Street Survival Skills Questionnaire (SSSQ) for evaluating the adult adaptive behavior of criminal defendants with intellectual disability claims. *Intellectual and Developmental Disabilities, 46,* 144–149.

Doane, B. M., & Salekin, K. L. (2009). Susceptibility of current adaptive behavior measures to feigned deficits. *Law and Human Behavior, 33*(4), 329–343.

Doll, E. A. (1936). *The Vineland Social Maturity Scale.* Vineland, NJ: Vineland Training School.

Doll, E. A. (1953). *Measurement of Social Competence: A Manual for the Vineland Social Maturity Scale.* Circle Pines, MN: American Guidance Service.

Everington, C., & Olley, J. G. (2008). Implications of *Atkins v. Virginia:* Issues in defining and diagnosing mental retardation. *Journal of Forensic Psychology Practice, 8*(1), 1–23.

Ex parte Briseño, 135 S.W. 3d 1 (2004).

Felce, D., de-Kock., U., Thomans, M., & Saxby, H. (1986). Change in adaptive behavior of severely and profoundly mentally handicapped adults in different residential settings. *British Journal of Psychology, 77,* 489–501.

Fine, M. A., Tangeman, P. J., & Woodard, J. (1990). Changes in adaptive behavior of older adults with mental retardation following deinstitutionalization. *American Journal on Mental Retardation, 94,* 661–668.

Fletcher, R. J., Barnhill, J., & Cooper, S. A. (2016) *Diagnostic Manual for Individuals with Intellectual Disabilities: A Textbook of Diagnosis of Mental Disorders in Persons with Intellectual Disability.* Kingston, NY: NADD Press.

Gottfredson, L. (1997). Mainstream science on intelligence: An editorial with 52 signatories, history, and bibliography. *Intelligence, 24,* 13–23.

Greenspan, S. (2015). The *Briseño* factors (pp. 219–231). In E. A. Polloway (Ed.), *The Death Penalty and Intellectual Disability.* Washington, DC: American Association on Intellectual and Developmental Disabilities.

Greenspan, S., Loughlin, G., & Black, R. (2001). Credulity and gullibility in people with developmental disorders: A framework for future research (Vol. 24, pp. 101–135). In L. M. Glidden (Ed.), *International Review of Research in Mental Retardation.* New York: Academic Press.

Greenspan, S., Switzky, H. N., & Woods, G. W. (2011). Intelligence involves risk-awareness and intellectual disability involves risk-unawareness: Implications of a theory of common sense. *Journal of Intellectual and Developmental Disability, 36*(4), 246–257.

Grissom, Brandi. (2011). Psychologists who cleared death row inmates is reprimanded. *The Texas Tribune,* April 14, 2010.

Hagan, L. D., Drogin, E. Y., & Guilmette, T. J. (2016). Assessing adaptive functioning in death penalty cases after Hall and DSM-5. *Journal of the American Academy of Psychiatry and the Law Online, 44*(1), 96–105.

Hall v. Florida, 134 S. Ct. 1986 (2014).

Harrison, P. L., & Oakland, T. (2003). *Adaptive Behavior Assessment System Second Edition: Manual.* San Antonio: Harcourt Assessment.

Harrison, P. L., & Oakland, T. (2015). *Adaptive Behavior Assessment System Third Edition (ABAS-III): Manual.* San Antonio: Pearson.

Heber, R. (1959). A manual on terminology and classification in mental retardation: A monograph supplement. *American Journal of Mental Deficiency, 64,* 1–111.

Heber, R. (1961). *A Manual on Terminology and Classification in Mental Retardation* (Revised Edition). Washington, DC: American Association on Mental Deficiency.

Holland, T., Clare, I. C. H., & Mukhopadhyay, T. (2002). Prevalence of "criminal offending" by men and women with intellectual disability and the characteristics of "offenders": Implications for research and service development. *Journal of Intellectual Disability Research, 46,* 6–20.

Hull, J. T., & Thompson, J. C. (1980). Predicting adaptive functioning of mentally retarded persons in community settings. *American Journal of Mental Deficiency, 85,* 253–261.

Keith, T. Z., Fehrmann, P. G., & Harrison, P., & Pottebaum, S. M. (1987). The relationship between adaptive behavior and intelligence: Testing alternative explanations. *Journal of School Psychology, 25,* 31–43.

Lakin, K. C., Larson, S. A., & Kim, S. (2011). *Behavioral Outcomes of Deinstitutionalization for People with Intellectual and/or Developmental Disabilities: Third Decennial Review of US Studies, 1977–2010.* Minneapolis: Research and Training Center on Community Living, Institute on Community Integration, University of Minnesota.

Linkenhoker, D. & McCarron, L. (1993). *Adaptive Behavior: The Street Survival Skills Questionnaire.* Dallas: McCarron-Dial Systems.

Luckasson, R., Borthwick-Duffy, S., Buntinx, W. H. E., Coulter, D. L., Craig, E. M., Schalock, R. L., Snell, M. E., Spitalnik, D. M., Spreat, S., & Tassé, M. J. (2002). *Mental Retardation: Definition, Classification, and Systems of Supports* (10th Edition). Washington, DC: American Association on Mental Retardation,

Macvaugh, G. S., & Cunningham, M. D. (2009). *Atkins v. Virginia:* Implications and recommendations for forensic practice. *Journal of Psychiatry & Law, 37,* 131–187.

McGillivray, J. A., & Moore, M. R. (2001). Substance use by offenders with mild intellectual disability. *Journal of Intellectual and Developmental Disability, 26*(4), 297–310.

McGrew, K. S., & Bruininks, R. H. (1990). Defining adaptive and maladaptive behavior within a model of personal competence. *School Psychology Review, 19,* 53–73.

Moore v. Texas, 137 S. Ct. 1039, 1045 (2017).

Olley, J. G. (2015). Adaptive behavior instruments (pp. 187–200). In E. Polloway (Ed.), *The Death Penalty and Intellectual Disability*. Washington, DC: American Association on Intellectual and Developmental Disabilities.

Olley, J. G., & Cox, A. W. (2008). Assessment of adaptive behavior in adult forensic cases: The use of the ABAS-II (pp. 381–398). In T. Oakland & P. L. Harrison (Eds.), *ABAS-II: Clinical Use and Interpretation*. San Diego: Academic Press.

Pearson, N. A., Patton, J. R., & Mruzek, D. W. (2016). *Adaptive Behavior Diagnostic Scale: Examiner's Manual*. Austin: PRO-ED.

Reiss, S. (1994). *Handbook of Challenging Behavior: Mental Health Aspects of Mental Retardation*. Columbus, OH: IDS Publishing.

Rojahn, J., & Tassé, M. J. (1996). Psychopathology in mental retardation (pp. 147–156). In J. W. Jacobson & J. A. Mulick (Eds.), *Manual of diagnosis and professional practice in Mental Retardation*. Washington, DC: American Psychological Association.

Rush, S. C., Major-Sanabria, M., & Corcoran, S. (2008). Using the ABAS-II with adolescents and young adults (pp. 313–332). In T. Oakland & P. L. Harrison (Eds.), *ABAS-II: Clinical Use and Interpretation*. San Diego: Academic Press.

Sattler, J. M. (2002). *Assessment of Children: Behavioral and Clinical Applications* (4th Edition). La Mesa, CA: Jerome M. Sattler, Publisher.

Schalock, R. L., Buntinx, W. H. E., Borthwick-Duffy, S., Bradley, V., Craig, E. M., Coulter, D. L., Gomez, S. C., Lachapelle, Y., Luckasson, R. A., Reeve, A., Shogren, K. A., Snell, M. E., Spreat, S., Tassé, M. J., Thompson, J. R., Verdugo, M. A., Wehmeyer, M. L., & Yeager, M. H. (2010). *Intellectual Disability: Definition, Classification, and System of Supports* (11th Edition). Washington, DC: American Association on Intellectual and Developmental Disabilities.

Schalock, R. L., & Luckasson, R. (2014). *Clinical Judgment* (2nd Edition). Washington, DC: American Association on Intellectual and Developmental Disabilities.

Schalock, R. L., Luckasson, R. A., Bradley, V., Buntinx, W. H. E., Lachapelle, Y., Shogren, K. A., Snell, M. E., Tassé, M. J., Thompson, J. R., Verdugo, M. A., & Wehmeyer, M. L. (2012). *Intellectual Disability: Definition, Classification, and System of Supports (11th Edition)—User's Guide*. Washington, DC: American Association on Intellectual and Developmental Disabilities.

Silverman, W. P., Silver, E. J., Sersen, E. A., Lubin, R. A., & Schwartz, A. A. (1986). Factors related to adaptive behavior changes among profoundly mentally retarded, physically disabled persons. *American Journal of Mental Deficiency, 90*, 651–658.

Sparrow, S. S., Balla, D. A., & Cicchetti, D. V. (1984). *Vineland: Vineland Adaptive Behavior Scales*. Circle Pines, MN: American Guidance Service.

Sparrow, S. S., Balla, D. A., & Cicchetti, D. V. (2005). *Vineland-II: Vineland Adaptive Behavior Scales* (2nd Edition). Minneapolis: Pearson Assessments.

Tassé, M. J. (2009). Adaptive behavior assessment and the diagnosis of mental retardation in capital cases. *Applied Neuropsychology, 16,* 114–123.

Tassé, M. J., & Grover, M. D. (2013). American Association on Intellectual and Developmental Disabilities (pp. 122–125). In F. R. Volkmar (Ed.), *Encyclopedia of Autism Spectrum Disorders.* New York: Springer.

Tassé, M. J., Luckasson, R., & Schalock, R. L. (2016). The relation between intellectual functioning and adaptive behavior in the diagnosis of intellectual disability. *Intellectual Developmental Disabilities, 54,* 381–390.

Tassé, M. J., Schalock, R. L., Balboni, G., Bersani, H., Borthwick-Duffy, S. A., Spreat, S., Thissen, D. T., Widaman, K. F., & Zhang, D. (2012). The Construct of Adaptive Behavior: Its Conceptualization, Measurement, and Use in the Field of Intellectual Disability. *American Journal on Intellectual and Developmental Disabilities, 117,* 291–303.

Tassé, M. J., Schalock, R. L., Balboni, G., Spreat, S., & Navas, P. (2016). Validity and reliability of the Diagnostic Adaptive Behavior Scale. *Journal of Intellectual Disability Research, 60,* 80–88.

Tassé, M. J., Schalock, R. L., Thissen, D., Balboni, G., Bersani, H. A., Borthwick-Duffy, S. A., Spreat, S., Widaman, K. F., Zhang, D., & Navas, P. (2016). The development and standardization of the Diagnostic Adaptive Behavior Scale: The application of item response theory to the assessment of adaptive behavior. *American Journal on Intellectual and Developmental Disabilities, 121,* 79–94.

World Health Organization (WHO). (1992). *The International Classification of Diseases* (10th Revision; ICD-10). Geneva: Author.

CHAPTER SEVEN

Assessing the Age of Onset

The third prong of the three-prong diagnostic criteria of intellectual disability is the age of onset of significant deficits in intellectual functioning and adaptive behavior. Onset is defined in the *Merriam-Webster* dictionary as the time or age at which the disorder began (*Merriam-Webster*, 2017). This is an important distinction because this third prong refers to the developmental nature of the condition and is used to differentiate between deficits in intellectual functioning and adaptive behavior that are associated with intellectual disability versus other disorders that have an adult onset (e.g., schizophrenia, dementia). When making a determination of intellectual disability, the clinician must establish that the individual's functioning is significantly subaverage in both intellectual functioning and adaptive behavior and also that these deficits manifested during the developmental period. An important point to be made here is that a "diagnosis" of intellectual disability does not necessarily need to be made during this period but rather that it must be established that the deficits in intellectual functioning and adaptive behavior were present during the developmental period. A large number of risk factors and causes of intellectual disability are present prenatally (e.g., genetic anomaly), perinatally (e.g., anoxia at birth), or postnatally (e.g., exposure to teratogens). Some risk factors and causes (e.g., malnutrition and other factors associated with poverty) of intellectual disability might have a gradual deleterious effect on individual functioning, and for this reason the age of onset has historically been set at the end of the developmental period, or approximately before the 18th birthday (Schalock et al., 2010).

Although the current age of onset criterion has been set at 18 years old for more than four decades, this has not always been the case. In 1968, the DSM-II (American Psychiatric Association (APA), 1968) used simply the term "developmental period." From 1959 to the early 1970s, AAIDD used the age of 16 years as the end of the developmental period (Heber, 1959, 1961). However, for the past 40 years, both the *DSM* and the AAIDD had operationally defined the developmental period and age of onset criterion to be before the age of 18 years (APA, 1980, 1987, 1994, 2000; Grossman, 1973, 1977, 1983; Luckasson et al., 1992, 2002; Schalock et al., 2010). Interestingly, in its most recent revision to the DSM, the American Psychiatric Association chose to return to the broader expression "developmental period" and eliminated its mention of a specific age of onset (APA, 2013). It seems that this change was made in part because there is evidence that the brain has not completed its develop until the approximate age of 25 years (Arain et al., 2013) and in part because of the APA's attempt to align its diagnostic criteria with the broader and more global system of the World Health Organization (WHO) and its eleventh edition of the *International Classification of Diseases (ICD-11)* (WHO, in press). It is understandable that the WHO not adopt a precise chronological age to demark the end of the developmental period in its ICD system because the ICD system is developed for use in almost 200 countries around the world, including many low- and moderate-income countries. It is likely out of a recognition that human development does not progress at the same rate in some more underdeveloped countries of the world that the WHO does not use a specific age of onset, leaving it to the clinical judgment of the professional to make the determination.

In the United States, many diagnoses of intellectual disability are made between birth and the end of the elementary school period. Typically, an assessment of intellectual functioning and adaptive behavior is done contemporaneously. However, in the forensic arena, this is not frequently the case. Often, the individual asserting intellectual disability as a bar to execution was not previously diagnosed with intellectual disability, or records that may support their claim of intellectual disability may not be readily available. In these situations, one must conduct a comprehensive evaluation of the individual's intellectual functioning (see Chapter 5 of this volume) and adaptive behavior (see Chapter 6) and, if there is evidence of significant deficits in both intellectual functioning and adaptive behavior, establish that these deficits were present before the age of 18 years. The age of onset determination can be established with information related to the individual's childhood functioning in the form of medical records, school records, school or other psychological evaluations, interviews with family members, neighbors, teachers, counselors, or other individuals who may have interacted with the individual during the developmental period. This may also require a retrospective assessment in situations where there may not be a documented assessment of adaptive behavior prior to age 18. We will discuss how to conduct a reliable retrospective assessment in making an intellectual disability determination.

Retrospective Assessment

A retrospective assessment or diagnosis is needed in forensic cases where the individual was not formally diagnosed before the age of 18 years and/or the individual has been incarcerated for a number of years and Prong 3 (age of onset of significant deficits in intellectual functioning and adaptive behavior) must be clearly established (Everington, 2014). The individual's school and medical records may be difficult to locate or have likely already been shredded; parents and other relatives are getting older, may have moved away, or may be ill or dead. Reschly (2009) reminded us of the important principle of collecting information from multiple sources and respondents and using convergent validity in analyzing all the information to inform one's clinical judgment in determining Prong 3. Obtaining information from multiple sources and employing a convergence-of-data approach is a key element to conducting a retrospective evaluation.

You will recall that the diagnosis of intellectual disability explicitly requires two conditions: (1) Limitations in present adaptive functioning (2) were considered within the context of community environments typical of the individual's peers and culture (Schalock et al., 2010). Conducting an assessment of the individual's present intellectual functioning does not generally pose a problem, even for an individual who is currently incarcerated. This is fortunate because administering a standardized test of intelligence retrospectively is impossible. The standardized adaptive behavior scales discussed in Chapter 6 have all been standardized using contemporary use of the scales. However, many items on standardized adaptive behavior scales would be impossible to assess in a prison context (see Chapter 6 for a review), the contemporaneous administration of an adaptive behavior scale with a person who has observed the individual's behavior in prison (e.g., correctional officer, prison staff) would not produce a valid assessment (Olley, 2015). The assessment of the individual's "present functioning" in terms of adaptive behavior, however, is challenging if the assessed individual is incarcerated and has been for a length of time. These two aforementioned conditions of present functioning and community environment are at odds with one another in death penalty cases where the individual's "present" adaptive behavior can only be assessed against life in a prison or on death row. Prison life and prison expectations for adaptive behavior cannot be substituted for society's expectations in making the determination of the individual's everyday functioning in the general community (Olley, 2013). Assessing adaptive behavior is best done based on the individual's functioning in the community (Tassé, 2009). As such, one must conduct a retrospective evaluation of the individual's adaptive behavior during a period of time prior to incarceration and when the individual was living in the community.

Although some authors have cautioned experts regarding the pitfalls of conducting a retrospective adaptive behavior assessment (Stevens & Price, 2006), the authors of this book agree with others (Macvaugh & Cunningham, 2009; Olley & Cox, 2008) that, with proper precautions and critical considerations, experts are able to use retrospective assessments when making an intellectual disability determination in death penalty cases. If the retrospective evaluation time period is set to be before the age of 18 years, then the evaluation can accomplish two important aspects of the intellectual disability determination: (1) establish whether significant deficits in adaptive behavior were present (i.e., Prong 2) and (2) establish that these deficits were present before age 18 (i.e., Prong 3). Conducting a retrospective assessment of adaptive behavior and diagnosis of intellectual disability is not exclusive to *Atkins* hearings. Retrospective assessments are at times necessary in clinical situations where a person presents for services as an adult, having lived with his or her parents or other family members, and is unknown to the state developmental disabilities service system (see Chafetz, 2015; Reschly, Myers, & Hartel, 2002; Schalock et al., 2010; Schalock et al., 2012). Conducting a retrospective assessment should be done with caution and under proper conditions to ensure the reliability of the conclusions (i.e., ruling in or ruling out of the diagnosis). The AAIDD's *Terminology and Classification Manual* (Schalock et al., 2010) supports the use of a retrospective assessment/diagnosis of intellectual disability. In addition to all the key guidelines presented in Chapter 6, here are some elements to consider during a retrospective assessment (see Keyes & Freedman, 2015; Schalock et al., 2012; Tassé, 2009):

1. Conduct a thorough social history.
2. Conduct a thorough review of all records (e.g., birth, medical, school, social and child protection records, social security administration, department of corrections, previous psychological or educational evaluations).
3. Assess adaptive behavior:
    *   Use multiple informants and multiple contexts;
    *   Recognize that limitations in present functioning must be considered within the context of community environments typical of the individual's peers and culture;

- Be aware that many important social behavioral skills, such as gullibility and naïveté, are not measured on current adaptive behavior scales;

- Use an adaptive behavior scale that assesses behaviors that are currently viewed as developmentally and socially expected for the person;

- Understand that adaptive behavior and problem behavior are independent constructs and not opposite poles of a continuum; and

- Realize that adaptive behavior refers to typical and actual functioning and not to capacity or maximum functioning.

4. When conducting an adaptive behavior interview retrospectively:

    - Identify a clear time period during which you want the respondent to focus his or her report of the individual's adaptive behavior. For example, you might instruct the respondent to recall the assessed individual before incarceration or identify some salient benchmarks to help ground the respondent to a specific time or period, such as living on a specific street, a life event (death of a family member, birth of a child), working at a specific job or location.

    - Build rapport and ask the respondent to think about where the assessed person was living at that specified time, working, and so on. These reference points in time will be important to assist the respondent in remaining focused in that time frame and to recall the assessed person's behavior during that time period.

    - Periodically remind the respondent that the aim is to assess the individual's adaptive behavior in that specific time period. Establish that the respondent is able to recall the person's behavior and to inform the evaluator as to whether the assessment is a "guess" or informed on observation and recollection.

There are situations where variations from standardization procedures may be necessary and advisable (American Educational Research Association (AERA), 2014). The Standards for Educational and Psychological Testing acknowledged that there are situations when the assessor might need to break standardization. Conducting a retrospective assessment using an adaptive behavior scale is one such departure from standardization. Hence, some caution is needed when interpreting the results obtained through a retrospective adaptive behavior assessment because of the variation from the standardization procedures and no research is available to inform us as to the possible error rate of adaptive behavior assessments obtained retrospectively (Tassé, 2009). The authors of this book believe these situations warrant such variations from the typical administration protocol of adaptive behavior because the recommended administration procedure would not yield a valid current assessment of the individual's adaptive behavior in a community setting. In short, prison is simply not a community setting.

As always, the adaptive behavior information obtained from any respondent, including during a retrospective evaluation, should be closely examined for any possible bias (Chafetz, 2015). As much as a parent, grandparent, aunt, older sibling, or other knowledgeable respondent might assert having a clear memory of the individual as a teenager or child, the clinician should be wary of the possibility that the respondent's specific memory regarding the individual's adaptive behavior may be fallible. Hence, the respondent should use clinical judgment (see Schalock & Luckasson, 2014) in assessing the consistency of the informant's information and routinely remind the respondent to inform the clinician when his or her ratings are based on a guess rather than clear recollection.

In summary, evaluating the age of onset of significant deficits in intellectual functioning and adaptive behavior is easily accomplished when the person being assessed is under the age of 18 years. When this is not the case, a review of records (e.g., school, medical, social security administration, employment) for prior psychological evaluations and diagnoses will contain important information permitting the ascertainment of onset during the developmental period. If the person was never diagnosed with intellectual disability prior to the age 18 and no prior evaluations are available, a rigorous retrospective assessment is warranted.

References

American Educational Research Association (AERA), American Psychological Association, and the National Council on Measurement in Education. (2014). *Standards for Educational and Psychological Testing*. Washington: Author.

American Psychiatric Association (APA). (1968). *Diagnostic and Statistical Manual of Mental Disorders* (2nd Edition). Washington, DC: Author.

American Psychiatric Association. (1980). *Diagnostic and Statistical Manual of Mental Disorders* (3rd Edition; *DSM-III*). Washington, DC: Author.

American Psychiatric Association. (1987). *Diagnostic and Statistical Manual of Mental Disorders* (3rd Edition, revised; *DSM-III-R*). Washington, DC: Author.

American Psychiatric Association. (1994). *Diagnostic and Statistical Manual of Mental Disorders* (4th Edition; *DSM-IV*). Washington, DC: Author.

American Psychiatric Association (APA). (2000). *Diagnostic and Statistical Manual of Mental Disorders* (4th Edition, text revised). Washington, DC: Author.

American Psychiatric Association APA). (2013). *Diagnostic and Statistical Manual of Mental Disorders* (5th Edition). Arlington, VA: American Psychiatric Publishing.

Arain, M., Haque, M., Johal, L., Mathur, P., Nel, W., Rais, A., Sandhu, R., & Sharma, S. (2013). Maturation of the adolescent brain. *Neuropsychiatric Disease and Treatment, 9,* 449–461. DOI: 10.2147/NDT.S39776

Chafetz, M. (2015). *Intellectual Disability: Civil and Criminal Forensic Issues.* New York: Oxford University Press.

Everington, C. (2014). Challenges of conveying intellectual disabilities to judge and jury. *William & Mary Bill of Rights Journal, 23,* 467–485.

Grossman, H. J. (Ed.). (1973). *Manual on Terminology and Classification in Mental Retardation.* Washington, DC: American Association on Mental Deficiency.

Grossman, H. J. (Ed.). (1977). *Manual on Terminology and Classification in Mental Retardation.* Washington, DC: American Association on Mental Deficiency.

Grossman, H. J. (Ed.). (1983). *Classification in Mental Retardation.* Washington, DC: American Association on Mental Deficiency.

Heber, R. (1959). A manual on terminology and classification in mental retardation: A monograph supplement. *American Journal of Mental Deficiency, 64,* 1–111.

Heber, R. (1961). *A Manual on Terminology and Classification in Mental Retardation* (Revised Edition). Washington, DC: American Association on Mental Deficiency.

Keyes, D. W., & Freedman (2015). Retrospective diagnosis and malingering (pp. 263–277). In E. A. Polloway (Ed.), *The Death Penalty and Intellectual Disability.* Washington, DC: American Association on Intellectual and Developmental Disabilities.

Luckasson, R., Coulter, D. L., Polloway, E. A., Reiss, S., Schalock, R. L., Snell, M. E., Spitalnik, D. M., & Stark, J. A. (1992). *Mental Retardation: Definition, Classification, and Systems of Supports* (9th Edition). Washington, DC: American Association on Mental Retardation.

Luckasson, R., Borthwick-Duffy, S., Buntinx, W. H. E., Coulter, D. L., Craig, E. M., Reeve, A., Schalock, R. L., Snell, M. E., Spitalnik, D. M., Spreat, S., & Tassé, M. J. (2002). *Mental Retardation: Definition, Classification, and Systems of Supports* (10th Edition). Washington, DC: American Association on Mental Retardation.

Macvaugh, G. S. & Cunningham, M. D. (2009). *Atkins v. Virginia:* Implications and recommendations for forensic practice. *Journal of Psychiatry & Law, 37,* 131–187.

Merriam-Webster (2017). *Merriam-Webster Online Dictionary.* https://www.merriam -webster.com/dictionary/onset

Olley, J. G. (2013). Definition of intellectual disability in criminal court cases. *Intellectual and Developmental Disabilities, 51,* 117–121.

Olley, J. G. (2015). Adaptive behavior instruments. In E. A. Polloway (Ed.), *The Death Penalty and Intellectual Disability* (pp. 187–200). Washington, DC: American Association on Intellectual and Developmental Disabilities.

Olley, J. G., & Cox, A. W. (2008). Assessment of adaptive behavior in adult forensic cases. The use of the adaptive behavior assessment System-II. In

T. Oakland & P. L. Harrison (Eds.), *Adaptive Behavior Assessment System-II* (pp. 381–397). San Diego, CA: Academic Press.

Reschly, D. J. (2009). Documenting the developmental origins of mild mental retardation. *Applied Neuropsychology, 16*, 124–134.

Reschly, D. J., Myers, T., G., & Hartel, C. R. (2002). *Mental Retardation: Determining Eligibility for Social Security Benefits.* Washington, DC: National Academy Press.

Schalock, R. L., Buntinx, W. H. E., Borthwick-Duffy, S., Bradley, V., Craig, E. M., Coulter, D. L., Gomez, S. C., Lachapelle, Y., Luckasson, R. A., Reeve, A., Shogren, K. A., Snell, M. E., Spreat, S., Tassé, M. J., Thompson, J. R., Verdugo, M. A., Wehmeyer, M. L., & Yeager, M. H. (2010). *Intellectual Disability: Definition, Classification, and System of Supports* (11th Edition). Washington, DC: American Association on Intellectual and Developmental Disabilities.

Schalock, R. L. & Luckasson, R. (2014). *Clinical Judgment* (2nd Edition). Washington, DC: American Association on Intellectual and Developmental Disabilities.

Schalock, R. L., Luckasson, R. A., Bradley, V., Buntinx, W. H. E., Lachapelle, Y., Shogren, K. A., Snell, M. E., Tassé, M. J., Thompson, J. R., Verdugo, M. A., & Wehmeyer, M. L. (2012). *Intellectual Disability: Definition, Classification, and System of Supports (11th Edition)—User's Guide.* Washington, DC: American Association on Intellectual and Developmental Disabilities.

Stevens, K. B. & Price, J. R. (2006). Adaptive behavior, mental retardation, and the death penalty. *Journal of Forensic Psychology Practice, 6*, 1–29.

Tassé, M. J. (2009). Adaptive behavior assessment and the diagnosis of mental retardation in capital cases. *Applied Neuropsychology, 16*, 114–123.

World Health Organization (WHO). (1992). *The International Classification of Diseases* (10th Revision; ICD-10). Geneva: Author.

CHAPTER EIGHT

Expert Witnesses

Most persons called as witnesses at trial can testify only to facts that they have personally observed; the rules of evidence do not generally allow witnesses to speculate or offer their opinion(s).[1] Expert witnesses, however, are treated differently by the rules of evidence. Every state allows expert witnesses to offer their opinions based on their knowledge and experience. Federal Rule of Evidence 702, for example, states that a "witness who is qualified by knowledge, skill, experience, training or education may testify in the form of an opinion, . . . if the expert's scientific, technical or other specialized knowledge will help the trier of fact understand the evidence or determine a fact in issue." Intellectual disability is an area about which experts are allowed to opine. They are permitted to draw inferences and offer their opinions about intellectual disability in general and whether a capital defendant or death row inmate is (or is not) a person with intellectual disability (Rogers & Shuman, 2005).

> An expert witness is different from a lay witness in several ways. Lay witnesses describe all individuals not qualified as experts, and they are allowed to testify only on what they personally have seen and heard (or in special instances, felt, tasted, touched). Expert witnesses are given a privileged status in the courtroom. They are allowed to give opinions. (Brodsky, 2013; p. 170)

An *Atkins* hearing, by necessity, is a proceeding that intersects criminal justice and the clinical field of intellectual disability. It is the only issue in the criminal justice system where a diagnosis determines whether a person can be executed. Thus, given the issue to be decided and the stakes involved, capital cases where intellectual disability is raised as a bar to the death penalty raise challenging issues regarding who is the best qualified expert witness. This chapter will speak to the required qualifications for expert witnesses, the roles that expert witnesses play in *Atkins* cases, and the importance of clinical judgment in informing a determination of intellectual disability.

As one of the authors and others have previously pointed out, forensic psychologists, neuropsychologists, and psychiatrists frequently lack the necessary training, professional experience, and clinical judgment required to make a thorough and reliable intellectual disability determination. Intellectual disability experts, on the other hand, often lack sufficient forensic training and adequate familiarity with the adversarial system to be an effective witness in an *Atkins* hearing (Macvaugh, Cunningham, & Tassé, 2015). Typically, experienced attorneys involved in *Atkins* cases will attempt to retain a mental health expert who has it all: extensive training and experience in forensic assessments, individual psychological evaluations, and the field of intellectual disability. Because such a person is often not easy to find, counsel may need to secure the services of more than one mental health professional in order to obtain complementary skills and competence. Given that most death row inmates and capital defendants are indigent, however, their ability to do so can be dependent on the court approving funding. Thus, the reality is that funding and other factors may limit attorneys to hiring one person to do an *Atkins* assessment who, hopefully, will be able to competently do it all.

Few traditional mental health experts have specialized graduate education and practical training in both forensic psychology/psychiatry and intellectual disability (Fabian, Thompson, & Lazarus, 2011; Keyes, Edwards, & Derning, 1998; Olley, 2009). Macvaugh and his colleagues (2015) summarized an unpublished study done by Macvaugh and Grosso in which they reported that fewer than half of the forensic experts surveyed had any formal ID training, approximately half reported having had some formal training in forensic assessments, and only one out of the 20 respondents reported having had training in both ID and forensic psychology. Olley (2009) opined that not only should an expert doing an *Atkins* assessment have extensive professional experience working with individuals with intellectual disability, but they also should have extensive experience specifically with individuals in the "mild range" of intellectual disability and be informed of the current research in the field of intellectual disability.

What adds to the complexities of intellectual disability determinations in *Atkins* cases is that almost all involve individuals who have (relatively speaking) mild deficits in intellectual functioning and/or adaptive behavior rather than individuals with more severe forms of the disability (Reschly, 2009). This adds to the complexity of the evaluation because assessment instruments are not perfect and error of measurement plays an even more critical role in determining the outcome of the final determination. Additionally, individuals with significant but milder severity of deficits in intellectual functioning and adaptive behavior will have more relative strengths and abilities that may confound even the most experienced clinician. It is important to note that not all mental health experts are equally competent and experienced in conducting an intellectual disability determination with individuals in the mild range of intellectual disability. In fact, making a diagnosis of intellectual disability near the range of functioning that is bordering on the −2 standard deviations from the population mean is a very challenging situation and should be conducted only by highly qualified professionals with expertise in intellectual disability (Schalock et al., 2010). The reality is that individuals with intellectual disability in the mild range will have any number of strengths and areas of ability (e.g., read books, drive a car, get and keep paid employment, play chess, etc.), and these strengths may confound a layperson or a mental health professional with limited clinical experience with this clinical population (Tassé, 2009). Persons, even highly trained mental health professionals, who do not have sufficient experience and expertise interacting with and evaluating people with mild intellectual disability often erroneously assume that these pockets of strengths and skills are inconsistent with a diagnosis of intellectual disability, ignore the findings from a comprehensive individualized evaluation, and therefore favor their misconceptions regarding what someone with intellectual disability can or cannot do (Tassé, 2009). This selective attention to misconceptions drives inaccurate belief systems regarding the diagnosis of intellectual disability that may lead some individuals to ignore or place less importance on the comprehensive assessment results obtained from a comprehensive evaluation of the person's intellectual functioning and adaptive behavior.

In addition to having proper training, qualifications, and experience, experts working on *Atkins* cases (like all mental health experts) must be prepared to present and defend their mental health/psychological data and conclusions with rigor and objectivity. As Hagan and his colleagues recently noted, mental health experts have an obligation to assist the trier of fact by using scientific procedures and data-supported findings and not be an advocate for a predefined outcome (Hagan, Drogin, & Guilmette, 2016). Others have also identified the struggle faced by experts in the forensic world to remain neutral and impartial and the need for them to advocate for data and the best science while not allowing outside factors that are independent of the data shape their professional opinion (Brodsky & Galloway, 2003; Macvaugh et al., 2015; Neal, 2016). Unlike prosecutors and defense attorneys, who are advocates in an adversarial system, retained or court-appointed mental health experts must faithfully adhere to best clinical practices, make as objective and thorough an intellectual disability determination as possible, and render their opinion accordingly (Neal, 2016).

Minimum Qualifications of Experts

As discussed in Chapter 3, the Supreme Court of the United States in *Atkins v. Virginia* did not specifically define intellectual disability, nor did it define what expert qualifications were needed to make a determination of intellectual disability. Nevertheless, the Court has consistently pointed to the national clinical consensus in the field of intellectual disability, namely the American Association on Intellectual and Developmental Disabilities (AAIDD) and the American Psychiatric Association (APA), for guidance regarding the established national consensus on the diagnostic criteria for intellectual disability (*Atkins v. Virginia*; *Hall v. Florida*; and, *Moore v. Texas*). Hence, mental health experts involved in *Atkins* cases should be (or become) familiar with the most current version of the *AAIDD Terminology and Classification Manual* (Schalock et al., 2010) and the *Diagnostic and Statistical Manual of Mental Disorders* (*DSM-5*) (American Psychiatric Association (APA), 2013), as well as the relevant state statute defining intellectual disability. The reader is referred to these following references for a review of existing state definitions of "intellectual disability" in states that have the death penalty (DeMatteo, Marczyk, & Pich (2007; Duvall and Morris, 2006; Wood, Packman, Howell, & Bongar, 2014).

Mental health experts should verify with their respective state licensing board to ensure that they have the proper professional license to conduct the evaluations needed to make a determination of intellectual disability. Macvaugh and his colleagues (2015) provided a number of excellent recommendations for mental health experts conducting *Atkins* evaluations, including ensuring that experts involved in cases outside their jurisdiction (i.e., state licensure) can practice psychology (e.g., conducting a psychological evaluation for the purpose of making an intellectual disability determination) in the state of jurisdiction of the case.

Mental health experts working in *Atkins* hearings should get a copy of all state statutes relevant to the case at hand (e.g., the state statute defining intellectual disability). Some state statutes specifically set forth who will be the fact finder who determines whether or not the *Atkins* claimant has satisfied his or her burden of proof; in most states, it is a judge (see Wood et al., 2014). Most state statutes do not specify precisely how the mental health expert should assess intellectual functioning or adaptive behavior, but at least five of the 31 states with a death penalty do impose some requirements about how experts should conduct their assessment for the purpose of making an ID determination (see Table 8.1) (Duvall and Morris (2006).

Some state statutes also stipulate who can be appointed as a mental health expert for the purposes of making an intellectual disability determination. For example, the State of Arizona stipulates in ARS § 13-753 K.2: "'Expert in intellectual disabilities' means a psychologist or physician licensed pursuant to title 32, Chapter 13, 17 or 19.1 with at least five years'

Table 8.1 State Statutes Prescribing How Experts Should Conduct Their ID Determination

Arizona (ARS 13-753 B): "[D]etermine the defendant's intelligence quotient using current community, nationally and culturally accepted intelligence testing procedures."

Florida (Florida Statute § 921.137 (1)): "The term 'significantly subaverage general intellectual functioning,' for the purpose of this section, means performance that is two or more standard deviations from the mean score on a standardized intelligence test specified in the rules of the Agency for Persons with Disabilities." The Florida Agency for Persons with Disabilities (APD) stipulates which tests of intelligence are accepted by the state of Florida [Florida State § 65G-4.017 (3) (c)] as follows: "Any standardized test may be submitted as proof, however the applicant must demonstrate that any test not presumptively accepted by the Agency is valid. The following are presumptively accepted standardized tests of intelligence to establish eligibility for mental retardation are: 1. Stanford-Binet Intelligence Test (all ages), 2. Wechsler Preschool and Primary Scale of Intelligence (under six years of age), 3. Differential Ability Scales—Preschool Edition (under six years of age), 4. Wechsler Intelligence Scale for Children (WISC) (children up to fifteen years, eleven months), 5. Differential Ability Scales (children up to fifteen years, eleven months), 6. Wechsler Adult Intelligence Scale (WAIS), 7. Test of Nonverbal Intelligence-3 (TONI-3), 8. Comprehensive Test of Nonverbal Intelligence-2 (C-TONI 2), 9. Universal Nonverbal Intelligence Test (UNIT), 10. Leiter International Performance Scale-Revised (Leiter-R)." Interestingly, the APD statute also provides a comparable list of accepted standardized tests to assess adaptive behavior, but Florida statute 921.137 (1) does not make any recommendation regarding the use of accepted standardized instruments for the assessment of adaptive behavior.

(continued)

Table 8.1   (*continued*)

Illinois (725 ILCS 5/114-15): "IQ tests and psychometric tests administered to the defendant must be the kind and type recognized by experts in the field of intellectual disabilities."

North Carolina (§ 15A-2005 (a) (2)): "An intelligence quotient of 70 or below on an individually administered, scientifically recognized standardized intelligence quotient test administered by a licensed psychiatrist or psychologist is evidence of significantly subaverage general intellectual functioning. . . . An intelligence quotient of 70, as described in this subdivision, is approximate and a higher score resulting from the application of the standard error of measurement to an intelligence quotient of 70 shall not preclude the defendant from being able to present additional evidence of intellectual disability, including testimony regarding adaptive deficits. Accepted clinical standards for diagnosing significant limitations in intellectual functioning and adaptive behavior shall be applied in the determination of intellectual disability."

Virginia (Virginia Statute § 19.2-264.3:1.1): "Assessment of intellectual functioning shall include administration of at least one standardized measure generally accepted by the field of psychological testing and appropriate for administration to the particular defendant being assessed, taking into account cultural, linguistic, sensory, motor, behavioral and other individual factors. All such measures shall be reported as a range of scores calculated by adding and subtracting the standard error of measurement identified by the test publisher to the defendant's earned score. Testing of intellectual functioning shall be carried out in conformity with accepted professional practice, and whenever indicated, the assessment shall include information from multiple sources. The Commissioner of Behavioral Health and Developmental Services shall maintain an exclusive list of standardized measures of intellectual functioning generally accepted by the field of psychological testing." The Virginia Department of Behavioral Health and Developmental Services compiles and maintains the "exclusive" list of intellectual assessment measures in accordance with §19.2-264.3:1.1(B)1 of the Code of Virginia. The list includes the following instruments: (1) Wechsler Adult Intelligence Scale-Fourth Edition (WAIS-IV; Wechsler, 2008); (2) Stanford-Binet Intelligence Test, Fifth Edition (SB5) (Roid, 2003); and (3) Reynolds Intellectual Assessment Scales—Second Edition (RIAS-2) (Reynolds & Kamphaus, 2015; Virginia Department of Behavioral Health and Developmental Disabilities, 2017). There is an important note on this document that stipulates: "Use of a test on this list does not preclude use of other psychological measures when conditions exist that make the use of these tests invalid or incomplete, such as language incompatibility or severe disabling conditions." Hence, the use of a different standardized test of intelligence may be preferred if the individual's circumstances justify doing so.

experience in the testing or testing assessment, evaluation and diagnosis of intellectual disabilities." The State of Virginia has very specific language in its statute regarding who can be appointed as a mental health expert in an *Atkins* hearing (§ 19.2-264.3:1.2):

> The mental health expert appointed pursuant to this section shall be (a) a psychiatrist, a clinical psychologist or an individual with a doctorate degree in clinical psychology, (b) skilled in the administration, scoring and interpretation of intelligence tests and measures of adaptive behavior and (c) qualified by experience and by specialized training, approved by the Commissioner of Behavioral Health and Developmental Services, to perform forensic evaluations. The defendant shall not be entitled to a mental health expert of the defendant's own choosing or to funds to employ such expert.

It is the responsibility of attorneys to know the relevant statutes and any specifications regarding who can be appointed as a mental health expert in their clients' cases. But it remains the responsibility and obligation of the mental health expert to review and comply with all aspects of the relevant state statute(s) governing the determination of intellectual disability in an *Atkins* hearing.

Board Certification

A licensed psychologist can legally practice without being board certified. Many choose to become board certified in their specialty area, if certification is available, to hold themselves to a higher standard of practice. The American Board of Professional Psychology (ABPP) certification is independent and above the state licensing requirements to be an independent practicing psychologist. The ABPP is a national organization that provides oversight and certification of psychologists to provide competent high-quality services in a number of specialty areas in psychology. To receive board certification through the ABPP, a licensed psychologist must have followed a specified course of education and training, have relevant professional experience in the specialty area, and demonstrate competence with the standards of practice within the specialty area. Board certification involves a three-step process: (1) a thorough review of professional credentials, (2) the submission of a work sample, and (3) an oral examination by trained examiners. Some boards (e.g., forensic psychology and child neuropsychology) also additionally require passing a written examination. Once board certified, a licensed psychologist can use the designation "ABPP." There are currently 15 specialty areas in psychology within which licensed psychologists can seek ABPP specialty certification (American Board of Professional Psychology (ABPP), 2017):

1. Clinical Child & Adolescent Psychology
2. Clinical Health Psychology
3. Clinical Neuropsychology
4. Clinical Psychology
5. Cognitive & Behavioral Psychology
6. Counseling Psychology
7. Couple & Family Psychology
8. Forensic Psychology
9. Geropsychology
10. Group Psychology
11. Organizational & Business Consulting Psychology
12. Police & Public Safety Psychology
13. Psychoanalysis in Psychology
14. Rehabilitation Psychology
15. School Psychology

There is no specialty certification for intellectual disability psychology. For work in *Atkins*-type cases, a licensed psychologist might obtain board certification in forensic psychology, but this is not required. Again, being board certified is not honorific but rather attests to a higher standard with regard to the psychologist's efforts and time devoted to a field of psychology for which certification is available (e.g., forensic psychology) (Fabian et al., 2011); however, it does not speak to the professional's training or competence in the area of making determinations of intellectual disability. Intellectual disability specialization is an entirely separate area of competence needed to work in *Atkins* cases. There may one day be an ABPP board certification for intellectual disability or some variant that includes intellectual disability psychology, but for now there is not. In lieu of intellectual disability board certification, *Atkins* experts may demonstrate a professional commitment to staying abreast of the field of intellectual disability by attending and/or participating at professional meetings in intellectual disability, as well as by belonging to professional organizations such as the American Psychological Association (including Division 33: Intellectual and Developmental Disabilities/Autism Spectrum Disorder) and/or the American Association on Intellectual and Developmental Disabilities (which is an interdisciplinary professional society focused on issues related to intellectual disability).

Admissible Scientific Evidence

It is largely the responsibility of mental health experts to select the most appropriate standardized assessment instruments and methods to use to best answer the questions before them and to ensure that the methods employed reflect accepted scientific practice. At this point in the ID determination process, experts must, in many cases, rely heavily on their clinical judgment. Although the *Frye* standard (*Frye v. United States*, 1923) stipulates that the methods upon which experts base their opinion must be sufficiently established to have gained general acceptance within the relevant field, this standard has been replaced in federal courts and most state courts by the more stringent *Daubert* standard to govern the admissibility of scientific evidence (Rogers & Shuman, 2005). The Supreme Court of the United States decision in *Daubert v. Merrell Dow Pharmaceuticals* (1993) provided the standards regarding the admissibility of scientific evidence based on the acceptance and reliability of the methods used by the expert. *Daubert* established the following factors for evaluating the validity of an expert witness's methodology: (1) testable theory or scientific method; (2) known error rate of the scientific method and use of accepted standards controlling the method; (3) the method used has been subjected to peer review and publication; and (4) the method has widespread acceptance within the relevant scientific community (Faigman, Monahan, & Slobogin, 2014). Hence, expert witnesses must be certain that their testimony and methods upon which it rests meet the relevant standards of admissibility.

There are a number of professional resources and materials to which all mental health experts involved in an intellectual disability determination must refer and adhere. These include the American Psychological Association's *Ethical Principles of Psychologists and Code of Conduct* (American Psychological Association, 2017) and *Specialty Guidelines for Forensic Psychology* (American Psychological Association's, 2013), as well as the *Standards for Educational and Psychological Testing* (American Educational Research Association (AERA), 2014). In addition, *Atkins* mental health experts should familiarize themselves with other resources that address specific diagnostic and practice issues related to intellectual disability, including AAIDD *Terminology and Classification Manual* (Schalock et al., 2010), the *DSM-5* (APA, 2013), *AAIDD User's Guide* (Schalock et al., 2012), and *The Death Penalty and Intellectual Disability* (Polloway, 2015).

Expert Witness Roles

In addition to the responsibility of educating themselves regarding what is intellectual disability and what goes into making a determination of intellectual disability, attorneys working on an *Atkins* case also have the responsibility of educating the trier of fact. If the attorneys themselves do not understand intellectual disability and what is needed to properly assess their client for intellectual disability, they are doing themselves and their clients a disservice. Attorneys must educate themselves and the trier of fact regarding the important elements associated with intellectual disability, the issues related to the assessment of intellectual functioning and adaptive behavior, the risk factors associated with ID, the common characteristics of intellectual disability, frequent misconceptions and faulty assumptions, and other related factors that would assist the trier of fact in rendering an informed decision (Fabian et al., 2011). Only when attorneys have an in-depth understanding of the issues related to the determination of ID will they be sufficiently informed to be able to select one or more experts who can assist with the case at hand. Expert witnesses will often play a critical role in conveying the relevant information to and facilitating understanding by the trier of fact.

Competency

Depending on the nature of the case, an expert witness may be called on to fulfill several roles when the defendant is suspected of having an intellectual disability. One such role may be assessing the individual's competency to stand trial (Siegert & Weiss, 2007). This role is obviously not limited to *Atkins* cases and is more often associated with defendants who may be presenting with serious mental illness. For the most part, adults with mild intellectual disability implicated in an *Atkins* hearing are likely to be competent to stand trial unless they have concomitant serious mental illness. Notwithstanding serious mental illness, intellectual disability, in and of itself, does not usually impact cognitive abilities implicated in competency matters, unless the person has a more severe form of intellectual disability.

A more common role that *Atkins* experts assume is that of conducting a psychological evaluation of defendants to assess their functioning in order to inform a determination of intellectual disability. This evaluation includes an assessment of intellectual functioning, adaptive behavior, age of onset, social and family history, and other relevant factors. The same expert (or additional experts) might also be asked to specifically address an issue related to defendants and their claim of intellectual disability. For example, a geneticist or other healthcare professional might testify about possible physiological, genetic, or other biologically based risk factors associated with intellectual disability. Other expert witness testimony might address school issues or special education programs and discuss relevant educational matters as they might relate to the case at hand. Finally, expert witnesses might be intellectual disability professionals (e.g., special education, psychology, medicine, etc.) who act as teaching experts. Testimony from a teaching expert informs the court about what is intellectual disability, and provides an overview of established practice around conducting a determination of intellectual disability and other relevant information. In the following sections, we will describe in more detail the role and required qualifications for expert witnesses who conduct evaluations, who give testimony on genetic etiologies, school performance, and other factors associated with ID, and who function as teaching experts. Finally, we will discuss the importance of clinical judgment in informing an intellectual disability determination.

Conducting Evaluation and Opining About ID

A single expert witness can conduct the entire ID evaluation (from assessment of intellectual functioning, adaptive behavior, age of onset, to rendering a final opinion about intellectual disability), or multiple expert witnesses can conduct different portions or complimentary portions of the evaluation. The selected expert(s) will need to be competent in reviewing previous evaluations and conducting a thorough intellectual disability assessment, including assessment of malingering and effort (see Chapter 5). Expert qualifications vary depending on the type of assessment. Licensed psychologists are generally qualified to administer standardized tests of intelligence and adaptive behavior; physicians and psychiatrists are not qualified to administer standardized tests of intelligence (Siegert & Weiss, 2007). A comprehensive evaluation of adaptive behavior requires a thorough review of all available case records (see Chapter 6 for a review). The mental health expert must interview multiple respondents as well as the individual being assessed. The mental health expert(s) conducting the adaptive behavior assessment need not be limited to licensed psychologists but can also include social workers, education specialists, developmental psychologists, and other professionals who are comfortable with conducting individual assessments, have experience with adaptive behavior evaluations, and have an in-depth knowledge of intellectual disability.

One or more mental health experts will need to review the issues and conduct a determination of the age of onset. In so doing, it is necessary to review the individual's family history and social history, conduct an exhaustive review of all available records (e.g., medical, school, employment, etc.), and examine the existence of risk factors. Although making a clear determination of the cause or origin of the intellectual disability is not essential, it may be helpful to the trier of fact to have a better understanding of existing risk factors experienced by the individual and such factors that might have contributed to the onset of intellectual disability. The precise determination of the cause(s) of an individual's intellectual disability remains a complex and puzzling endeavor where the exact etiology remains unknown in approximately 40% of all cases (Flint, 2001; Raymond, 2015).

Providing Information About Conditions Associated with ID

Whether other types of mental health experts might be needed depends on the individual being evaluated and the information available. These other expert witnesses might include different medical professionals, genetics experts, and/or bilingual and cross-cultural professionals. It may be relevant to consult with a geneticist or dysmorphologist (i.e., a sub-branch of genetics devoted to the study of malformations possibly associated with a genetic condition) in cases where there may be some indication the assessed individual may have a genetic disorder that might explain the intellectual disability. It may also be relevant to hire a genetics counselor or social worker to conduct a thorough family history if there is some suspected hereditary disease or presence of risk factors in the individual's ancestry. Any number of other medical experts might be consulted depending on the specifics of the individual's case, including a neurologist for seizure disorders or the assessment of fetal alcohol spectrum disorder, and so on.

If the assessed individual is a foreign national, it is essential to hire a mental health expert who speaks the defendant's native language. Attempting to conduct an assessment using an interpreter is a recipe for disaster. If the foreign national has limited spoken English, the mental health expert will need to make an informed clinical determination regarding the best standardized intelligence test to use. A number of challenges remain with many standardized tests of intellectual functioning in the assessment of non-native English speakers and foreign nationals. Interested readers are referred to several good reviews of these issues (Ferraro, 2016; Funes, Rodriguez, & Lopez, 2016; Suen & Greenspan, 2009;

Thaler & Jones-Forrester, 2013). The selection of a standardized adaptive behavior scale may also be challenging in these situations. Whatever is decided, the experts will need to justify that choice based on solid science and best clinical practices in their evaluation report.

Mental health experts will also need to be intimately familiar with the foreign national's culture and upbringing. This information is essential to accurately conducting and interpreting the assessment of the individual's adaptive behavior. Having to conduct an intellectual disability determination with a foreign national will also generally necessitate traveling to that individual's country or region of origin or childhood to interview respondents and understand the defendant's culture, age of onset, and risk factors.

Teaching Expert

Attorneys representing an individual with an *Atkins* claim should do everything they can to educate the trier of fact to enable him or her to be able to assimilate the complex information needed to make an intellectual disability determination. Attorneys representing an *Atkins* claimant will often rely on their mental health experts who have conducted the evaluations to provide key information about psychometrics, the psychometric properties of the tests they chose, and the diagnostic criteria of intellectual disability, in addition to explaining to the court their choice of evaluation instruments and selection process for the informants they relied upon. It is often helpful to have a teaching expert testify who is independent, who is not involved in the assessment, or who may not even have necessarily met the defendant. This intellectual disability professional can testify to best practices in making a determination of intellectual disability. This "teaching expert" role is not limited to a licensed psychologist. The teaching expert could very well be an education specialist, social worker, developmental psychologist, psychiatrist, pediatrician, or other professional who has documented knowledge, training, expertise, and/or relevant experience working with people with intellectual disability.

The teaching expert's role encompasses presenting to the trier of fact the established clinical practice regarding the determination of intellectual disability, including the assessment of intellectual functioning, assessment of adaptive behavior, and establishment of age of onset. The expert often addresses important psychometric and testing issues relevant in cases of ID determination, common risk factors associated with intellectual disability, common characteristics of people with intellectual disability, and common misconceptions and erroneous stereotypes associated with intellectual disability (e.g., academic abilities, physical features, capacity for independence, employability, strengths and weakness, etc.). Ideally, the teaching expert is neutral and has the sole responsibility of educating the trier of fact about current knowledge and practice regarding ID determination. The teaching expert is best used when she or he does not have access to the client's records or previous evaluations and is not asked to opine as to a diagnosis for the defendant.

Clinical Judgment

A determination of intellectual disability requires a comprehensive and individualized assessment of the person's intellectual functioning and adaptive behavior (APA, 2013; Schalock et al., 2010). It also requires a significant amount of clinical expertise and should not be considered mechanistic, where just any licensed psychologist or clinician qualified to administer standardized psychological tests can go out and interview a few family members, conduct a few clinical interviews, and administer a test of intelligence. Conducting a comprehensive clinical evaluation to rule in or rule out intellectual disability requires not only knowledge and ability that are inclusive of training and familiarity with individual psychological evaluation procedures and relevant standardized tests but also a level of competence and appropriate clinical judgment in the area of intellectual disability (Schalock & Luckasson, 2014). Mental health experts in *Atkins* hearings are being asked to conduct high-stakes evaluations and make important decisions and recommendations that require a high level of competence and clinical judgment in the field of intellectual disability (Schalock & Luckasson, 2014). To be absolutely clear, however, clinical judgment is not just someone's subjective professional opinion, and it is not acquired simply with the earning of a degree or professional license. Instead, clinical judgment is "a special type of judgment that is built upon respect for the person and emerges from the clinician's training and experience, specific knowledge of the person and his/her environments, extensive data, and use of critical thinking skills" (Schalock & Luckasson, 2014; p. 1). Hence, mental health experts might have clinical judgment in one area of clinical practice (e.g., guardianship, competency evaluation) but not in other areas (e.g., intellectual disability, autism).

The accuracy of ID determination is enhanced when (1) the diagnosis of ID is based on the person meeting three core criteria defined as significant limitations in intellectual functioning, significant limitations in adaptive behavior, and age of onset before age 18; (2) the individual's functioning level is assessed in typical (i.e., natural) community environments; (3) assessments are culturally and linguistically relevant and use psychometrically sound and individually administered instruments; (4) the evaluator has expertise and training regarding the construct of ID, assessment strategies, and familiarity with the person; and (5) the mental health expert has the prerequisite clinical judgment to make this complex clinical determination (Luckasson & Schalock, 2015; Schalock & Luckasson, 2014).

Conclusion

Professional standards for *Atkins* evaluations would promote greater uniformity of these evaluations (Macvaugh & Cunningham, 2009), but we have yet to heed Everington and Olley's (2008) call for the fields of forensic psychology and intellectual disability to join forces and provide leadership in developing practice guidelines for the diagnosis of intellectual disability in the *Atkins* context. The development of standards specific to conducting intellectual disability evaluations in a forensic case would illuminate what is generally accepted in the field, one of the factors governing the admissibility of scientific evidence (e.g., *Frye* and *Daubert* Standards) (Macvaugh et al., 2015). This book and other texts (e.g., Polloway, 2015) are not a formal set of professional guidelines, but hopefully they can serve as a basis and resource to inform mental health experts and attorneys involved in *Atkins* hearings.

In conclusion, a mental health expert with expertise in intellectual disability is essential to conducting an *Atkins* evaluation for the purpose of making an intellectual disability determination. Working with an intellectual disability expert who can learn and incorporate the important elements of forensic psychology as they relate to being able in order to effectively obtain, preserve, and present psychological data in a legal context that can withstand cross-examination is vital to ensuring that the trier of fact obtains that necessary information needed to make an informed, reliable decision. It would be extremely challenging for an *Atkins* evaluation to be conducted by a forensic or other mental health expert who has little direct professional experience working with people with intellectual disability or ID training. This expert would need to acquire this necessary expertise, experience, and clinical judgment to be able to conduct a valid intellectual disability determination.

Note

1. The rules of evidence vary from state to state (with most resembling the federal rules of evidence), but on this point the rules of evidence are in agreement nationwide.

References

American Board of Professional Psychology (ABPP). (2017, May 26). *The ABPP Certification Process: An Overview.* https://www.abpp.org/i4a/pages/index.cfm ?pageID=3299

American Educational Research Association (AERA), American Psychological Association, & National Council on Measurement in Education. (2014). *Standards for Educational and Psychological Testing* (5th Edition). Washington, DC: Author.

American Psychiatric Association (APA). (2013). *Diagnostic and Statistical Manual of Mental Disorders* (5th Edition). Arlington, VA: American Psychiatric Publishing.

American Psychological Association. (2013). Specialty guidelines in forensic psychology. *American Psychologist, 68,* 7–19.

American Psychological Association (2017). *Ethical Principles of Psychologists and Code of Conduct* (including 2010 and 2016 amendments). http://www.apa .org/ethics/code/index.aspx?item=4

Atkins v. Virginia, 536 U.S. 304 (2002).Brodsky, S. L. (2013). *Testifying in Court: Guidelines and Maxims for the Expert Witness.* Washington, DC: American Psychological Association.

Brodsky, S. L., & Galloway, V. A. (2003). Ethical and professional demands for forensic mental health professionals in the post-*Atkins* era. *Ethics & Behavior, 13*(1), 3–9.

Daubert v. Merrell Dow Pharmaceuticals, 509 U.S. 579 (1993).

DeMatteo, D., Marczyk, G., & Pich, M. (2007). A national survey of state legislation defining mental retardation: Implications for policy and practice after *Atkins. Behavioral Sciences and the Law, 25,* 781–802.

Duvall, J. C., & Morris, R. J. (2006). Assessing mental retardation in death penalty cases: Critical issues for psychology and psychological practice. *Professional Psychology: Research and Practice, 37,* 658–665.

Everington, A., & Olley, J. G. (2008). Implications of *Atkins v. Virginia*: Issues in defining and diagnosing mental retardation. *Journal of Forensic Psychology Practice, 8,* 1–23.

Fabian, J. M., Thompson, W. W., & Lazarus, J. B. (2011). Life, death, and IQ: It's much more than just a score: Understanding and utilizing forensic psychological and neuropsychological evaluations in *Atkins* intellectual disability/mental retardation cases. *Cleveland State Law Review, 59,* 399–430.

Faigman, D. L., Monahan, J., & Slobogin, C. (2014). Group to individual (G2i) inference in scientific expert testimony. *The University of Chicago Law Review, 81,* 417–480.

Ferraro, F. R. (2016). *Minority and Cross-Cultural Aspects of Neuropsychological Assessment: Enduring and Emerging Trends* (2nd Edition). New York: Taylor & Francis.

Flint, J. (2001). Genetic basis of cognitive disability. *Dialogues in Clinical Neuroscience, 3*(1), 37–46.

Frye v. United States, 293 F. 1013 (D.C. Cir 1923).

Funes, C. M., Rodriguez, J. H., & Lopez, S. R. (2016). Norm comparisons of the Spanish-language and English-language WAIS-III: Implications for clinical assessment and test adaptation. *Psychological Assessment, 28,* 1709–1715.

Hagan, L. D., Drogin, E. Y., & Guilmette, T. J. (2016). Assessing adaptive functioning in death penalty cases after *Hall* and DSM-5. *The Journal of the American Academy of Psychiatry and the Law, 44,* 96–105.

Hall v. Florida, 134 S. Ct. at 1986 (2014).

Keyes, D. W., Edwards, W. J., & Derning, T. J. (1998). Mitigating mental retardation in capital cases: Finding the "invisible" defendant. *Mental and Physical Disability Law Reporter, 22,* 529–539.

Luckasson, R., & Schalock, R. L. (2015). Standards to guide the use of clinical judgment in the field of intellectual disability. *Intellectual and Developmental Disabilities, 53*(3), 240–251.Macvaugh, G. S., & Cunningham, M. D. (2009). *Atkins v. Virginia*: Implications and recommendations for forensic practice. *Journal of Psychiatry & Law, 37,* 131–187.

Macvaugh, G. S., Cunningham, M. D., and Tassé, M. J. (2015). Professional practice (pp. 325–336). In E. A. Polloway (Ed.), *The Death Penalty and Intellectual Disability*. Washington, DC: American Association on Intellectual and Developmental Disabilities.

Moore v. Texas, 581 U.S. ____ (2017).

Neal, T. M. S. (2016). Are forensic experts already biased before adversarial legal parties hire them? *PLOS ONE, 11*(1), e0154434. https://doi.org/10.1371/journal.pone.0154434.

Olley, J. G. (2009). Knowledge and experience required for experts in Atkins cases. *Applied Neuropsychology, 16,* 135–140.

Polloway, E. A. (2015). *The Death Penalty and Intellectual Disability*. Washington, DC: American Association on Intellectual and Developmental Disabilities.

Raymond, F. L. (2015). Genetics and genomics of neuro-psychiatric diseases, V: Learning and behavioral disorders (pp. 530–540). In D. Kumar & C. Eng (Eds.), *Genomic Medicine: Principles and Practice* (2nd Edition). London: Oxford University Press.

Reschly, D. J. (2009). Documenting the developmental origins of mild mental retardation. *Applied Neuropsychology, 16,* 124–134.

Reynolds, C. R., & Kamphaus, R. W. (2015). *Reynolds Intellectual Assessment Scales (RIAS-2) and the Reynolds Intellectual Screening Test (RIST-2) Professional Manual*. Lutz, FL: Psychological Assessment Resources.

Rogers, R. & Shuman, D. W. (2005). *Fundamentals of Forensic Practice: Mental Health and Criminal Law*. New York: Springer Science+Business Media.

Roid, G. H. (2003). *Stanford-Binet Intelligence Scales, Fifth Edition: Technical Manual*. Itasca, IL: Riverside Publishing.

Schalock, R. L., Buntinx, W. H. E., Borthwick-Duffy, S., Bradley, V., Craig, E. M., Coulter, D. L., Gomez, S. C., Lachapelle, Y., Luckasson, R. A., Reeve, A., Shogren, K. A., Snell, M. E., Spreat, S., Tassé, M. J., Thompson, J. R., Verdugo, M. A., Wehmeyer, M. L., & Yeager, M. H. (2010). *Intellectual Disability: Definition, Classification, and System of Supports* (11th Edition). Washington, DC: American Association on Intellectual and Developmental Disabilities.

Schalock, R. L., & Luckasson, R. (2014). *Clinical Judgment* (2nd Edition). Washington, DC: American Association on Intellectual and Developmental Disabilities.

Schalock, R. L., Luckasson, R. A., Bradley, V., Buntinx, W. H. E., Lachapelle, Y., Shogren, K. A., Snell, M. E., Tassé, M. J., Thompson, J. R., Verdugo, M. A., & Wehmeyer, M. L. (2012). *Intellectual Disability: Definition, Classification, and System of Supports (11th Edition)—User's Guide.* Washington, DC: American Association on Intellectual and Developmental Disabilities.

Siegert, M. & Weiss, K. J. (2007). Who is an expert? Competency evaluations in mental retardation and borderline intelligence. *The Journal of the American Academy of Psychiatry and the Law, 35,* 346–349.

Suen, H. K., & Greenspan, S. (2009). Serious problems with the Mexican norms for the WAIS-III when assessing mental retardation in capital cases. *Applied Neuropsychology, 16*(3), 214–222.

Tassé, M. J. (2009). Adaptive behavior assessment and the diagnosis of mental retardation in capital cases. *Applied Neuropsychology, 16,* 114–123.

Thaler, N. S. & Jones-Forrester, S. (2013). IQ testing and the Hispanic client (pp. 81–98). In L. T. Benuto (Ed.), *Guide to Psychological Assessment with Hispanics.* New York: Springer.

Virginia Department of Behavioral Health and Developmental Disabilities (2017). *List of Standardized Measures of Intellectual Functioning.* http://www.dbhds .virginia.gov/professionals-and-service-providers/forensic-services/training -resources

Wechsler D. (2008). *Wechsler Adult Intelligence Scale–Fourth Edition: Administration and Scoring Manual.* San Antonio: Psychological Corporation.

Wood, S. E., Packman, W., Howell, S., & Bongar, B. (2014). A failure to implement: Analyzing state responses to the Supreme Court's directives in *Atkins v. Virginia* and suggestions for a national standard. *Psychiatry, Psychology and Law, 21,* 16–45.

CHAPTER NINE

The Future of *Atkins*

In this final chapter, we will briefly examine the future of the Supreme Court's exclusion from capital punishment for persons with intellectual disability, a categorical bar the Court created in *Atkins*, as well as the potential effect the Court's decision might have in other capital and noncapital contexts.

At least with respect to its core holding that persons with intellectual disability may not be executed, the future of *Atkins* is in the hands of its creator, the Supreme Court of the United States. And in broad strokes, the categorical bar seems to be on solid footing. In recent years, the Court has showed a continued commitment to *Atkins*, and it seems unlikely that, even if the Court's composition were to change due to justices retiring (or dying), the Supreme Court would do an about-face and return to the era when intellectual disability was merely a mitigating circumstance for the jury to consider in deciding whether a capital defendant should live or die.

As has been discussed elsewhere in this volume, the Court's categorical exclusion is (generally) being faithfully enforced in many, indeed most, death penalty jurisdictions. Nonetheless, even in the states that both adhere to clinical consensus in their definitions of intellectual disability and have not stacked the procedural deck against the person seeking exemption from capital punishment, there are, for lack of a better term, puzzling and in some instances tragic outcomes. As set forth in Chapter 4, strong, even very strong, cases of intellectual disability sometimes lose, and, although less commonly, weaker cases sometimes win. It is true, of course, that there is no error-proof system of legal adjudication. It is equally true that the uneven application of the Court's categorical rule is inevitable in an adversarial legal system, where fact finder predisposition, the varying quality of defense counsel, the variable level of access to funding for factual development and qualified experts to assess the *Atkins* claimant, a growing number of prosecution-oriented experts willing to dispute claims of intellectual disability on clinically rejected bases, and a host of other factors combine to foster significant variance in outcomes. We hope that this book is of assistance to both attorneys and clinicians in obtaining more reliable case outcomes in those states where there is reason to be at least cautiously optimistic about the future of *Atkins*.

On the other hand, the tragic reality is that, in other states, the Court's categorical bar has been effectively gutted. In these states, people who all but the most prosecution-oriented experts would agree have intellectual disability continue to be sentenced to death and even executed. Texas is the best example of this phenomenon, but there are other places (e.g., Alabama, Georgia, and Louisiana) where the Court's constitutional mandate has been nullified by state court recalcitrance, largely in the form of "glosses" to the generally accepted clinical definition of intellectual disability or by allowing prosecution experts to opine in ways that markedly deviate from clinical consensus. The previously mentioned *Briseño* factors, which the Texas Court of Criminal Appeals admittedly created to limit *Atkins'* applicability in Texas, not only allowed, but actually facilitated and encouraged, the rejection of many meritorious intellectual disability claims. The Supreme Court's recent repudiation of the *Briseño* factors in *Moore v. Texas* is surely of little consolation to the death row inmates who raised intellectual disability as a bar to execution but who were nevertheless put to death before the Court intervened.

Robert Ladd, for example, was executed by the state of Texas in January 2015. Although reviewing courts found that he had significantly subaverage intellectual functioning (and thus satisfied Prong 1, the Texas courts concluded that his conceded deficits in multiple areas of adaptive behavior were attributable to his antisocial personality disorder rather than his deficits in intellectual functioning (*Ladd v. Stephens*, 2014).[1] The courts' consideration of the *Briseño* factors confirmed the rejection of a diagnosis of intellectual disability. Ladd, who had been sent to the Gatesville State School for Children with Mental Handicaps as a child, tested with an IQ of 67, and was found to be "obviously retarded," should have (in our view) prevailed on his intellectual disability claim and would have done so in many other states that adhere to accepted clinical standards. But Ladd, along with so many other Texan death row inmates, was put to death after his intellectual disability claim was denied on bases contrary to clinical consensus.

Georgia's creation of the "guilty but mentally retarded" verdict, which requires that the defendant prove beyond a reasonable doubt that he or she is a person with intellectual disability, is an example of a different type of state resistance to *Atkins*. While Georgia's substantive definition of intellectual disability is in line with clinical consensus, the standard of proof beyond a reasonable doubt has not been adopted by any other jurisdiction. Given that the prosecution can easily create suspicions of malingering (and therefore reasonable doubt) even in the most airtight cases of intellectual disability, it is no surprise that virtually all assertions of intellectual disability raised by capital defendants in Georgia fail. Kenneth Fults, who was executed in Georgia in April of 2016, was put to death despite presenting a case for intellectual disability that would have prevailed in most death penalty jurisdictions. Despite multiple IQ scores below the intellectual disability threshold, Fults's claim failed to satisfy the jury beyond a reasonable doubt. An expert for the prosecution had opined that Fults was "street smart" and could make some choices for himself and thus did not have significantly subaverage intellectual functioning (*Fults v. GDCP Warden*, 2014).[2]

Whether the High Court will continue to allow these outlier states to nullify *Atkins*' impact remains to be seen. *Hall v. Florida* (2014) and *Moore v. Texas* (2017), discussed in detail in Chapter 3, indicate that it will not, at least when confronted with flagrant state attempts to "end-run" the Court's constitutional mandate. Nevertheless, the story of *Atkins*' future in some states remains unwritten, and in the meantime persons with intellectual disability continue to be sentenced to death and executed.

We could discuss numerous cases to make this point, but at present and in the capital punishment context, intellectual disability is a clinical condition with a clinical definition that means one thing in Texas and another in North Carolina. We think it unlikely in creating the categorical bar that the Supreme Court envisioned people like Robert Ladd and Kenneth Fults being executed in Texas or Georgia but not in North Carolina or Pennsylvania. Tragically, this is nonetheless the current lay of the legal landscape, and the future of *Atkins* is uncertain (and uneven) until courts take seriously their responsibility to protect all persons with intellectual disability.

The future of *Atkins* is particularly uncertain for Hispanics—*Atkins* claimants of Hispanic descent lose at disproportionately high rates. In fact, "disproportionate" is an understatement: Even very strong cases of intellectual disability made by Hispanics, especially those of Mexican descent, are routinely rejected. Whether this is the result of implicit bias or cultural and other forms of stereotyping is unclear, although both seem, from our review of the cases, to be at work here. But regardless of the reasons, the risk of wrongful execution persists for those individuals accused or convicted of capital crimes who assert intellectual disability. Take, for example, the case of Ramiro Hernandez-Llanas. Hernandez-Llanas was executed in Texas in 2015 despite uncontradicted evidence that his IQ scores on five tests were all in the intellectual disability range. However, The Texas state courts concluded that the scores were the results of malingering (again despite expert testimony to the contrary) and that his "true" IQ was reflected by his score on a brief screening test administered by the Texas Department of Criminal Justice. When the federal courts reviewed Hernandez-Llanas's case, they concluded that his IQ scores were "undermined" by the fact that "[w]hen scaled to Mexican norms, [he] scored exactly 70 on the one full-scale WAIS-III test" (*Hernandez v. Stephens*, 2013). This ignored the fact that, at the time, the WAIS-III test was the *only* full-scale IQ test that was appropriate to administer to Hernandez-Llanas (and also that his score on that test was clearly within the mentally retarded range).[3] The state and federal courts likewise rejected overwhelming evidence of adaptive functioning deficits (e.g., he could not make change, follow directions, or run simple errands), crediting a clearly unqualified state expert's testimony that Hernandez-Llanas's limitations were normal for his Mexican "cultural group" (*Hernandez v. Thaler,* 2012).[4]

On a more positive note, the future of *Atkins* may well also involve the creation of new categories of people exempted from the death penalty. As discussed in Chapter 3, the primary concerns that led six justices to conclude that intellectual disability should be a categorical bar to execution, rather than a mitigating consideration for jurors on a case-by-case basis, were maintaining the proportionality of punishment and controlling the risk of wrongful execution. As to proportionality, which is at bottom concerned with human dignity, the Court found the death penalty wanting for people with intellectual disability because it did not legitimately further either deterrence or retribution due to their lesser culpability and the compromised ability to premeditate, deliberate, and appreciate the consequences of their conduct (*Atkins v. Virginia*, 2002). Furthermore, the Court concluded that due to their impairments, persons with intellectual disability were at a heightened (and inacceptable) risk of wrongful execution. Noting the higher incidence of false confessions, difficulties communicating favorable information to counsel, a lesser ability to testify effectively on their own behalf, and demeanor issues that could incorrectly be equated with lack of remorse, the Court concluded that capital punishment was not an appropriate punishment (*Atkins v. Virginia*, 2002).

Many commentators and some judges have recognized that there are other categories of offenders who are arguably, and for many of the same reasons, equally at risk of wrongful execution and for whom the deterrence and retribution interests that legitimize executing persons for murder are similarly not served. These proposed categorical exclusions include persons with severe mental illness, fetal alcohol syndrome, or autism spectrum disorders; combat veterans; and persons who meet Prongs 1 (i.e., subaverage intellectual functioning) and 2 (i.e., subaverage adaptive behavior) of the intellectual disability criteria but, because of traumatic brain injury or some other insult that occurred in the postdevelopmental period, do not meet the criteria for a diagnosis of intellectual disability but have similar functioning.

First, we will address this last category, persons who cannot satisfy Prong 3 (i.e., age of onset before age 18). As discussed in earlier chapters, an individual who has significantly subaverage intellectual functioning and deficits in adaptive behavior may still not be a person with intellectual disability if the etiology of both was some postdevelopmental period incident, such as a head injury in a car accident at age 30. That is because intellectual disability is considered a developmental-period disorder. Many, including an American Bar Association Task Force on Mental Disabilities, have suggested that such persons should also be exempt from capital punishment because there is no significant difference in the moral culpability of someone who has identical limitations in their cognitive abilities and adaptive behavior from birth and someone who has an accident later in life. Others, based on our continually updated understanding of juvenile brain development, have called for extending the developmental period to age 21 or 25. This notion appears to have been endorsed by the American Psychiatric Association in their most recent version of the *DSM*, which removed the upper age boundary from the definition of the third prong for an intellectual disability diagnosis (American Psychiatric Association, 2013). However, such cases are rare (in the *Atkins* context), and only a handful of courts have squarely confronted the issue.

The most frequently discussed additional categorical exemption from capital punishment would be for people with severe mental illness. Jamie Wilson, for example, has been mentally ill since childhood and has been hospitalized numerous times. After a hospital refused to accept him due to his father's lapsed insurance, he entered a school and killed two children. All the mental health experts who evaluated him, including the prosecution's psychiatrist, agreed that Wilson was so mentally ill at the time of the crime that he lacked the capacity to confirm his conduct to the requirements of the law. Wilson was nevertheless sentenced to death (Blume & Johnson, 2003).[5] While Wilson is an extreme example of someone whom the law does not currently protect from execution, many people on death row were profoundly mentally ill at the time they committed the crimes that led to their death sentences (American Bar Association, 2016).[6] A significant challenge, however, in creating a categorical exemption for such people is defining the category. Mental illness encompasses a broad range of deficiencies and disorders, and defining with precision who is sufficiently mentally ill to warrant exemption from capital punishment is a difficult (although we do not believe impossible) endeavor.

Individuals with fetal alcohol syndrome (FAS) and autism spectrum disorder (ASD) are other potential categories of excludable offenders. Many individuals who meet the criteria for either FAS or ASD have many, if not all, of the difficulties with judgment, impaired cognitive abilities, and impaired impulse control identified in persons with intellectual disability. Brandy Holmes was convicted of murder and sentenced to death in Louisiana, despite uncontradicted evidence that she had FAS (Fanning, 2010–2011). Her mother admitted drinking heavily throughout her pregnancy and then named her daughter after her favorite type of liquor. Experts testified that Holmes had an IQ of 77 and brain damage consistent with FAS and was "impulsive" and "emotionally reactive." Because her IQ was above the intellectual disability cutoff of 70, her *Atkins* claim was rejected by the state courts, who also refused to extend *Atkins* to persons with FAS.

To be clear, in this and the other contexts discussed, we are not suggesting that the definition of intellectual disability should be altered to encompass any of these other conditions. That would blur intellectual disability's clear diagnostic criteria. We are merely saying that many of the reasons given by the Court for exempting people with intellectual disability from capital punishment also apply to people with severe mental illness, traumatic brain injury, FAS, and ASD.

Finally, the future of *Atkins* is inevitably intermeshed with the future of the American death penalty. The post-*Atkins* era has coincided with a steady decline in death sentences, executions and, likely related, public support for capital punishment. From the high-water mark of 1999 when 295 persons were sentenced to death and 98 death row inmates were executed, the numbers of both new death sentences and executions have steadily declined. In 2016, for example, there were only 30 new death sentences and 20 executions (Death Penalty Information Center, n.d.). According to recent polling data, a majority of Americans now favor life without parole as a sentencing option when given the choice between lifetime incarceration and the death penalty (Death Penalty Information Center, n.d.). The number of states that retain the death penalty is in decline, with states such as Connecticut, New Jersey, New Mexico, New York, and Maryland abolishing capital punishment in recent years. Capital punishment repeal efforts are under way in a significant number of states that retain the death penalty, and in those and other states that retain it, the death penalty is never used in practice, even though it is legally available in theory. As discussed in Chapter 2, some members of the Supreme Court have also started to question the soundness of the death penalty's legal foundation. In the final analysis, then, *Atkins* may become just a footnote, albeit a very important one, in the history of the demise of capital punishment in the United States.

Notes

1. The court agreed Ladd had deficits in functional academics, social skills, work, and communication but credited a prosecution expert who said that the deficits were "properly attributed to his anti-social personality disorder." *Ladd v. Stephens*, 748 F.3d 637, 646 (5th Cir. 2014).

2. The state's expert acknowledged that Fults' IQ scores on appropriate, individual IQ tests were 68, 72, and 74, and thus within the confidence interval for subaverage intellectual functioning is generally determined. However, she testified his claims failed prong 1 because he was "street smart." *Fults v. GDCP Warden*, 764 F. 3d 1311 (11th Cir. 2014).

3. Furthermore, unlike U.S. norms, Mexican norms were developed from an inadequate sample and therefore tend to *overestimate* IQ by an average of 12 points. On the Mexican WAIS, scored with *American* norms, Hernandez-Llanas scored a 62.

4. This expert did not speak Spanish and admitted he had no independent knowledge of Hernandez-Llanas's "cultural group." *Hernandez v. Thaler*, No. SA-08-CA-805-XR, 2012 WL 394597, p. *18 (W.D. Tex. Feb. 6, 2012).

5. Wilson is still on death row due to his incompetency to be executed.

6. See American Bar Association Death Penalty Due Process Review Project, Severe Mental Illness and the Death Penalty, 19–21 (Dec. 2016) (detailing cases where persons found insane and not competent to stand trial were nonetheless executed, and noting that "existing procedures do not adequately protect individuals with severe mental illness from being sentenced to death or executed, . . . and can . . . allow people with profound impairments to slip through the cracks").

References

American Bar Association Death Penalty Due Process Review Project, Severe Mental Illness and the Death Penalty, 19–21 (Dec. 2016) https://www.americanbar.org/content/dam/aba/images/crsj/DPDPRP/SevereMentalIllnessandtheDeathPenalty_WhitePaper.pdf

American Psychiatric Association (APA). (2013). *Diagnostic and Statistical Manual of Mental Disorders* (5th Edition). Arlington, VA: American Psychiatric Publishing.

Blume, J. H. & Johnson, S. L. (2003). Killing the non-willing: *Atkins*, the volitionally incapacitated, and the death penalty. *South Carolina Law Review*, 55, 93–143.

Death Penalty Information Center, Facts About the Death Penalty [nonperiodic web document]. http://www.deathpenaltyinfo.org/documents/FactSheet .pdf

Fanning, C. (2010–2011). Defining intellectual disability: Fetal alcohol spectrum disorder and capital punishment. *Rutgers Law Record*, 38, 97–111.

Fults v. GDCP Warden, 764 F. 3d 1311 (11th Cir. 2014).

Hernandez v. Stephens, 537 F. App'x 531, 539 (5th Cir. 2013).

Hernandez v. Thaler, No. SA-08-CA-805-XR, 2012 WL 394597 18 (W.D. Tex. Feb. 6, 2012).

Ladd v. Stephens, 748 F.3d 637, 646 (5th Cir. 2014).

Index

About the Authors

Dr. Marc J. Tassé is a Professor of Psychology and Psychiatry and the Director of The Ohio State University Nisonger Center, a University Center for Excellence in Developmental Disabilities. Dr. Tassé's experience includes 25 years of conducting research and providing clinical services in the field of intellectual disability (ID), autism spectrum disorder (ASD), and related developmental disabilities (DD). He has conducted more than 240 trainings, workshops, and presentations related to ID, ASD, and related developmental disabilities. His publications include more than 130 articles in peer-reviewed journals, chapters, and books in the area of intellectual and developmental disabilities. Dr. Tassé is a coauthor of the *AAIDD Terminology and Classification Manual* (Luckasson et al., 2002; Schalock et al., 2010) and *AAIDD User's Guide* (with Schalock et al., 2012), as well as senior author on the *Diagnostic Adaptive Behavior Scale*. He has also coauthored several other published standardized tests in the field of intellectual and developmental disabilities, including the assessment of adaptive behavior, problem behavior, and support needs. Dr. Tassé is a fellow of the American Association on Intellectual and Developmental Disabilities (AAIDD), American Psychological Association (APA), and International Association for the Scientific Study of Intellectual and Developmental Disabilities (IASSIDD). He previously served as an associate editor for the *American Journal on Intellectual and Developmental Disabilities*. He has consulted and testified in a number of capital cases involving intellectual disability determination. Dr. Tassé is a past president of the American Association on Intellectual and Developmental Disabilities.

John H. Blume is the Samuel F. Leibowitz Professor of Trial Techniques at Cornell Law School. A 1978 graduate of the University of North Carolina at Chapel Hill, a 1982 graduate of Yale Divinity School, and a 1984 graduate of Yale Law School, clerked for the Hon. Thomas A. Clark (U.S. Court of Appeals for the Eleventh Circuit) after graduating from law school. Following several years in private practice, Professor Blume became the Executive Director of the South Carolina Death Penalty Resource Center, a position that he held until joining the Cornell Law School faculty. Professor Blume is a coauthor (with Rick Lempert, Sam Gross, James Liebman, Steve Landsman, and Fred Lederer) of *A Modern Approach to Evidence*, the coauthor (with Keir Weyble) of the *Federal Habeas Corpus Update*, and the coeditor (with Jordan Steiker) of *Death Penalty Stories*. He has also published numerous book chapters and law review articles in the fields of capital punishment, habeas corpus, criminal procedure, and evidence.

Professor Blume has argued eight cases in the Supreme Court of the United States and has been cocounsel or amicus curiae counsel in numerous other Supreme Court cases. Additionally, he has argued cases in the United States Court of Appeals for the Second, Fourth, Fifth, Seventh, Ninth, and Eleventh Circuits, and he has litigated more than 50 capital cases at trial, on direct appeal, and in state and federal postconviction proceedings. He has served since 1996 as Habeas Assistance and Training Counsel and in that capacity consults with the Defender Services Division of the United States Courts on matters related to capital habeas representation. Professor Blume teaches Criminal Procedure, Evidence, and Federal Appellate Practice and supervises the Capital Punishment and Juvenile Justice Clinics.